The Value of Business Analytics

Wiley & SAS Business Series

The Wiley & SAS Business Series presents books that help senior-level managers with their critical management decisions.

Titles in the Wiley & SAS Business Series include:

For more information on any of the above titles, please visit www.wiley.com.

The Value of Business Analytics

Identifying the Path to Profitability

Evan Stubbs

WILEY

John Wiley & Sons, Inc.

Published by John Wiley & Sons, Inc., Hoboken, New Jersey.

Published simultaneously in Canada.

For general information on our other products and services or for technical support, please contact our Customer Care Department within the United States at (800) 762-2974, outside the United States at (317) 572-3993 or fax (317) 572-4002.

Wiley also publishes its books in a variety of electronic formats. Some content that appears in print may not be available in electronic books. For more information about Wiley products, visit our web site at www.wiley.com.

Library of Congress Cataloging-in-Publication Data:

Stubbs, Evan.
   The value of business analytics: identifying the path to profitability / Evan Stubbs.
      p. cm.
   ISBN 978-1-118-01239-0 (hardback); ISBN 978-1-118-09338-2 (ebk);
   ISBN 978-1-118-09340-5 (ebk);   ISBN 978-1-118-09341-2 (ebk)
   1. Business planning.   2. Strategic planning.   3. Decision making.   4. Industrial management–Statistical methods.   I. Title.
   HD30.28.S787 2011
   658.4′01–dc22

                                   2011012037

10 9 8 7 6 5 4 3 2 1

Contents

Preface

One of the most awkward conversations I have ever had was with someone who simply refused to believe that anything as abstract as "analytics" could possibly be real. The conversation culminated in his rather backhanded compliment that, and I paraphrase, "I was lucky to have ended up in an industry where it was so easy to make things up."

Despite what I knew, it was hard to convince him otherwise. While that was possibly the most extreme example I have ever experienced, it is unfortunate how often we seem to struggle to convince the rest of the world of the value business analytics brings. This book is a response to that. I hope it will help others take advantage of what has taken me over 10 years to realize and understand.

HOW TO READ THIS BOOK

This book consolidates more than a decade of experience. In practice, success often comes down to understanding the role analytics plays in creating competitive advantage and the reasons why many teams fail. Given this groundwork, selling the value of analytics involves four key activities:

1. Defining the value
2. Communicating the value
3. Committing to the execution
4. Measuring success

This book provides guidance on each of these based on hands-on experience. When applied, these activities help managers strengthen their ability to sell the value of analytics within any organization.

While the chapters can be read in any order, readers will find it helpful to read them sequentially. This is because each chapter builds on the insights and terminology defined in the previous chapters. However, experienced managers may find it useful to skip ahead to their areas of greatest interest.

Although the subject matter can be highly technical, this book tries wherever possible to make the content as approachable as possible. What is important is not the technical detail but an understanding of how organizational dynamics can help or hurt success. Practical examples are provided wherever possible; the most effective learning comes from understanding how things work in practice, and not merely in theory.

UNDERSTANDING THE STRUCTURE

Our starting point is how analytics creates competitive advantage. Mapping tactical activities to strategic outcomes makes it is easier not only to create a vision but also to get management aligned with that vision. Chapter 2 focuses on the role analytics plays within strategic planning processes. Regardless of how planning is executed, analytics can almost inevitably play a significant role in creating sustainable competitive advantage. This chapter will be of most interest to those who are anxious to develop an understanding of the role analytics plays within the development of strategy.

From there, we consider how teams can understand and overcome tactical challenges. Setting a vision is critical. Equally important is delivering that vision and avoiding common execution issues. Chapter 3 focuses on the tactical application of analytics and why teams often struggle. It introduces the core vocabulary used throughout this book and outlines common organizational structures and team roles. It outlines the most common challenges faced by a business analytics team. This chapter will be of most interest to those who need to understand the practical side of business analytics without getting into the numerical detail.

Chapter 4 focuses on how to define the value of analytics. Decisions and commitment are made based on projected outcomes. When the value is unclear, commitment is hard to obtain. Chapter 4 focuses on a variety of strategies to help define the value of business analytics. It outlines the different meanings of *value* and provides a number of ways of quantifying the value created through business analytics, paying attention to both tangible and intangible value. This chapter will be of most interest to those who want to build an understanding of how to quantify the value of their planned work.

The next chapter focuses on how to communicate the value of analytics. Defining the value is not enough; not only does it need to be quantified, it needs to be communicated. Chapter 5 focuses on the elements managers should consider when communicating the value of their work. It outlines why communication breakdowns occur and identifies how to overcome such challenges. It pays specific attention to how organizational culture, environmental culture, and personal psychology impact understanding, helping managers to build a holistic communication strategy. This chapter will be of most interest to those interested in building a tailored communication strategy to help generate organizational support.

From there, we discuss how to create a delivery plan. Once commitment has been obtained, managers must deliver the value they have said they will deliver. Chapter 6 focuses on building a successful execution plan and delivering returns. It outlines the various activities most analytics teams are involved in and how to effectively plan around them. It also introduces the concept of *tactical revolution*, an invaluable tool that assists managers to overcome often significant resourcing challenges. Finally, it provides managers with various essential planning considerations. This chapter will be of most interest to those who must overcome a lack of resources or who are tasked with creating delivery plans.

The penultimate chapter focuses on how to establish a measurement framework. Because trust requires history, Chapter 7 focuses on how to measure the team's successes and activities. This gives the team the ability to demonstrate value, build trust, and optimize processes. It focuses on a variety of useful measures, how they can be used in practice, and the benefits from establishing a dedicated measurement platform. It also provides some guidance on building best-practice measurement processes. This chapter will be of most interest to those trying to optimize their existing activities or quantify the value of the work they are doing.

Finally, we consider a hypothetical example of how to bring everything together. Chapter 8 synthesizes a variety of real-world examples into a single narrative, demonstrating how the lessons learned in this book might be applied in practice.

SOME FINAL THOUGHTS

Analytics is one of the most exciting fields available today. History has conspired to create an opportunity like no other for those skilled in selling the value and executing on their findings. It is rare for any discipline to offer such a significant strategic impact and deliver such substantial tactical efficiencies. Because of the renewable value that analytics offers, people who are skilled in acting as change agents with the ability to transform their organizations into analytically enabled competitors will be among the most sought after in the market.

While reading this book, you should remember the following:

- Although executive management commitment is important, change often comes down to the effectiveness of the manager responsible for execution.
- Quantifying the value that business analytics brings is the first and most important step and, when effectively communicated, overcomes most challenges.
- Trust and credibility overcome whatever is left, but unless you deliver and can measure what you have delivered, it is unlikely you will get them.

Acknowledgments

This book would have been impossible without the phenomenal support of so many people. Every author says that, but it is hard to appreciate how much people are willing to give until you have been humbled by their generosity. Without Shelley Sessoms's kind help in putting together my pitch and supporting the idea, it is unlikely anything would have happened in the first place. Stacey Hamilton's help throughout the writing process was invaluable in making sure I actually finished everything on time!

Thanks are due to Natalie Mendes, Peter Kokinakos, and Annelies Tjetjep for putting aside their valuable personal time to review content as it was written. Greg Wood deserves special recognition for his enviable ability to ask such simple and yet poignant questions that they led to a relatively substantial rewrite of certain chapters. I would especially like to thank Anne Milley for her support and excellent recommendations on research material, much of which greatly expanded the scope of this book.

Two people are owed such gratitude that I question whether I will ever be able to repay them. The first is Sarah Agius for her extensive, critical, and priceless feedback. Not only did she repeatedly go through the entire manuscript with a fine-toothed comb, she correctly pointed out innumerable ways the content could be improved. Without her help, I sincerely feel the book would have been a pale version of its final form. The second is Vicki Batten. Despite not having any background (or, possibly, interest!) in the topic, she happily read the manuscript from cover to cover in record time, helping me to no end by providing a much-needed sanity check on whether what I had written actually made any sense!

Most of all, I would like to thank my wife, daughter, and son: my wife, Vanessa, for tirelessly trying to make sense out of what I was writing and picking up a multitude of things I would never have thought of—words cannot describe the effort she put in to support me in what must have seemed like a fool's errand at times; my daughter, Amélie, for making sure I didn't work too hard; and my son, Calvin, for joining us halfway along our journey.

CHAPTER 1

Introduction and Background

THE POWER OF INFORMATION

Revolutions come and revolutions go; while their influence may be obvious in retrospect, it is rare that we appreciate their impact at the time. The one thing they have in common is disruption at all levels of society. First, the agricultural revolution; then the industrial revolution; and now, 60 years into the latter, we have the information revolution.

Information has always been power, but the past few decades have seen a subtle shift occur, fundamentally altering the way we perceive it. It has been only relatively recently that the amount of data available to us has outstripped our ability to investigate that data. At one point in time, it was arguably possible to have read every written word ever set on parchment or papyrus. While the true number will never be known, it is said that King Ptolemy II Philadelphus set the Library of Alexandria a target of 500,000 scrolls. At the time, this represented the largest collection of knowledge in the known world.

Things change. At the time of this book's publication, the United States Library of Congress had over 33 million books (including other printed material) and 63 million manuscripts. The Internet Archive, capturing only a subset of all the information contained on the Web, has already cataloged almost 2 petabytes of text and is growing at approximately 20 terabytes a month, in itself a larger amount of information than that held by the Library of Congress.

A little over 2,000 years have passed between King Philadelphus and now. Things are accelerating at such a rate that in another 20 years our staggering statistics will probably be considered equally quaint.

This tsunami of information is a real challenge at every level in society. At a personal level, we struggle to keep on top of everything that is happening around us. Alvin Toffler coined the term "future shock" as early as 1970 to describe the overwhelming and disorienting impact of information overload.[1] And, at a professional level, where we once struggled with a paucity of information we now struggle to pick which pieces of information are important out of the millions of measures at our fingertips. Regardless of where you start, this ever-increasing amount of information has changed the way we view the world, the way we live, and the way we do business.

Dealing with this data deluge requires being smarter. It requires developing the ability to selectively process information based on value, not sequence. It requires, more than anything, the realization that brute force and manual effort are, in the long run, an impossible solution. Quite simply, it requires the effective application of analytics.

Getting to this point has not happened overnight—it has taken decades of research and thought. Among others, Claude Shannon led the charge when he published his seminal work, "A Mathematical Theory of Communication": His proof that information could be quantified and measured was both innovative and revolutionary.[2] Without his research, our world would be vastly different. Among other things, it is unlikely that Voyager would have launched or that the Internet would exist.

Treating information as a measurable quantity has changed the world. While statistics had always been concerned with extracting useful knowledge from raw data, information theory helped encourage the perception that information was more than just insight.

Instead, it could legitimately be seen as an asset in its own right, something of real (and comparable) value.

This intersection of statistically based insight and the realization that information can be an asset has had and will continue to have serious reverberations in the business world. Being smarter has always meant being successful; as far back as the nineteenth century, analytics was already generating competitive advantage.

William Gosset, employed by Guinness, had been struggling to identify the varieties of barley that had the best productive yield. Like medical researchers and biometricians, he was forced to deal with extremely small samples, often as little as 30 or fewer observations. Through a combination of rigorous research and trial and error, he identified a new distribution to help model likely population means, something that gave Guinness a significant competitive advantage through optimizing production efficiencies. By using his distribution to better predict crop yields, Guinness was able to gain a cost advantage over its competitors.

An interesting side note is that despite Guinness having prohibited employees from publishing their discoveries (given their understanding of the importance of analytics as a competitive advantage), Gosset published his work anyway. However, in the interests of keeping his job, he published it under a pseudonym, giving us the well-known "Student's t-distribution" that we work with today.

MODERN-DAY MAGICIANS

Today, we face the opposite of Gosset's challenge. While we still sometimes have to deal with fewer observations than we would like, the growing challenge is working out how to deal with the massive amounts of information we do have. As Moore's law suggests, we have seen the number of transistors we can fit inexpensively on an integrated circuit double roughly every two years. Although it is not an exact relationship, we have seen roughly exponential growth in processing power since the early 1950s.

Importantly, processing power is not the only area that has grown by leaps and bounds. Kryder's law suggests that disk storage density doubles annually, a pattern that has largely held true since the mid-1990s, when it was first suggested. And Butters's law suggests that the amount of data carried by a single optical fiber doubles every nine months.

Combined, these create our future. We have the storage capacity to track ever-increasing amounts of information, often referred to as "big data." We have the bandwidth to support the transfer of this information as needed. And, we have the processing power to extract insight from this data.

Because of this, we are drowning in data. For the first time ever, we have more data than we have storage capacity. In 2008, International Data Corporation (IDC) estimated that the amount of data being generated exceeded our total aggregate storage. Organizations such as eBay have repositories in the petabytes, and there are no signs that this accelerated rate of data retention is going to slow.

The answer does not lie in better processes. Enterprise resource planning (ERP) systems play a critical role in standardizing operational processes, but they do not create competitive advantage or insight. Their focus is instead on establishing process efficiencies. There are obvious advantages to this, one of the biggest being that it reduces cost in the long run. However, because they rely on standardizing processes between organizations, at best they simply set a minimum benchmark. *It is impossible to differentiate yourself if you use exactly the same processes as everyone else.*

Instead, competitive advantage comes from capitalizing on what makes you unique. Every organization is different, and every organization has the potential to exploit that exact uniqueness in a way that no one else can match. Doing this means taking advantage of their single biggest resource: their data.

The people who know how to manage this data deluge are our future. Hal Varian, Google's chief economist, summed it up best: "I keep saying that the sexy job in the next ten years will be statisticians."[3] Being able to translate massive amounts of data into real insight is beyond magic—it is competitive advantage distilled. Nothing else offers an equivalent level of agility, productivity improvement, or renewable value. Being "smarter" than your competitors is not just hyperbole; it is a real description of how significant the impact of applied analytics can be. If yours is an organization like Zappos.com, trying to understand what over a million people are telling you every day through social media, it is simply impossible to do business without leveraging advanced analytics for text mining and sentiment analysis.

Today, we stand on the cusp of transformation. The organizations that successfully extract the maximum amount of useful information from their ever-increasing data repositories and act on their insights are on the path to success. Those that do not are inevitably set on a track toward mediocrity at best, and abject failure at worst. Much as Henry Ford's assembly line forced handmade production into a niche, the organizations that successfully apply business analytics will increasingly reduce the relevancy of those that do not.

However, success requires more than just knowledge of statistics or ways of dealing with big data. Execution is essential, but without a plan and commitment, little happens. It also requires an understanding of how analytics translates to competitive advantage. It requires an ability to enact change within an organization. And, it requires managers to sell the value of analytics.

While analytics has a long and hallowed history of creating organizational value, it remains a relatively opaque discipline. For many organizations, the insights created by advanced analytics are often tied to individuals, not processes, making it hard for them to extend the value to other areas of the business. While there is rarely any disagreement that any organization should be smarter in its decision making, the linkage between numerical analysis and value creation is rarely understood. When it comes to investing in building these capabilities, many organizations are reluctant to take the leap of faith that is apparently necessary.

It does not need to be that way.

THE SECRET OF SUCCESS

When one looks globally, some organizations seem not to mistrust analytics. Somehow, they seem to create renewable value through applying their competencies across many different business problems. Somehow, they succeed, not once, but repeatedly. And somehow, they translate their experience and skills into sustainable competitive advantage. Whether one is looking at Marriott, Canada Post, Sainsbury's, or Telstra, some organizations consistently manage to deliver significant returns through their application of business analytics.

Possibly the best-guarded secret in business analytics is that in practice, their success comes down not only to organizational culture but also to the ability of their managers to successfully sell the value of analytics. As researchers such as Thomas Davenport and Jeanne Harris have rightly pointed out, overall success can often be linked to a variety of factors, including organizational structure, management commitment, and successful strategic planning. However, it is often "where the rubber hits the road" that the greatest impact can occur.

Change comes from two directions: top down or bottom up. If the organization already has the right management culture, using insight as a competitive advantage is relatively straightforward. As Jack Welch is reputed to have said, "An organization's ability to learn, and translate that learning into action rapidly, is the ultimate competitive advantage."

In these organizations, applying business analytics is relatively easy. There is management commitment to the use of insight, there is an understanding of the role analytics plays in creating competitive advantage, and there is often a culture of continuous improvement. For those of us lucky enough to work in this context, life is easy.

Unfortunately, most of us do not work with these types of organizations. Instead, we work in environments that are unfamiliar with the use of analytics. Environments that struggle to differentiate between intuition and fact, often taking pride in making decisions based on "gut feel." Environments that, as frustrating as it can be, cannot understand the value that business analytics provides.

This book is written to help those who want to change the environment in which they operate.

Analytics is a multidisciplinary activity: The value from insight comes not from the activity but from the execution. Often, this crosses a variety of departments within an organization. Few analytics groups have responsibility for both the insight creation and the execution of that insight. Because of this, selling the value of analytics is not just an aspirational goal for managers; it is a necessary criterion for success.

For many managers, this can be challenging. Despite broad interest in business analytics as a discipline, there exist few useful sources that help managers with the practicality of getting organizational commitment to using business analytics. This book aims to fill that knowledge gap.

NOTES

1. A. Toffler, *Future Shock* (New York: Random House, 1970).
2. C. Shannon, "A Mathematical Theory of Communication," *Bell System Technical Journal* 27 (July–October 1948): 379–423.
3. J. Manyika, "Hal Varian on How the Web Challenges Managers," *McKinsey Quarterly* (January 2009), www.mckinseyquarterly.com/Hal_Varian_on_how_the_Web_challenges_managers_2286.

CHAPTER 2

The Importance of Business Analytics

INTRODUCTION

Business analytics, when successfully executed, plays multiple roles within an organization. It:

- Supports strategic planning
- Creates competitive advantage
- Delivers tactical value

Everything needs a starting point. While we will get into detail of how to successfully overcome common barriers in later chapters, this chapter is primarily focused on giving a basic grounding as to why business analytics almost inevitably forms a cornerstone strategic enabler.

Within this chapter we will examine the key driver of market success: the ability to develop competitive differentiation. To do this, we will review four different perspectives on how organizations create competitive advantage through strategic planning:

1. The Traditional Perspective: SWOT Analysis
2. The External Perspective: Porter's Five Forces

3. The Internal Perspective: The Resource-Based View of the Firm

4. The Market Perspective: Wilde and Hax's Delta Model

Each of these approaches provides a structured process to identify and nurture competitive differentiation. By examining the assumptions behind and execution of these different perspectives, we will uncover the critical role business analytics invariably plays within each. And, by doing so, managers can consciously map their tactical activities into strategic outcomes, raising the profile of their work within the organization.

After establishing the importance of business analytics in effective strategic planning, we will look into how it supports innovation, invention, and agility. And finally, we will briefly review the biggest reason why business analytics is different from most initiatives: its ability to deliver constant incremental returns with relatively low investment.

BUSINESS ANALYTICS: A DEFINITION

Before we start examining the role of the organization in an economic context, it is important to quickly review what is meant by "business analytics" and why it is different from pure analytics or "advanced analytics."

The cornerstone of business analytics is pure analytics. Although it is a very broad definition, *analytics* can be considered *any data-driven process that provides insight*. It may report on historical information or it may provide predictions about future events; the end-goal of analytics is to add value through insight and turn data into information.

Common examples of analytics include:

- *Reporting:* the summarization of historical data
- *Trending:* the identification of underlying patterns in time series data
- *Segmentation:* the identification of similarities within data
- *Predictive modeling:* the prediction of future events using historical data

All of these applications of analytics have a number of common characteristics:

- They are based on data (as opposed to opinion).
- They apply various mathematical techniques to transform and summarize the raw data.
- They add value to the original data and transform it into knowledge.

Broadly speaking, various applications of analytics can be divided into two categories. Activities such as *business intelligence, reporting,* and *performance management* tend to focus on *what happened*—they analyze and present historical information.

Advanced analytics, however, aims to identify:

- Why things are happening
- What will happen next
- What is the best possible course of action

The distinguishing characteristic between advanced analytics and reporting is the use of higher-order statistical and mathematical techniques such as:

- Operations research
- Parametric or nonparametric statistics
- Multivariate analysis
- Algorithm-based predictive models (such as decision trees, gradient boosting, regressions, or transfer functions)

Business analytics in turn *leverages all forms of analytics to achieve business outcomes.* It seems a quibbling difference, but it is an important one—business analytics adds to analytics by requiring:

- Business relevancy
- Actionable insight
- Performance measurement and value measurement

There is a great deal of knowledge that can be created through applying various forms of analytics. Business analytics, however, makes a distinction between *relevant* knowledge and *irrelevant* knowledge. A significant part of business analytics is identifying the insights that would be valuable (in a real and measurable way) given the business's strategic and tactical objectives. If analytics is often about finding "interesting" things in large amounts of data, business analytics is about making sure that this information has contextual relevancy and delivers real value.

Once created, this knowledge must be acted on in some form for value to be created. Whereas analytics focuses primarily on the creation of the insight and not necessarily on what should be done with the insight once created, business analytics recognizes that creating the insight is only one small step in a larger value chain. Equally important (if not more so) is that the insight be *used* to realize the value.

This *operational* and *actionable* point of view can create substantially different outcomes when compared to applying pure analytics. If the insight is considered in isolation, it is quite easy to develop a series of outcomes that are impossible to execute on within the broader organizational context. For example, a series of models may be developed that, although extremely accurate, are impossible to integrate into the organization's operational systems. If the tools that created the models are not compatible with the organization's inventory management systems, customer relationship management systems, or other operational systems, the value of the insight may be high but the realized value negligible.

By approaching the same problem from a business analytics perspective, the same organization may be willing to sacrifice model accuracy for ease of execution, ensuring that economic value is delivered even though the models may not have as high a standard as they otherwise could have. A model that is 80 percent accurate but can be acted on creates far more value than an extremely accurate model that cannot be deployed.

This operational aspect forms another key distinction between analytics and business analytics. More often than not, analytics is about answering a question at a point in time. Business analytics, however, is about sustained value delivery. Tracking value and measuring performance therefore become critical elements of ensuring long-term value from business analytics.

ROLE OF THE ORGANIZATION

To understand how business analytics helps create competitive advantage, it helps to revisit the role of the organization in the market and society. Because business analytics requires *business relevancy*, creating real competitive differentiation requires a strong comprehension of *why* organizations exist. By understanding these drivers, one uncovers the critical role analytics plays in enabling competitive advantage.

Private Sector Perspective

There are multiple perspectives on the role of the organization in the private sector. Some of the most common reasons include:

- To increase the efficiency of converting inputs into value-added outputs
- To deliver a return to shareholders
- To jointly benefit stakeholders

Organizations do not exist within a vacuum. They operate in what is often a highly complex interexchange with other organizations, individuals, and regulatory forces. Not surprisingly, a great deal of research has been conducted into why organizations form in the first place.

Value-Added Transformation

In principle, all of the elements necessary to produce a given output already exist in the market (in an economic sense). If this is the case, why should organizations appear?

One of the original (and most influential) perspectives on why this formation takes place was developed by Ronald Coase in the early twentieth century.[1] Coase's argument was that the formation of an organization is an economically efficient outcome where there exists the opportunity to benefit from longer-term arrangements but the market cannot support such an arrangement. This holds true within the neoclassical perspective of the market, where decisions are instantaneous and isolated.

Fundamentally, the role of organizations within this context is to achieve prices lower than the market would generate in equilibrium through reducing (or eliminating) market-based transactional costs. Although it has been generally acknowledged since that this is somewhat of an oversimplification and that the neoclassical view of the market has various limitations, it is still an important perspective in that it emphasizes the importance of internal efficiencies in economic success.

Profit-Making Enterprise

Another common perspective is that the role of the firm is to maximize shareholder value. This perspective, often supported within the value-based management field, emphasizes the role of the firm as an instrument of its owners to deliver sustainable economic return. Quantitative (and often financial) measures such as revenue, working capital, and the duration of competitive advantage are identified as success criteria.

Importantly, maximizing shareholder value within this point of view does not necessarily mean purely short-term economic benefits: Factors such as reputation, trust, and longer-term investments can and should play a significant role in decision-making processes. For example, taking advantage of limitations in foreign regulation around managing toxic assets may lead to a short-term reduction in manufacturing costs. However, this short-term cost efficiency advantage could turn into a longer-term brand and value issue should these toxic assets create health concerns in the general public.

Balancing these and understanding the longer-term picture (and not just the short-term opportunities) is a critical component of effective value-based management. One of the critical elements of this point of view is the emphasis it places on market performance.

Maximizing Stakeholder Value

A final perspective is that the role of the firm is to maximize stakeholder value. A key distinction is made between *shareholder* value and *stakeholder* value: Within this point of view, while shareholders are a key stakeholder, they are not the only stakeholder. Equally important is ensuring that all involved stakeholders (employees, partners, and society in general) benefit. This perspective is heavily normative and emphasizes social responsibility over profitability; it argues that sustainable profitability is a natural byproduct of pursuing stakeholders' joint interests.

This point of view reinforces a final critical component of the firm: the role and satisfaction of stakeholders in achieving success. If the role of the organization is to increase aggregate social welfare, benefiting all involved stakeholders is the most efficient way of maximizing total utility. By doing this, the organization works toward Pareto optimality, a situation where no individual can be made better off without making another individual worse off.

Public Sector Perspective

The role of the public sector has a similarly varied series of perspectives. Some of the most common reasons for the existence of public sector organizations include:

- To intervene to mediate and resolve various forms of market failure
- To increase social welfare
- To provide for national security and economic stability

Prevention of Market Failure

The free market has a wide variety of advantages. As Adam Smith identified over 200 years ago, it is a highly efficient mechanism for moving toward optimal pricing efficiency. And while the ideals of a Walrasian auction (where perfect equilibrium is achieved between supply and demand) are arguably impractical, prices do tend to exhibit greater efficiency where the conditions of a free market are met.

However, not every situation allows for these characteristics. An organization may produce pollution as a byproduct of manufacturing, impacting society as a whole. As this hidden cost (also known as a *negative externality*) is not explicitly carried by the organization in a free market, society as a whole is made worse off. Equally, imbalances in access to information (also known as *information asymmetries*) can lead to inefficient pricing where one party takes advantage of the other.

One perspective is that the role of public sector organizations is to minimize the occurrence and impact of these market failures. Through appropriate application of regulation and public investment, market failures can and should be prevented. This perspective emphasizes efficiency in the form of interference only where necessary. If the net impact of a policy would have created a disproportionate cost in policy creation and administration when compared against market efficiency improvements, the policy should not have been enacted in the first place. Within this context, efficiency is key: The role of the government is both to operate efficiently and to ensure the market is operating efficiently.

Welfare and Net Utility Creation

Another perspective, one highly grounded in normative economics, is that the role of the public sector is to maximize social welfare, often through minimizing income inequalities for the broader good. *Social welfare* within this context is often defined as the aggregation of individual measures of welfare, emphasizing measures including wealth, utility, or more recently, estimates of life satisfaction and happiness.

Within this point of view, the role of the public sector is to actively shape the market to maximize social welfare. Pareto efficiency is the end goal, where no individual can be made better off without making another individual worse off. A wide range of outcomes are targeted, including minimizing market failure, limiting income inequalities, and focus public sector investment on ensuring macro- and microeconomic stability and growth.

This point of view emphasizes effective information management and policy consideration. Without excellent access to various measurement devices and market indicators, it is impossible to track welfare gains. By measuring welfare gains in the form of industry concentration, well-being, or any other number of social elements, policies can be individually assessed in terms of their positive or negative influence on society as a whole. Policy is often created through multiple instruments in a relatively complex manner and considering the interactions between these instruments is critical.

Security and Stability

A final commonly held view of the role of the public sector is that it is an agent of growth and stability. Threats exist nationally and internationally across both economic and security spheres of activity and the role of the public sector is to identify, mitigate, and eliminate these risks where possible. This may take the form of macroeconomic policy focused on encouraging investment, the creation of domestic and internationally focused security agencies and military operations, or targeted market regulation or deregulation to generate competitive efficiencies and regional centers of excellence.

This point of view emphasizes the role of the public sector as caretaker and strategic visionary, tasked with identifying strategic direction and minimizing risk. Macroeconomic and risk modeling is a key element in this approach, as limited resources must be deployed for maximum gains.

REASONS BEHIND STRATEGIC PLANNING

At the highest level, these reasons are fairly straightforward. As is commonly the case, the devil lies in the details—achieving these outcomes is rarely guaranteed. Success requires a plan.

Developing a Plan

As a rule, we are a fairly motivated species, regardless of whether one is talking about individual performance or organizational performance. As individuals, we typically seek opportunities for professional or personal advancement. As organizations, we typically seek opportunities for financial or social improvement. In both situations, we leverage the resources that are available to us in order to achieve our desired outcomes.

However, success does not normally occur without effort. At an individual level, we deal with personal limitations and environmental challenges that have the potential to undermine our success. At an organizational level, we face competitive challenges and regulatory constraints. The opportunities in front of us are often real; the difficulty is in determining the best route to achieving them.

To help identify this path to profitability, we need a plan of some form. And that, fundamentally, is the role of strategic planning within an organization. Through applying the principles of strategic management, leaders aim to:

- Identify longer-term opportunities
- Understand their current advantages and limitations
- Develop a plan to achieve their target opportunities
- Manage challenges in such a way as to limit or negate them

In the private sector, these are often steps toward developing a sustainable competitive advantage in some form. In the public sector, they are often steps toward achieving particular policy outcomes or production efficiencies when benchmarked against comparable peers. In both cases, however, planning is a means to an end: It articulates a series of steps that, if taken, will hopefully lead the organization to a stronger position.

Success Requires Change

By definition, successfully achieving this outcome almost always involves change in some form. Part of effective strategic planning therefore involves understanding the impact of these changes, providing the organization with sufficient compelling reasons to make those changes, and managing the change as it happens. Because of this, strategic planning can also be seen as a process to create organizational transformations and identify sources of competitive and comparative advantages.

The specifics behind this planning process vary by organization, culture, and philosophical alignment. Some of the most common models include:

- *The traditional view*, represented by SWOT analysis
- *The external view*, represented by Porter's Five Forces and generic strategies
- *The internal view*, represented by the resource-based view of the firm
- *The market view*, represented by the Delta model

One of the biggest reasons for the importance of business analytics is that it inevitably has a role as an enabler in creating sustainable competitive advantage, regardless of which perspective (or combination of perspectives) is used.

An essential point leading from this is that a tight relationship often exists between the application of business analytics and the creation of competitive advantage. Because of this, effective use of business analytics almost inevitably means relating it back to *specific organizational objectives*. In other words, *what works for one firm may not work for another*. Different organizations have different business models, different focuses, and different cultures—because of this, it is rare that exactly the same application of analytics will work as effectively in two different contexts. Competitive advantage comes from differentiation, not replication.

Retailers provide an excellent example of how significant a difference this can be. One retailer may have built its differentiation around being the lowest-cost provider in the market. To achieve this, it may have deployed a variety of supply-chain management and cost-monitoring solutions, focusing on logistics and using technologies such as radio-frequency identification (RFID) to assist with low-cost/high-visibility goods monitoring. In this retailer's context, leveraging operations research to support supply-chain optimization may make a great deal of sense: There is a strong culture of cost minimization, the retailer has the required supporting operational systems to facilitate model deployment, and it builds on the retailer's existing competitive advantage.

Another retailer may have a focus on customer engagement, using that to seek higher prices in the market. It may put a priority on one-to-one customer relationship marketing, providing highly personalized offers and seeking customer loyalty and overall share of wallet. In this retailer's context, it may find significant benefits in using segmentation and cross-sell/up-sell models to increase offer relevancy across its customer base. Using this approach will likely fit in well with this retailer's already-in-place campaign execution systems and will require relatively minimal cultural change.

While each organization would benefit from trying to transplant the other's analytical application, they are each also likely to

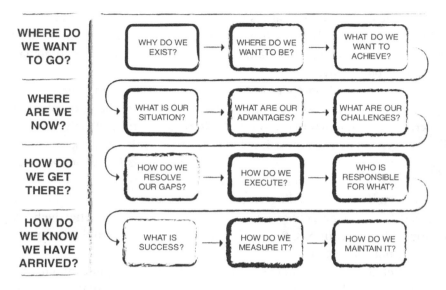

Figure 2.1 Strategic Planning Process

experience a harder time achieving success. This is not because the analytics approach does not add value; it is because the organizations are operating in different contexts. Understanding this context and ensuring the analytical application fits well within the organization's unique competencies and focus are essential.

In practice, each of these models is leveraged within a generally stereotypical planning process, as shown in Figure 2.1.

Equally important as identifying which planning approach to use is identifying the appropriate level at which planning will take place.

Strategic Planning Occurs at Multiple Levels

Planning is needed within every area of the organization. Within the context of creating deliberate organizational change, it is useful to consider planning as occurring at three levels:

1. Organizational

2. Business

3. Functional

The relationships between these and their target outcomes are described in Figure 2.2.

Organizational Planning

At the highest level is *organizational planning*. Within the private sector, this level typically focuses on identifying the markets where the organization will or will not compete, targeting acquisitions or creating key competencies and cultures. For example, a bank may have a strategic objective of increasing its footprint within a particular geographic region. Or, a telecommunications company may have a strategic objective to expand its role within the information value chain.

Within the public sector, the focus tends to be on policy objectives and the high-level allocation of resources for public benefit. For example, a department tasked with ensuring state-level or national competitive efficiency might set an objective of minimizing monopoly rents to maximize public welfare. At this level, the planning process is normally the responsibility of the most senior individuals within the organization.

Business Planning

Strategic planning at the business level focuses more on the individual strategies that will lead to the broader organizational strategies. *Business planning* may include the creation of competitive differentiation, cost minimization, or vertical integration. It is normally focused more on identifying ways of achieving levels of competitive or comparative advantage and less on deploying and managing operational units.

Within the private sector, business-level strategic planning identifies the actions needed in the market to achieve competitive dominance. For the same bank discussed earlier, its primary business-level strategy may involve identifying and building a dominant retail

TARGET OUTCOMES

- Company vision
- Key markets
- Target culture
- Organizational structure

- Competitive differentiation
- Environmental response
- Sustainability
- Target outcomes

- Operational planning
- Business execution
- Resource management
- Departmental management

ORGANIZATION PLANNING

BUSINESS PLANNING

FUNCTIONAL PLANNING

Figure 2.2 Levels of Strategic Planning

network leveraging joint-investment partners in the region it is interested in growing. For the telecommunications company, it may be around consolidating its position within the information consumption chain by providing value-added information matchmaking services.

Within the public sector, the focus is often on the programs and policy needed to achieve various outcomes. For the same department discussed earlier, it may involve focusing on specific industries with heavy capital investment (such as telecommunications or the electrical utilities). Whereas competitive advantage is often a driving factor in the private sector, relative efficiencies compared to peers is often used as a primary measure within the public sector. At this level, the planning process is often owned by the more senior individuals within the organization but developed jointly with functional or departmental heads.

Functional Planning

Strategic planning at the functional level focuses on the operational activities needed to achieve the objectives outlined at the business level. *Functional planning* normally revolves around processes and resources. Activities at this level are the most specific, often dealing with detailed execution plans and individual resources. For the same bank, the plan may involve conducting a series of location studies to identify comparative market potentials, developing a series of partner engagement models, and starting a series of jointly funded capital works programs. For the telecommunications company, it may be the progressive creation of content, an investment in automated content categorization and information matchmaking technology, along with a series of targeted campaigns aimed at delivering relevant content to high-potential users.

At this level, the target outcomes from strategic planning are largely similar within the public sector. Our competitive efficiency department may focus on delivering a project to identify relative levels of market concentration within global markets, a progressive benchmarking of local companies along with assessments of relative market power, and then a series of policy recommendations aimed at improving overall competition levels. Planning at this level is typically owned by functional or departmental heads.

Intentional versus Opportunistic Planning

Developing these plans can be a relatively complicated process, especially given the varying levels of internal and external uncertainty many organizations experience. For organizations dealing with stable markets, planning may be easy; the future will likely look much like the past.

Alternatively, for organizations dealing with highly volatile markets or goods that cross multiple segments, accurately predicting market outcomes over a typical planning horizon can be extremely challenging. This is especially true when organizations deal with products that are going through high levels of convergence. The relatively fast rise and fall of PDAs when smartphones blurred the boundaries of the two markets provides a very real example of how difficult planning can be!

Regardless of where the organization sits, every organization needs a plan. These strategic plans are often created in two ways: *intentional* planning and *opportunistic* planning.

Intentional planning follows a deliberate methodology and remains the focus of this chapter. Depending on the perspective chosen, this methodology may vary. However, its key characteristics include a series of normally predefined planning steps, a deliberate consideration of various influences, and a horizon that extends relatively far into the future.

A key advantage in using this approach is that substantial change over relatively long periods of time can be explicitly defined and worked toward; effective intentional strategic planning coupled with deliberate execution can grow and transform an organization. A key weakness, however, is the degree to which short-term opportunities can be overlooked by focusing too heavily on the desired end state.

Opportunistic planning forgoes this level of long-term intention for flexibility and tactical delivery. Instead of following a predefined methodology and identifying a desired end state relatively far into the future, managers seek incremental tactical improvements that broadly lead toward an often generally described end state. For example, rather than strictly defining desired outcomes in specific regions or markets, an opportunistic plan may be driven on "grow revenues by a set percentage."

This approach tends to work well in situations where outcomes are highly subject to change due to prevailing market conditions, where internal stability is insufficient to plan beyond a relatively short horizon, or where management commitment to longer-term goals is relatively weak. However, a key trade-off in using this approach is that it is easy to be diverted; by planning on such short horizons, it is difficult to maintain direction for significant periods of time.

Regardless of whether intentional or opportunistic planning is used, the end goal of strategic planning is normally to create a competitive or comparative advantage of some form. As such, for the remainder of this chapter we will consider a variety of models that provide structure around strategic planning and discuss how business analytics inevitably acts as a source of competitive advantage within each of these models.

BUSINESS ANALYTICS AND THE TRADITIONAL VIEW

The classic view of strategic planning involves a fairly standard process that:

- Establishes a desired end-state
- Profiles the organization's current context
- Creates a plan

The first step of this process typically involves identifying high-level organizational target outcomes. The planning process then focuses understanding where the organization sits relative to its environment. This situational analysis then drives the creation and execution of a strategy to achieve the identified targets, creating organizational change as an implicit requirement.

SWOT Analysis

This situational planning involves considering a variety of internal and external factors in turn, each of which has the potential to either create or destroy value within the organization. Often called a *SWOT analysis*, this process focuses on identifying organizational:

- Strengths
- Weaknesses
- Opportunities
- Threats

The organization's strengths are competencies and assets that can be leveraged to create competitive advantage. Common examples include brand, production efficiencies, research and development capabilities, and access to unique resources. If effectively leveraged, these are often the driving force behind effective product differentiation.

The organization's weaknesses are often either the counterbalancing force against a strength or a gap in competency. Common examples include a large organization's lack of agility, an inability to effectively capitalize on the information assets owned by the firm, or an overly complex supply chain leading to high costs. If not appropriately managed, weaknesses create opportunities for other firms to create competitive advantage.

The organization's opportunities are external conditions that, if appropriately realized, lead to success in some form. This success may be market growth, it may be increased revenue streams, or it may be improved policy outcomes such as lower rates of criminality within society. Opportunities represent areas of potentially successful outcomes.

The organization's threats are potential changes in the external environment that, if they occur, may prevent the organization from achieving the opportunities it has identified. Common examples include a new entrant into the market, a shift in consumer preferences, or a significant change in macroeconomic conditions.

THE IMPORTANCE OF BUSINESS ANALYTICS ◄ 27

Strategic Planning Using SWOT Analysis

Once these factors have been considered and enumerated, the organization goes through a process of matching and converting to develop a variety of value-creating strategies. "Matching" involves mapping strengths to opportunities, looking for ways to establish a competitive advantage. For example, a heavily vertically integrated bricks-and-mortar retail organization with strong supply-chain efficiency through automation might have significant success moving into the online market, leveraging its experience in logistics to automate shipping given a customer order.

"Converting" involves identifying strategies that transform weaknesses or threats into strengths or opportunities. At best, these strategies aim to overcome these value-destroying factors. At worst, they aim to neutralize them. For example, an organization that is facing potential profitability issues due to national economic conditions might consider expanding its sphere of operations to regional markets, minimizing its risk through spreading its investment portfolio over multiple uncorrelated markets.

Identifying the Ideal Strategy

Underpinning this approach is an implicit philosophy that the ideal strategy is determined by the environment (also known as environmental determinism). As external factors are considered fixed by default, a variety of complementary methodologies have been developed to help consider how the organization's actions can alter the reality in which it deals.

Additionally, this approach emphasizes pursuing strategies that lead to competitive advantage; while some opportunities may be significant, it is often the case that most sustainable strategies involve matching unique organizational strengths to market opportunities. The harder a particular strength is to replicate, the greater the competitive advantage conferred when leveraged to achieve a matching opportunity.

Assuming the organization uses the traditional model as its planning framework, business analytics inevitably has a key role to play in creating competitive or comparative advantage. As described earlier, business analytics seeks to apply various forms of data-driven decision making to create business value.

Business Analytics as a Critical Enabler

Leveraging business analytics is one of the most direct paths to creating strengths and neutralizing weaknesses. Because business analytics is highly generalizable and can be applied across multiple problems, it is rare that judicious consideration cannot identify ways of applying business analytics that support matching or converting strategies. For an organization focused on market growth, business analytics may allow flexible and relevant pricing structures, one-to-one marketing, or risk-driven pricing. For an organization focused on lowering rates of criminality, business analytics may help optimize allocation of resources to maximize detection rates.

Equally, business analytics helps support modeling the potential impact of various threats. Techniques such as simulation modeling, stress testing, and constraints analysis all help predict the upper and lower impacts based on what is known by the organization at that point in time. By leveraging business analytics, the organization is able to prioritize threats within its planning process and add focus where it is needed.

These applications often form the core of competitive advantage; by being smarter or faster than their competitors within the context of a given opportunity, private sector organizations create sustainable competitive advantage. And, by effectively modeling the potential impact of various threats, organizations can better develop matching strategies to mitigate or neutralize threats.

BUSINESS ANALYTICS AND THE EXTERNAL VIEW

An alternative approach, suggested by Michael Porter, is to consider the external factors that influence the attractiveness of a given market. This is often referred to as the "positioning approach" due to the importance of positioning the organization within the broader external environment.

Porter's Five Forces

Within this context, attractiveness is considered to be closely aligned with overall industry profitability. By considering the major external drivers of profitability within a given market, strategic planners can develop a series of strategies that aim to mitigate or manage these forces.

Porter identified five major forces that influence market attractiveness:

1. The threat of new market entrants
2. The threat of substitutable products
3. Competitive rivalry
4. The bargaining power of suppliers
5. The bargaining power of customers

The interrelationships among these factors are shown in Figure 2.3.

New Entrants

New entrants create a significant force against market attractiveness: They may drive prices down in the interest of gaining market share, they reduce mindshare in consumers, and they dilute profitability. Barriers to entry act as a constraining force against new entrants, but their threat is real. New entrants may pose an especially significant threat if products are largely undifferentiated and substitutable. Equally, the lower the start-up costs associated with market entry, the higher the odds of new competitors entering the market. And, the simpler the processes used by incumbents, the easier it is for a new entrant to replicate their activities.

Substitutable Products

The degree to which products can be substituted within a given industry also forms a powerful force against attractiveness. The

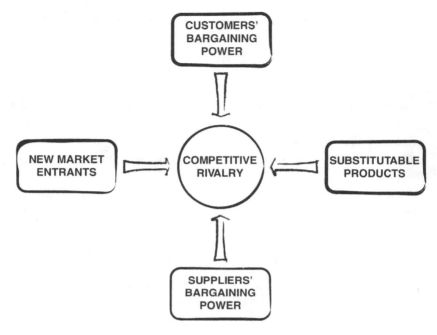

Figure 2.3 Porter's Five Forces. *Source: Adapted from Michael Porter,* Competitive Strategy *(New York: Free Press, 1980).*

greater the degree of product substitutability in a given market, the harder it becomes to maintain profitability. In aggregate, these substitutes create a de facto price ceiling under which all market participants are constrained. Example factors that affect product substitutability include the level of differentiation provided by a particular firm and the contribution of non-price considerations to purchasing decisions. In the presence of commodity products, the ability of a firm to increase price within the market is limited, if not eliminated.

Competitive Rivalry

Competitive rivalry is traditionally the strongest of the five forces. However, its influence will vary significantly from one industry to the next. One way to consider this force is to view it as the aggressiveness with which market participants pursue market success, focusing their attention on various playing fields such as price, bundling, value-add, or customer engagement. Cultural and technological factors can have a significant influence on the level of competitive rivalry in a given market; markets characterized by high levels of innovation or market volatility (either positive or negative) may exhibit high levels of competitive rivalry. Failure to adequately plan for this force can lead to losses in market share and potentially exiting the market.

Suppliers

Suppliers also form a major force in influencing market attractiveness. This influence can manifest in a wide variety of ways. For example, a small number of upstream suppliers can make identifying alternative sources of raw inputs extremely difficult. Or an organization's suppliers may operate their own retail network, reducing the importance of the organization in the value chain. These different forms of supplier lock-in and market control all reduce the ability of an organization to capture market rents.

Customers

Just as suppliers form a major force in market attractiveness, so do customers (also referred to as "buyers" by Porter). For example, as the concentration of customers increases, the ability of the organization to exert market control decreases. As this concentration increases, so does the level of exposure faced by the organization should a customer move to a competitor. Similarly, the greater the cost of the good to the customers proportional to their overall budget, the more price sensitive they are likely to become, increasing the odds of their shopping around for a more competitive offering.

Strategic Planning Using Porter's Five Forces

Similar to a SWOT analysis, this perspective emphasizes the importance of the external environment in determining strategy. However, unlike with SWOT analysis, strengths and weaknesses are not explicitly considered. Rather than focus on innate capabilities, the focus is instead on identifying ways of dealing with the five forces.

Strengths and weaknesses are implicit within the planning process, but by avoiding focusing on them, the intent of the planning process moves away from the current environment and instead toward the desired outcome. Because of this, Porter's Five Forces are often used to augment a SWOT analysis by providing a less constrained field of view.

As macroeconomic conditions often determine the overarching strength of these forces, modifying these forces is usually beyond the capability of the organization. Instead, the whole point of the planning process is to determine strategies that will manage these forces effectively. Competitive success comes from minimizing the impact of these forces on the organization and competitive advantage comes from developing unique competencies or assets to deal with these forces.

Porter's Generic Strategies

Leading from these five forces are Porter's *generic strategies*, shown in Figure 2.4. Porter suggests that there exist two primary dimensions to any strategic plan:

Figure 2.4 Porter's Generic Strategies

1. *Strategic scope*, focused on the size and composition of the market to be targeted

2. *Strategic strength*, focused on the core competency to be leveraged within the strategy

In considering all the possible combinations of these dimensions, Porter identified three commonly effective strategies:

1. A differentiation strategy

2. A cost leadership strategy

3. A segmentation strategy

One argument is that by restricting focus to a single strategy, organizations avoid the trap of trying to "be everything to everyone." However, a common criticism of this approach is that it paints a relatively single-dimensional view of customer value perception. Both positions have validity; regardless of which position is taken, business analytics is often a key enabler in delivering successful generic strategies.

Differentiation as a Strategy

A differentiation strategy focuses on building unique competitive differentiators within the broader market. This differentiation can then be leveraged to charge higher prices, increase customer loyalty, or otherwise create barriers against competitors. Often, these focus on unique features, proprietary technology, brand appeal, or positive network externalities and customer lock-in. This strategy tends to be most effective in highly saturated markets characterized by relative price insensitivity.

Cost Leadership as a Strategy

A cost leadership strategy takes the alternative approach and instead focuses on achieving the lowest perceived market price (taking into account the value received from the good). Often, this strategy is heavily aligned to achieving supply chain efficiencies, economies of scale or scope in production, and high sales volumes; given the lower margins implicit with this approach, profitability comes from increasing turnover or reducing costs. Inputs and production efficiencies are therefore typically a key component of this strategy.

Segmentation as a Strategy

A segmentation strategy, also known as a focus strategy, attempts to deliver success by identifying subgroups within the market and treating these groups differently. One could argue that in many mature industries, it is the natural progression for organizations keen to increase their profitability; by segmenting their customers and building product and offer differentiation into their customer engagement models, they not only increase their relevancy within each segment but also increase their overall segment attractiveness.

Business Analytics as a Critical Enabler

For an organization intent on pursuing a cost leadership strategy, business analytics provides numerous ways of reducing cost. By focusing on competencies such as pricing analytics, supply chain optimization, and hedonic pricing analysis, organizations can:

- Identify the ideal balance between price and demand
- Drive cost out of their supply chain
- Prioritize features to maximize customer perceived value at minimum cost

Equally, for an organization intent on pursuing a differentiation strategy, business analytics provides numerous ways of creating customer loyalty and perceived value. By focusing on competencies such as retention analytics, direct marketing analytics, and up-sell modeling, organizations can:

- Discourage customers from moving to other providers
- Improve product or service relevancy to their customer base
- Increase overall share of wallet through positioning appropriate value-added offers

Finally, delivering a segmentation strategy requires a thorough understanding of customers' similarities. Segmentation modeling is often one of the most effective ways of developing this understanding, especially when dealing with highly complex, multidimensional information. If the only things the organization considers are levels of spend, product preferences, and geographic distribution, a simple rules-based segmentation model may suffice.

However, when additional factors such as behavioral patterns, changes in preferences, and sociodemographic information are also included, rules-based models become increasing unwieldy, increasing the attractiveness of analytics-based segmentation models. Algorithm-based segmentation models have no issues with scaling to deal with large sets of customer information. Where a rules-based model might be able to consider only a handful of customer characteristics in defining a segment, algorithm-based models often deal with hundreds or thousands of factors when identifying what makes customers similar.

In practice, business analytics becomes a strong counteracting force against Porter's Five Forces, allowing organizations to:

- Better target distinct groupings of customers
- Increase differentiation in customer treatment patterns
- Optimize pricing structures
- Reduce costs by increasing automation and efficiencies
- Scale to deal with increasingly complex market strategies

Although business analytics is not the only way of delivering these generic strategies, it is often an extremely cost-effective choice. And, it can often be delivered faster than other enabling options.

BUSINESS ANALYTICS AND THE INTERNAL VIEW

Another point of view is to derive strategy based on the internal characteristics of an organization. While this approach is often seen as a direct alternative to Porter's Five Forces, it is arguably better viewed as a complementary position.

Resource-Based View of the Firm

Rather than start with the assumption that the external environment dictates organizational strategy, this perspective argues that an organization is a construct of resources and competencies. Because of this, competitive advantage comes from reconfiguring these internal factors in a way to add value or differentiate the organization from other competitors.

While the external environment still has a role to play in dictating what level of differentiation is needed to achieve competitive advantage, strategic planning in this context is more focused on identifying the best allocation of resources, the ideal internal processes, and the most important competencies to develop. Success in the market requires leveraging tangible and intangible resources through core competencies to create distinctive capabilities that lead to sustainable competitive advantage.

One of the most effective ways of creating this sustainable competitive advantage is to focus on acquiring or developing resources that are:

- **V**aluable
- **R**are
- **I**nimitable
- **N**onsubstitutable

These are sometimes referred to as *VRIN* resources.

Valuable resources are resources that allow an organization to achieve improvements in efficiency and effectiveness if leveraged. Similar to the perspective used within a SWOT analysis, valuable resources allow organizations to either create a strength or mitigate a weakness.

Rare resources are held only by the organization in question and are difficult to source by other organizations. By definition, if a resource is available to many organizations within a given market, it is unlikely that it will lead to sustainable competitive advantage.

Inimitable resources cannot be easily replicated by other organizations; they represent a uniqueness that leads directly to competitive advantage. They may come from location, experience, or any other number of factors; what is important is that they are hard to copy. Three common reasons for this uniqueness are:

1. History
2. Causal ambiguity
3. Social complexity

The historical choices made by an organization may lead directly to a unique resource. Without replicating the entire history of the organization exactly, it may be impossible to develop the same resource.

Equally, the organization itself may not know how it developed the resource in question; the resource may have been accidentally created through a series of fortunate choices. Creating a positive culture is a common example: An organization may experience success through innovation, encouraging ideas, and just "having the right attitude." Although there are often lots of theories as to why this culture may have developed, it is extremely hard to replicate. This causal ambiguity makes it extremely difficult, if not impossible, for other organizations to replicate the resource.

Finally, the resource may have been created through various complex social interactions, such as a particular combination of skill sets carried by internal resources. Having the right combination of organizational structure, highly unique skill sets, and the right supporting processes can sometimes create highly inimitable resources.

The final necessary condition is that the resource be nonsubstitutable. While a particular resource (such as a leadership team) may be valuable, rare, and inimitable, it is not necessarily nonsubstitutable—by hiring another team with similar capabilities, another organization may be able to replicate the same strategic outcomes without having access to a directly equivalent resource.

Sustainable competitive advantage arises from acquiring or developing resources that meet all these characteristics. They represent a strong focus on the uniqueness of the organization itself as a source of competitive advantage.

Strategic Planning Using the Resource-Based View of the Firm

As this approach emphasizes competitive advantage coming from within, strategic planning involves five core steps:

1. Understand the resources available within the organization, especially those that are valuable, rare, inimitable, and nonsubstitutable.

2. Identify the organization's competencies and core capabilities.

3. Profile the profit-making capacity of resources and competencies in terms of their potential for competitive advantage and their ability to generate revenue streams.

4. Develop a strategy based on these findings that best leverages the resources and competencies available within the organization.

5. Identify any resource or competency gaps and invest in strengthening or creating these.

While comparisons against competitors and the external environment are not explicitly conducted, they are implicit in resources meeting VRIN criteria.

Business Analytics as a Critical Enabler

Because of this internal focus, business analytics forms a direct enabler when applying the resource-based view of strategic planning. Business analytics creates both competencies *and* resources that, when effectively executed, meet the requirements for VRIN resources. One of the reasons for this is the high level of alignment between good use of business analytics and unique organizational characteristics; whereas the technology and resources are often highly portable between organizations, the execution and use of these resources can vary significantly and meet the core requirements for either historical dependency or social complexity.

For example, a market analytics team may develop their competencies and processes over a number of years, tailoring them heavily to the organization's unique information ecosystem. These competencies could include specific segmentation, market insight, predictive modeling, and deployment skills. And, the resources development may include individuals, technology platforms, and organizational structures and cross-team relationships that facilitate this approach to customer engagement.

By leveraging the unique set of total technology available to it through sustained effort, the organization may be able to achieve faster-than-market-average time to execute campaign activities, which will create a competitive advantage around its ability to bring new products to market as well as increase customer communication relevancy regardless of changing environmental characteristics.

Getting to this point requires navigating significant social complexity. It often involves working with a large number of discrete teams within the organization spanning multiple business units. And, creating these processes is often a byproduct of a sustained history of many incremental improvements, making it extremely difficult for other firms to replicate.

It is important to note that this execution in its own right does not create sustainable competitive advantage; given enough time, competitors could possibly replicate these benefits through creating substitutable resources. Instead, sustainable competitive advantage comes from creating an organizational culture that focuses on leveraging business analytics within a large variety of processes. By transforming the organization, business analytics creates a culture of smarter, faster, and more effective decision making, a distinct competitive advantage in its own right.

BUSINESS ANALYTICS AND THE CUSTOMER VIEW

A final perspective on strategic planning is to put the customer at the forefront of strategy. Within this context, competitive advantage comes from establishing a high level of customer bonding, thereby discouraging them from moving to the competition.

Wilde and Hax's Delta Model

Successfully achieving this level of bonding comes through three possible strategies:

1. Best product
2. Total customer solutions
3. System lock-in

These represent points on a spectrum, as shown in Figure 2.5.

Best product is closely aligned to Porter's generic strategies; using this strategy requires achieving either a high level of product

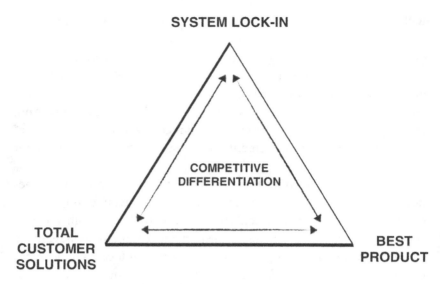

Figure 2.5 Wilde and Hax's Delta Model. *Source: Adapted from Alfonso Hax*, The Delta Model *(New York: Springer, 2010).*

differentiation or becoming the cost leader. This competitive advantage may stem from innovation, economies of scale, or any other number of commonly cited economic factors.

A key criticism against this approach is that differentiation is dynamic and rarely sustainable in isolation—once a product is available in the market, it is often only a matter of time until competitors duplicate its value proposition. Ongoing dominance through differentiation requires a culture of continuous innovation, something that is frequently hard to develop. This perspective therefore suggests that the outcome is more often than not commoditization when this strategy is used.

A second possible strategy involves offering *total customer solutions*. Practically, this means achieving three things:

1. Relevancy and understanding of your customers, through *segmentation*

2. Making things easier for your customers than they would have been otherwise, through *effective delivery*

3. Increasing the breadth of dealings with your customers, through *horizontal breadth*

By understanding the patterns of what its customers are looking for, the organization can better establish a unique value proposition for each of these groups. If the organization is more effective in solving customers' problems than they are, customers will prefer to engage in a relationship. And by expanding the breadth of this relationship to as wide a portfolio as possible, the organization decreases transaction costs and increases value proportionally.

This strategy hinges on providing what is effectively a "one-stop-shop" for a customer and focusing on cooperation and relationships over acquisition and competition. Value comes from moving away from selling products and instead solving customers' problems, even if this means leveraging external partners within the value chain.

System lock-in involves establishing an ecosystem with such strong system economics that moving to alternative market offerings creates active economic disincentives. For example, one of the benefits of a dominant technology platform is that it is easy to source skills, find applications, and source developers. Apple's wildly successful App Store provides a prime example of how effective this strategy can be: Developers and consumers are linked through access to an attractive ecosystem that covers hardware, distribution, development, and commerce. While other platforms may be available, moving to them requires sacrificing ease of sourcing resources and support as well as increasing overall risk. In Apple's case, moving to any other mobile platform means sacrificing access to a large set of consumers from the developer's perspective and access to a wide variety of highly functional apps from the consumer's perspective. These directly discourage customers from migrating, even if they are unhappy with their current platform.

Not every organization has the potential to deliver this strategy; many industries lack sufficient network externalities to allow such a strategy to succeed. Organizations that form one small part of an overall value network may find it impossible to achieve system lock-in. However, by understanding the power of system lock-in as a strategy and actively looking for ways to encourage it, even non-network-based organizations can sometimes increase their overall value proposition to a customer. For example, an organization can focus on the creation of industry standards or vertical integration through acquisition or exclusionary contracts.

In practice, these three strategies are not mutually exclusive— many organizations balance between two of these approaches. Importantly, however, each of these is focused on the *customer's perception of value*, not the *product design*. Competitive advantage stems from developing and executing strategies that achieve a high level of customer bonding, regardless of which of the three approaches is adopted.

Strategic Planning Using the Delta Model

In many situations, this is an iterative process; assumptions are made, tested, and refined based on further research. Planners start by considering the organization's current and desired strategic position within the three core bonding strategies. For some organizations, this may identify a desire to move from a best-product position to a hybrid best-product/total-customer-solutions position with the intention of increasing margins and growing revenues through cross-selling multiple services.

Once a desired strategic position has been identified, planners define the mission of the business, the scope of markets it will be competing in, and the competencies required to support these activities. It may seem somewhat counterintuitive to consider this *after* identifying the preferred strategic position, but the reason for doing it in this order is simple: Focusing on how the organization wants to interact with its customers helps clarify where it should be competing. If the mission and scope are defined before this interaction and value-creation preference, a primary source of competitive advantage may be eliminated.

From there, planners consider the production and external characteristics that define the positioning and context of the organization.

Profiling production activities that create profitability helps identify potential sources of competitive advantage and operational efficiencies. Importantly, though, these activities are not limited to a purely internal focus; as the strategies focus on the entire customer value proposition, it is essential to also consider the role of the system as a whole as well as the sum of all value-chain activities.

Profiling external activities often starts with Porter's Five Forces model but makes one important modification: It relaxes the requirement to consider competitive rivalry as the only dominant force. Instead, it may be more important to consider overall customer/value-provider bonding. For example, while a best-product strategy may encourage rivalry, a total-customer-solutions strategy may instead encourage complementary partnering or playing the role of a centralized value exchange *and* service provider.

Developing an Execution Plan

Once this profiling has been completed, planners develop an execution plan involving the following three factors, their relative importance and role having been defined by the context of their objectives and organizational context:

1. Operational effectiveness
2. Innovation
3. Customer targeting

Operational effectiveness covers all processes associated with delivering value to the customer. In a classic sense, this would normally include all internal production, supply chain, and service delivery activities. However, the Delta model goes a step further and looks at *all* value-chain activities, also covering suppliers, customer behaviors, and potential partners/complementors. As would be expected, the major focuses of this process are on capacity and efficiency.

Innovation revolves around the creation of new products and services to offer to the customer. In a classic sense, this would normally be limited to internal product development. However, the Delta model also includes considering how external parties can add value to the customer through various forms of complementary positioning. The major focus within this process is on the creation of differentiation and continuous business renewal.

Customer targeting focuses on the activities involved with attracting, acquiring, retaining, growing, and understanding new and existing customers. Effective segmentation forms a critical enabler within this process, as the ability to discriminate between high-value and low-value customers, reduce interaction and servicing costs appropriately, and engage effectively drives revenue growth and overall profitability.

Business Analytics as a Critical Enabler

Much like the other views of strategic planning, business analytics has the capability to both support strategy as well as provide competitive advantage. Regardless of which position is favored by the planners, business analytics has a role it can play in supporting all three processes within the execution plan.

For example, for an organization intent on pursuing a best-product strategy, business analytics can help achieve operational efficiencies in a wide variety of ways. These could include supply-chain optimization, process improvement through the application of six-sigma methodologies, and measuring total cost of service delivery.

For an organization intent on pursuing a total-customer-solutions strategy, business analytics can help improve customer targeting effectiveness in a wide variety of ways. These could include the application of segmentation models, customer profitability measurement, and the creation of cross-sell and up-sell models to improve horizontal breadth.

For an organization intent on pursuing a system-lock-in strategy, business analytics can help improve innovation effectiveness in a wide variety of ways. These could include highly scalable exchanges that automatically link potentially interested parties or large-scale test-and-learn strategies to identify highly marketable products.

Because the execution of these strategies requires a strong understanding of customer preferences, highly scalable systems support, and excellent access to information, business analytics becomes a significant driver for competitive advantage. Again, while it is not the only source of competitive advantage, it has a unique value proposition in that it can be applied to support multiple execution strategies, making it a competitive differentiator in its own right.

FOSTERING INNOVATION AND INVENTION

Innovation and invention play a critical role in creating competitive advantage. The difference between the two is important: Whereas invention makes ideas a tangible reality, innovation involves doing things differently. Invention may form an important part of delivering innovation, but it is not an essential part.

Innovation often plays a role within strategic planning processes. Whereas strategic planning may help identify a preferred path, innovation can act as a significant force to drive a favorable disequilibrium in the market. By doing things differently, organizations can increase their level of market differentiation and, by doing so, their overall market power. In practice, this often means greater revenue, higher profitability, or increased efficiencies.

Creating innovation is a challenging process; research suggests that the vast majority of innovation activities have little or no impact. However, if successful, innovation has the potential to create not only sustainable advantage but also a temporary monopoly, significantly increasing profits in the short term.

This market disruption can stem from a variety of sources. Technological advancement through research and development can drive significant changes but is hard to predict. Strategic innovation can stem from deliberately focusing on changing the external environment through activities such as:

- Creating a new market
- Developing new products
- Establishing new production methods

All of these objectives are made easier through the application of business analytics. By leveraging the information assets available within the organization, it can reduce uncertainty and improve clarity around target goals, two major reasons behind unsuccessful projects.

Creating a new market is challenging—by definition, the market does not exist. One approach is to launch and hope for the best. A better approach involves using various forms of advanced analytics to understand and model potential cannibalization levels, segment and size target markets, and model the rate of diffusion (and implied profitability) under different assumptions.

Similarly, developing new products is challenging, especially when it comes to understanding customer price sensitivities, the potential for product overlap, and market interest in bundled goods or services.

Again, business analytics has the potential to model these considerations prior to market launch, reducing uncertainty and helping to either redirect focus onto more profitable activities or adjust product design to better increase the odds of success.

Finally, establishing production efficiencies can be challenging without the aid of advanced analytics. It can be hard to understand the relationships between controllable factors and output quality or reliability in many complicated production processes. Techniques such as design of experiments can make this analysis simpler *and* more effective. And optimizing a multi-echelon supply chain can be close to impossible without the aid of advanced analytics; while it is often possible to achieve a *better* outcome through manual optimization, it is hard to know whether one has achieved the *best* outcome.

While business analytics may not always have the ability to create innovation in its own right, it is more often than not a key enabler in delivering innovation.

DELIVERING VALUE THROUGH RENEWABLE RETURN

A final reason behind why organizations are increasingly applying business analytics for competitive advantage has to do with its potential for regular incremental return. Unlike the typical investment model where a given investment delivers a one-off return (which may be staggered over a number of years), business analytics has the potential to generate new returns year on year with relatively minimal additional investment.

Because the competencies used within a business analytics team can be applied to multiple business problems, the organization has the potential to reuse these competencies to deliver new returns. And, because business analytics can be readily translated into operational processes, historical gains can be continually captured over time.

Analytics is one of the few areas in business that can truly deliver renewable returns. Unlike many business investments, the return on technology and skills investment is not limited to the project to which they are initially associated; by being linked to generalizable assets, the investment can be continually releveraged to give additional incremental returns.

A good example lies in the development of a predictive modeling competency. The first project may involve reducing customer churn rates; the total costs booked against this project include:

- Hiring and training of new staff
- Technology platform acquisition
- Systems integration work

On successful completion, the project will accrue various returns to the business. The processes developed by the team will be deployed for ongoing scoring, helping to ensure that the returns captured will continue to exist in the future. And, if properly managed for efficiency, the team will again become available to work on a new project.

This project might involve the creation of various up-sell and cross-sell models to help increase share of wallet and overall sales volumes. It is here that the value of business analytics shines: Despite its being a fundamentally new problem with different requirements and no overlapping value potential, *the organization requires virtually no incremental investment to deliver it.*

The same team, using the same technology and the same processes, can help deliver direct economic value in a totally new way. This potential for constantly renewable returns at relatively low cost cannot be underestimated as a platform for growth.

A Practical Example: The ERP Approach

It is useful to contrast an investment in analytics with an investment in a traditional enterprise resource planning (ERP) system. Both require an investment in technology, people, process, and data. And both require changing how business is conducted to varying degrees, largely dependent on the maturity of the organization. However, that is where the similarities end.

As most organizations will attest, embarking on an ERP transformation is a nontrivial task; project life cycles are typically measured in the order of years. Operational and transactional management are the focus, and strictly defined processes are the norm. Most importantly within the context of this book, the benefits (while often large and real) are typically one-off and linked to the completion of the implementation.

A good practical example is the implementation of an improved ordering and inventory planning system. Within most retail organizations, inventory management and ordering is the lifeblood that keeps the heart pumping. If the right stock is not in the right place at the right time, orders go unfilled. One of the most painful things a seller can possibly see is an interested customer walking out to a competitor simply because the product she was interested in is not on the shelf at that point in time!

By implementing a more efficient ordering system, store managers often have greater time to spend analyzing stock flows, seasonal patterns, and future product releases—and, by doing so (the theory goes), make better orders. These better orders may have a number of benefits, including:

- Increasing the speed at which products on shelves move (leading to better revenue)
- Allowing the manager to focus on goods that offer higher margins (improving profitability)
- Allowing the manager to reduce stocks of slow-moving goods (reducing capital investment and improving liquidity)

All of these are real financial benefits, but once the ERP system goes live and is embedded within normal ordering processes, that is *it*. Because the ERP system is built and tailored to improve a specific process, the benefits are capped to that specific process. Once things are better, that is the end of it; additional benefits require additional investment in new technology, people, process, and (often) data.

Analytics is different. Although a good analytics project is still tightly aligned to a specific business problem, the technology, people, process, and data are far more generalizable to other business problems. In practice, significant percentages of these capabilities can be reused to solve other business problems, leading to ongoing incremental returns on investment.

A Counterexample: The Analytics Approach

Solving that same inventory management and ordering problem using analytics might involve a slightly different approach; the same organization might focus on augmenting its ordering and inventory management processes by applying forecasting and stock optimization techniques. By using analytical forecasting, it might be able to isolate seasonal factors, model the effects of promotional activity on sales, and improve aggregate baseline forecast accuracy through sheer computational scalability. By applying optimization, it might be able to dynamically adjust safety stock levels based on underlying demand, ensuring that the probability that the organization has a stock-out remains below a certain desired level. This may even take into account differing levels of profitability by product, allowing every product to have a different safety stock level that varies automatically throughout the year as the underlying demand patterns change.

As with the ERP system, these benefits are realized only once; after the processes are embedded and management efficiencies have been accrued, all of the project benefits have been capitalized. However, that is where the similarity ends.

How Business Analytics Delivers Renewable Value

As it turns out, the same organization may also have issues with its marketing efficiency. On a day-to-day basis, it may be contacting too many potential customers (incurring needless costs) or the wrong potential customers (causing those same customers to start shopping elsewhere), or not contacting the "right" customers at all (missing on out potential sales). The ERP approach would be to implement another parallel system to reduce marketing costs through making the overall process more efficient. It may involve leveraging additional, lower-cost channels such as e-mail, SMS, or targeted online advertisements. However, regardless of the approach used, the degree of overlap with the order management system already implemented is likely to be low.

Doing this through an ERP system will very likely require that additional investment be made into people, process, technology, and data. New processes will need to be defined along with supporting rules and activities. New people will need to be hired to manage and execute the processes. New tools will need to be purchased and implemented. New operational data structures will need to be put in place to support these new processes.

Analytics offers an alternative. At their core, both problems have a common root: the need to minimize use of a limited resource for maximal gain. For stock management, it is all about minimizing investment in stock while simultaneously trying to maximize sales. For marketing, it is all about minimizing marketing cost by communication channel (such as telephone versus e-mail) while maximizing customer purchasing patterns. As both problems share a common root, the same capability can be leveraged across both of them.

Importantly, it can be done through using common resources, minimizing additional investment in people, process, technology and data. Because the analytics approach leverages the existing customer contact platform, minimal additional processes are required. Because it leverages the same skills being used to support stock optimization, minimal additional resources are required. Because it uses the same optimization platform, minimal additional tools are required. And, because it uses existing data, minimal extensions are required to the organization's existing data stores!

This is not to say that ERP systems and analytics are replacements for each other; in practice, they are both necessary components in effective and efficient competition. Best-in-class organizations understand how to leverage both. However, the differences between them are why analytics is such a critical enabler for industry-leading performance: It allows organizations to achieve ongoing incremental return on investment with proportionally small reinvestment requirements.

What does this mean in practice? It means that unlike ERP systems, analytics creates renewable value. It means that the same capabilities developed to improve identifying which products to sell to which customers can be used to proactively identify potential occupational health and safety risks. It means that the same capabilities developed to predict how much product will be needed in a given month can also be used to assist in large-scale network planning. It means that the same capabilities developed to identify the minimum rate needed to be offered to retain a term deposit can be used to maximize collections of bad and doubtful debts.

Simply put, analytics offers business improvements unlike any other system, ones that have the potential to give new annualized returns, year after year.

SUMMARY

Within this chapter we have reviewed the importance of business analytics within a variety of strategic planning frameworks. Within each of the perspectives, business analytics has the potential to play a key enabling role regardless of where competitive advantage stems from. Equally, business analytics has the potential to act as a key enabler for innovation and an ability to deliver constantly growing incremental economic returns.

With all this going for it, it is not surprising that business analytics is seen as a key strategic enabler and differentiator by so many organizations. However, translating these strategic imperatives into tactical delivery plans is often challenging.

Over the next chapter we will move from a strategic view to a tactical view, looking specifically at:

- What business analytics means in practice
- Where barriers to success come from and why
- A high-level view of how to manage these challenges

NOTE

1. R. H. Coase, "The Nature of the Firm," *Economica* 4, no. 16 (1937): 386–405.

CHAPTER 3

The Challenges of Tactical Delivery

INTRODUCTION

In the previous chapter we covered the reasons behind the importance of business analytics as a path to competitive advantage. That it is a core enabler within a variety of strategic planning frameworks is not surprising; as we have already covered, business analytics is one of the few disciplines that can deliver incremental return with relatively minimal additional investment. However, even though it is broadly acknowledged that business analytics is both important and valuable, there is not as much guidance on why some teams are successful and some are not.

Davenport and Harris, through their research in *Competing on Analytics*, have shown that one of the key differentiators between organizations that are average or poor performers in their industry or segment and those that are considered leaders is their ability to make better decisions through applying business analytics.[1] However, it is important to distinguish between the actual *use* of analytics and an *intention* to apply analytics; reality is not kind enough to reward every company that announces a strong belief in business analytics as a competitive enabler.

In practice, not every team is successful. Even among those that are successful, the level of success varies significantly. Whereas some successfully transform the organization, others simply manage to stay afloat in what rapidly evolves into a highly challenging (and often frustrating) environment of firefighting with no strategic focus.

The reasons behind these successes can be both obvious and deceptively elusive. Although virtually every team has a strategy to deliver increased value, it is telling that many struggle, miss deadlines, and are constantly stymied by their own organizations. To understand why, within this chapter we cover:

- The vocabulary used throughout this book
- Team composition and how it fits within the organization
- The most common internal challenges that prevent a team from succeeding

CORE VOCABULARY

Throughout this book we will be using certain terms repeatedly; for clarity, we will spend some time here defining what they mean.

The Business Analytics Team

At its core, a *business analytics team* is charged with *creating value*. We will consider the many meanings of *value* in Chapter 4, but for now we will say that it is often *economic return* in some form. Common examples include revenue growth, profitability improvements, or cost reductions.

The team delivers this value through *leveraging competencies* within *specific roles*, using *tools* and in the process, *creating a series of assets*. Within this book, an asset is some form of *tangible or intangible object* that can be tracked, viewed, managed, and used. Much like the resource-based view of strategic planning, the team takes time, experience, and other resources and, through application, creates these assets, which then act as vehicles for value delivery.

To create these assets, the team leverages two environments within a single *analytics platform*: a discovery environment and an operational environment. These platforms offer standardized tools and allow the creation, reuse, and management of standardized assets. The team's discovery environment is used to generate insight and develop assets and its operational environment is used to turn these assets into operational processes.

Over the next few subsections, we will define each of these in greater detail.

Competencies

Developing *processes*, *models*, and other *assets* requires various *competencies*. A competency is a particular set of skills that can be applied across multiple business problems. Examples include:

- Predictive modeling using decision trees
- Operations research and optimization
- Text analytics to understand unstructured data

Importantly, a competency can be used within multiple contexts— building and interpreting decision trees, for example, can be used to aid customer segmentation, retention modeling, or cross-selling products. Social network analysis can be used for viral marketing, for preventing contagious churn, or for identifying fraud or collusion.

Competencies require the investment of *time*, the *right supporting roles*, and the *use of tools*; while technical understanding is a key part of developing a new competency, it is not the only part. Also important are:

- An understanding of how it can be applied for business value
- Awareness of how to transform results into an asset
- A plan for how to build it into an operational process

Tools

Tools are the basic building block with which most assets are created. They can be internally developed or purchased off the shelf, but without an appropriate set of purpose-built tools, a business analytics team is unable to create any new assets. A good analogy lies in building a house—regardless of how competent a builder is, without any tools he will be unable to construct a house. The rate of depreciation tools experience varies and is highly related to technological advancement.

Assets

Competencies are applied by the team using *tools* to create *assets*. The most common classes of assets within a business analytics team include:

- Strongly defined processes
- Datamarts
- Models
- Reports
- Documentation

Processes can be either strongly defined or weakly defined, as described in Figure 3.1. A *strongly defined process* is any series of steps that:

- Is clearly defined
- Is repeatable
- Can be automated
- Leads to the creation of value

Critically, it is not an asset if it cannot be automated or if it is not strictly repeatable by anyone else within the team. In contrast, although a weakly defined process may lead to value creation, it is a one-off activity that is neither generalizable nor repeatable by anyone else within the team.

A good example of a strongly defined process is a *scoring process*. A scoring process takes a set of input data, applies various transformation and imputations, applies a formula to the result, and delivers the resulting scores (such as propensity or risk estimations) to a defined location. The entire end-to-end process can be automated and

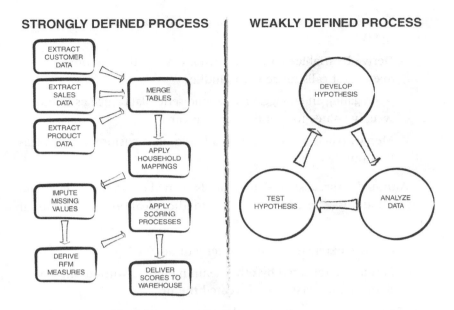

Figure 3.1 Strongly versus Weakly Defined Processes

deployed in such a way that it requires minimal (if any) manual interaction.

A *weakly defined process* has no such structure; it relies on the skill and ingenuity of the analyst to complete successfully. A good example is exploratory data analysis: Though the tools may be common across business problems, the actual process the analyst goes through to get to a point where she *can* create a standardized scoring process may vary significantly by both the business problem and the analyst doing the work. Although it is still a generally defined process that the analyst will go through, it is not an asset within this context because it has insufficient structure to be defined, tracked, monitored, repeated, and automated.

Within this overall class of processes, the principal ones of interest to a business analytics team are often *data management processes*. These are a series of well-defined steps that take data from several locations, potentially alter it, and deliver it to another location. Common alterations can include:

- Transformations (such as taking the natural logarithm of a field)
- Derived variables (such as calculating the three-month rolling average of calls made on a landline)
- Aggregating and disaggregating time-series data (such as summing weekly values to monthly or vice versa)
- Merges (such as joining tables based on a customer identification number)

Although spreadsheet-based tools can be used to do data transformations, these do not lead to the creation of an asset if they:

- Require extensive manual intervention
- Cannot be repeated by other team members without any oversight by the person who created the process
- Are incapable of tracking the resources consumed when creating and using them

Data management processes often leverage *datamarts*. Datamarts are centralized repositories containing source and value-added information to be used by other business analytics assets. The specific architecture and data structures can vary, but they promote the core concepts of:

- Data reuse
- Trusted data
- High-quality data (relevant, accurate, and complete)
- Pragmatic storage minimization

As data is a foundational building block for the business analytics team, often the only alternative is to store the requisite data on individual PCs. This inevitably leads to a number of significant inefficiencies, including:

- Excessive time spent duplicating data management processes between team members

- Reductions in accuracy and timeliness of delivery due to varying levels of data quality
- Delays in deployment due to differences in process definition and data sourcing
- High risk of operational failure or loss of IP when systems fail

Data management processes and data from datamarts are combined to create various *models* and *reports*. Within the context of business analytics, models are abstractions that describe reality in various useful ways. They may be *rules-based* or they may be *algorithmically based*, but critically, they can be applied to data contained within datamarts. There is an extremely wide variety of models that can be created and applied, but the most common types of models and their usages are described in Table 3.1.

Table 3.1 Common Model Types

Type	Usage	Example Application
Grouping models	Group data into specific categories	Segmenting customers into groups that display common behaviors
Propensity models	Predict a probabilistic outcome	Predicting the likelihood of someone buying a given product
Relational models	Identify strength and significance of relationships	Predicting the likelihood of two goods being sold together
Optimization models	Identify the best possible combination of inputs to maximize or minimize a target outcome	Identifying the most efficient route for a delivery truck to take within a network
Simplification models	Collapse highly dimensional information into more manageable bits of information	Identifying and extracting the entities described in articles to make it easier to find information

At a practical level, these models typically take the form of logical rules or formulas that when applied create various scores or assessments against data elements such as customers, accounts, or documents.

These models are assets only when they can be used in an ongoing manner. If they cannot be applied to new data as it becomes available, they are not assets. In the case of a retention model, it is only an asset if it can be applied on a regular basis to identify existing customers who are likely to churn. If it cannot, it may still have added value, but it is fundamentally a research outcome, something we will cover shortly.

Reports are similar to models in that they take a set of input data and apply various transformation processes to it, but instead of creating a prediction or classification, *they present insight in a visually appealing and informative manner.* Simply, they are the visual presentation of insight, created through a repeatable data management process. Common examples include management reporting, model degradation reports, and customer activity reports. As with other assets, a key characteristic is that they can be automated and are repeatable.

The Analytical Platform

These assets do not exist within a vacuum; they are created within an *analytical platform* of some form. This platform is a technical necessity to support the tools used, and to provide an area for data storage and a platform for asset creation. The traditional view of an analytical platform is one that goes through a fairly standard maturity model, described in Figure 3.2.

At the lowest level is *unstructured chaos*. Multiple tools are used, licenses are primarily desktop based, and tool usage varies from team member to team member. Though an enterprise-level datamart may or may not exist, the business analytics team will definitely lack a standardized data management model—every team member maintains his or her own set of data according to the individual's storage and usage requirements. Process inefficiencies are high, competencies

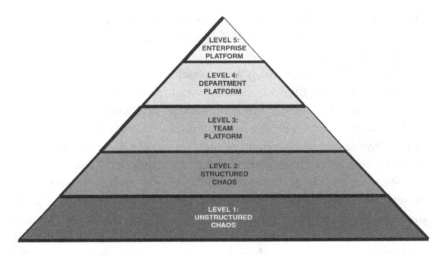

Figure 3.2 The Analytical Platform Maturity Model

are rarely shared between team members, and repeatability is extremely low.

Needless to say, this introduces a significant number of inefficiencies:

- Knowledge and capability vary from individual to individual and, because different tools are used by different individuals, mentoring is extremely difficult.

- Data management processes are typically repeated across individuals, wasting significant amounts of time.

- Assets are rare as no platform exists to provide robust automation or generalizability among team members.

The movement to the second level, *structured chaos*, involves standardizing on a subset of tools. These are still PC based and often somewhat loosely defined, but the team at least makes an effort to limit the number of tools the members are using to a common minimum. Some degree of collaboration exists, but this is driven primarily by individuals, not culture or management. Many of the challenges associated with operating at level 1 still exist, but the team moves to a slightly higher level of process commonality due to selection of a single subset of tools.

The third level of maturity is the establishment of a *team platform*. Typically, this takes the form of movement from a PC-based licensing model to a server-based licensing model. However, this move is limited to the team level; the broader organization is either unaware of or unwilling to apply analytics more generally. Data is often standardized into a single analytical datamart, the team typically starts the standardization of its data extraction and transformation processes, and competencies are often held by more than one team member by virtue of common access to tool sets. However, scoring processes are rarely integrated into the broader organization and competencies are rarely shared or leveraged by the rest of the business.

The fourth level of maturity is the creation of a *departmental platform*. Typically, this occurs in parallel with an increasing internal recognition of the value that business analytics brings as well as a cultural shift encouraging the application of business analytics wherever possible. The same approach used by the team is spread across an entire department.

The fifth, and highest, level of maturity is an *enterprise platform*. This is normally aligned with a top-down commitment to using business analytics as a cornerstone of competitive advantage. At this level, the organization often applies analytics across every business process, including logistics, pricing, marketing, and even sometimes occupational health and safety as well as human resources.

Various indicators of analytical platform maturity across the key dimensions of tools, data management processes, datamarts, and competencies are shown in Table 3.2.

Discovery and Operational Environments

Within this overall platform exist two environments: a *discovery environment* and an *operational environment*. The discovery environment

Table 3.2 Analytical Platform Maturity Indicators

	Tools	Datamart	Processes	Competencies
Level 1: Unstructured Chaos	Wide variety of desktop-based tools	Data often exists in tabular format on individual PCs and no sharing occurs.	Processes are undefined.	Individuals are explicitly linked to competencies, which are applied only where individuals "own" the project.
Level 2: Structured Chaos	Common desktop-based tools	Data often exists in tabular format on shared network drives and some sharing occurs.	Processes are weakly defined at best.	Individuals are explicitly linked to competencies, but these are applied across multiple projects.
Level 3: Dominant Team Platform	Common team-level server-based environment	Data exists in a common team-level datamart and sharing regularly occurs.	Strongly and weakly defined processes exist within the team, as appropriate.	Competencies are held by the team, not by individuals, and lineage planning/up-skilling occurs at a team-level.
Level 4: Dominant Departmental Platform	Common department-level server-based environment	Data exists in a common department-level datamart and cross-functional sharing occurs.	Strongly and weakly defined processes exist at a departmental level; execution processes are well understood.	Competencies are recognized by the department and applied across multiple projects.
Level 5: Dominant Enterprise Platform	Common enterprise-level server-based environment	Data exists in departmental datamarts and cross-functional sharing and linkages regularly occur.	Strongly and weakly defined processes exist across multiple departments; interconnections are well understood.	Competencies are recognized by the organization and contribute to competitive differentiation.

is primarily used to create assets and generate insight—it is often referred to as a "playpen," a workbench, or a modeling environment.

Supporting this is the counterpart to the discovery environment: the operational environment. This gives organizations the ability to deploy models into production and, by doing so, integrate analytics into operational processes. Once a model or report has been built, it needs to be used in an ongoing process. In the lower levels of maturity, many organizations are unaware of the importance of an operational environment and often conduct both discovery and operational activities in the same environment.

The relationship between a discovery and an operational environment is described in Figure 3.3.

The distinction between a discovery environment and an operational environment is a critical one. Broadly speaking, a discovery environment is normally designed to support analytical development and insight creation activities. In most cases, this includes:

- One-off research projects
- Model development activities
- Exploratory data analysis

At the highest level, the activities conducted in a discovery environment focus on insight over operational execution. Specifically, these activities have:

- *No strict requirements around how long jobs take to complete.* Often, "sometime today" is good enough. Whether a processing job takes five minutes or an hour is often of little importance as long as it is fast enough to answer the business question in a reasonable amount of time.

- *Minimal impact on the business through short-term environment downtimes.* It normally matters little whether the answer is provided in the morning or the afternoon—as long as it is provided in a reasonably timely manner, it is good enough.

- *Relatively low data redundancy and availability requirements.* Although it may be somewhat irritating for the team,

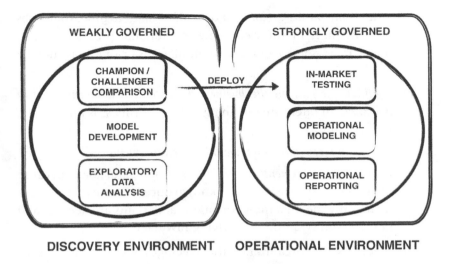

Figure 3.3 Discovery and Operational Environments

having the environment go down inconveniences no one but the direct users.

■ *High storage requirements, primarily for exploratory purposes.* Often, highly granular data is needed because the team members may not know in advance which specific transformation or derivation they will need.

By contrast, an operational environment is designed to support operational business processes. In practice, it could include:

■ Direct integration with outbound campaign delivery processes to provide cross-sell and up-sell propensity scores by customer

■ Real-time identification of potentially fraudulent behaviors in credit card transactional processing facilities

■ Behaviorally based matchmaking media delivery services

Activities conducted in an operational environment have a number of common characteristics. These are:

- *Strict requirements around job-completion time.* If processing jobs do not finish in sufficient time, operational processes halt—offers may not go out or financial transactions may not be processed.

- *Significant impact on the business through short-term environment downtime.* If offers are not going out, the business is not making money.

- *High data redundancy and availability requirements.*

- *Low storage requirements, primarily for scoring input datasets.* Because the model structure is already known once it is ready for deployment, only the final transformations and inputs are needed, and not necessarily all the underlying raw data.

By necessity, any organization that leverages business analytics for operational business value requires an operational environment. The reason these environments must be separated is simple: Discovery environments allow significantly more leeway when it comes to environmental performance. In a business context, this leeway almost directly equates to cost; the lower the tolerances for platform availability issues, the greater the maintenance costs. Architectural choices such as high-availability storage with fast-restore options, highly redundant architectures, and guaranteed runtime completions all increase costs.

When both are run within the same environment, there is no easy way to prevent discovery processes from impacting operational processes. A bad query, a complex application of business analytics, or simple environmental misuse can directly impact the execution of outbound campaigns or fraud detection processes. This is almost always a serious problem—halting operational processes costs real money.

COMMON TEAM STRUCTURES

Organizational structures supporting the use of business analytics tend to follow one of three general patterns, described in Figure 3.4. The most common team structure is *functionally aligned and narrowly focused*. It is normally tasked with meeting a specific vertical requirement

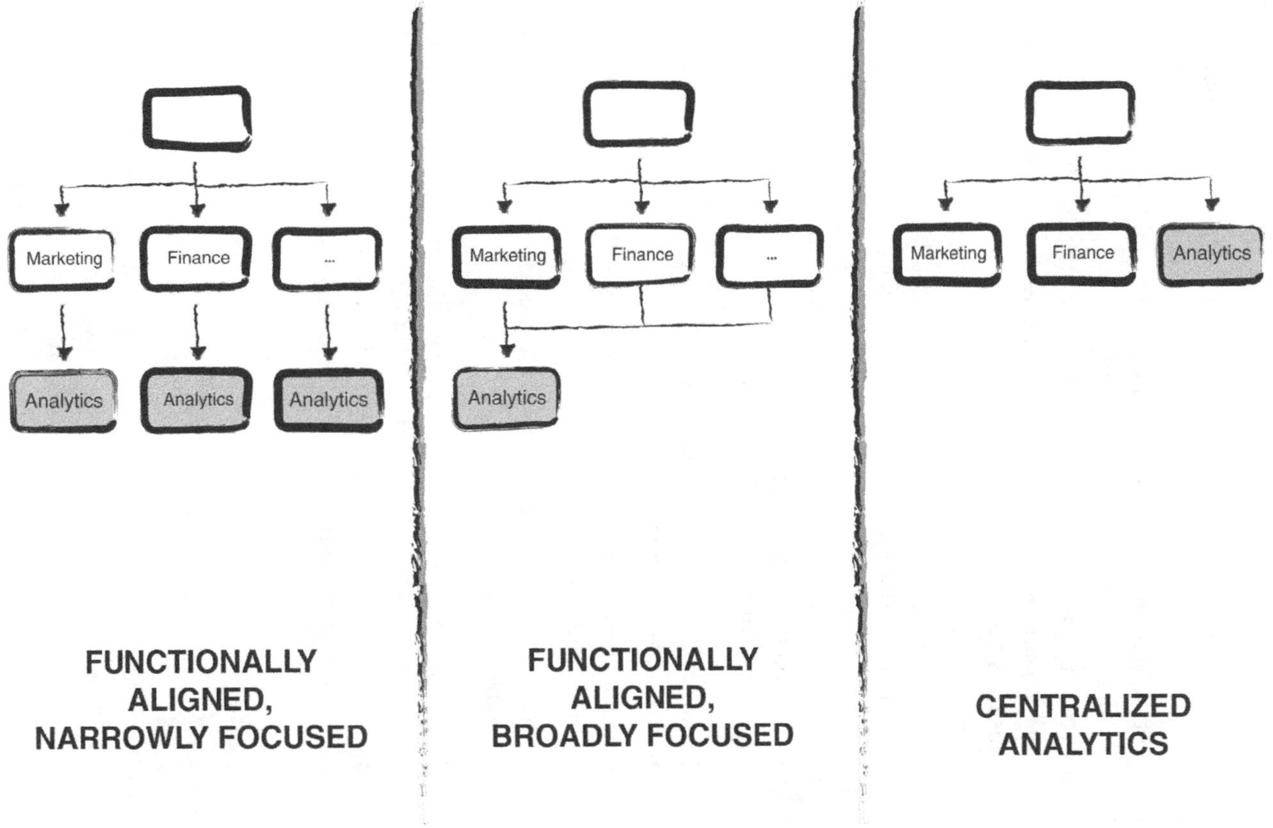

Figure 3.4 Team Structures

within the business, such as identifying fraud or providing market insight. The size of team will often vary, ranging from a few individuals to a large team covering a wide variety of roles and responsibilities. One of the major characteristics of this model is the narrow focus; although the team may have competencies that could be applied elsewhere, it is rare that the team will do so.

This structure may evolve over time into one that is *functionally aligned and broadly focused*. The team will normally report to a single line of business but, due to internal recognition of the value of business analytics, it will also provide support to other lines of business interested in leveraging business analytics within their own processes. The team in this situation tends to be a larger group with a fairly comprehensive set of roles identified.

The most mature structure involves the centralization of business analytics capabilities. The exact nature of this centralization can vary. Common models include:

- *Consultancy*, where the group is cross-charged for their services against other business units
- *Center of excellence*, where the team reports both to a single owner and to "home" business units in a matrix structure
- *Formally centralized*, where the team exists as a business unit in its own right

The centralized model usually involves the team leveraging its competencies across all aspects of the business, focused through either internal demand or strategic imperative. The team in this situation tends to be a larger group with a very comprehensive set of roles identified.

ROLES AND RESPONSIBILITIES

Regardless of whether the team is operating under a centralized or a functional model, building an analytics team is not quite as easy as simply hiring a bunch of smart people and hoping for the best. As with most things, doing it well is somewhat more complex. To turn an economic phrase, people with excellent analytics abilities are a necessary but not sufficient condition for success.

At first, this seems counterintuitive—after all, isn't business analytics all about doing analytics? By that logic, hiring a top-notch statistician should be all that is needed. Although intuitively appealing, that position is true only if applying algorithms is all you do. Within the context of pure research, that is often the case; the outcome of applying analytics is frequently the answer. However, within the commercial and public sector, analytics is always a means to an end; it is a small word, but the inclusion of *business* in "business analytics" changes the focus.

In the professional realm, *the value of analytics is in the action taken from the insight*, whether it be new customers acquired or children saved from domestic violence. Because of this, analytics forms only part of the overall picture. Equally important is the ability of the team to:

- Translate its results into insight and recommended actions
- Make its processes operational
- Generate trust through transparency and evangelism
- Establish efficient processes

Just like any multifunctional team within an organization, an effective analytics team requires more than just statisticians. However, as many analytics teams start relatively small, it is also important to balance the need for multiple roles and responsibilities against what is often a fairly restrictive resource count. In practice, *this often means individuals need to perform more than one function within their role.* So, while the list may seem fairly daunting, it is only the largest organizations that often need every role to be filled by at least one individual. For most organizations, it is simply enough to ensure that they have adequate role coverage across their existing team.

Although not an exhaustive list, the roles (and the value they provide) summarized in Table 3.3 form a useful starting point to establish a core set of capabilities covered by an effective analytics team.

Table 3.3 Core Roles within an Analytics Team

Role	Core Focus	Likely Background	Value Provided
Analytics Team Lead	Lead the team and define strategic direction.	Analytics management	Ensure value creation and interface with management.
Advanced Analytics Modeler	Develop and maintain predictive models.	Statistics, business analytics	Deliver insight through predictive models.
Ad Hoc Analytics Analyst	Respond to ad hoc queries from the business.	Reporting	Assist the business with ongoing insight.
Domain Expert	Provide business-level experience and acumen.	Business	Ensure relevancy of insight.
Data Steward	Standardize analytical data and encourage automation.	Data modeling, Data warehousing	Minimize data management overhead.
Analytics Process Designer	Create and enforce reusable and common processes.	Management consulting	Increase repeatability and reduce execution time.
Monitoring/ Validation Analyst	Establish and enforce common measures within the measurement platform.	Performance management/ finance, business analytics	Measure value and optimize focus.
Deployment Specialist	Ensure fast and robust model deployment.	Data warehousing	Reduce time to market and interface with IT.

Analytics Team Lead

A team is nothing without a leader to define direction; the role of the Analytics Team Lead is to provide this clarity of direction. However, it is more than that; it is also to ensure that the team is presented with sufficient:

- Challenges to keep them interested
- Opportunities to keep them engaged
- Protection to shield them from the sometime excessive demands of the business

Analytics Team Leads ideally play a far greater role in management and mentoring than in modeling. They will often have strong numerical backgrounds, but their skills are best applied to identifying a road map, ensuring value is being delivered to the business, and growing the skills offered by their team.

The role of Analytics Team Leads is to ensure that:

- A strategic plan on how business analytics will deliver competitive advantage is defined and achieved
- They maintain a high level of retention within their team
- Measurable value is regularly being delivered to the organization

Their core capabilities often include:

- Strong people management, mentoring, and coaching skills
- Strategic thinking and planning
- Practical modeling experience in multiple fields

The background of Analytics Team Leads spans both people management and practical business analytics; although it is of lesser importance that they have a strong understanding of everything analytics, it is still essential that they maintain a strong working knowledge of technical information. As the primary interface point between the analytics team and the rest of the organization, they are responsible for ensuring regular growth in value delivery while balancing against the dangers of limiting team activities to business as usual.

Good Analytics Team Leads are not necessarily the best analytics modelers; while there are some skills in common, an excellent analytics modeler does not necessarily make an excellent Analytics Team Lead. The reason for this has much to do with the different skill sets required to build models compared to leading a team. We will cover this in greater detail in Chapter 5 when we discuss various communication and thinking preferences; suffice it to say at this point that often the detailed focus required to do effective predictive modeling and analytics runs contrary to the skills required for developing a team.

A team *can* be hampered by too heavy an analytical focus from its manager. Typically, this is because the best-performing individual within the team is promoted into the Team Lead position without adequate awareness on either the individual's or the organization's side of the skills that need to be developed to perform successfully.

This does not mean analytical managers are incapable of developing the right skill sets; in practice quite the opposite is true! However, these skills are not necessarily a given and, if they do not exist, they need to be developed.

Advanced Analytics Modeler

When it comes to building an analytics team, this is the person most recruiters assume will form the core of the team. The role of the Advanced Analytics Modeler is to answer business needs through the use of various advanced analytics assets.

These individuals tend to have very strong advanced analytics capabilities, often with some degree of specialization in a particular field. Some examples of these specializations could include:

- Time-series analysis
- Optimization and linear programming,
- Cross-sectional modeling
- Risk simulation
- Ratemaking

Typically, their primary role involves developing advanced models to help solve business problems. The defining characteristic of these models is that they are normally intended to be made operational in some form, whether it be a fraud detection process or a monthly cross-sell identification process. These are different from models developed for one-off purposes, such as those used to generate insight or understanding.

As such, the models developed by these team members generally need to be designed in such a way that they can be deployed as a standardized scoring process, often controlled and maintained by other individuals within the organization.

The role of Advanced Analytics Modelers is to ensure that:

- Business problems are defined to a point where a model can be built
- Predictive and classification models are developed to an appropriately accurate and robust level
- Results are communicated in a comprehensible (and not necessarily technical) manner
- Models in deployment are monitored for excessive levels of degradation

Their core capabilities often include:

- A mathematical, statistical, or econometric background with practical business experience
- Strong communications skills
- Familiarity with requirements gathering
- An understanding of project management and methodology definition
- Curiosity and creative thinking

The background of Advanced Analytics Modelers is often quite technical, although the best modelers also have experience that cuts across other fields. Communication skills are a critical component of good modelers; as they are the interface between technical analysis and business outcomes, it is essential that they be able to translate the results of various forms of advanced analytics into something a layperson can understand.

Good modelers come from a variety of backgrounds; as the skills are generally fairly transferable to new business problems, they will often make the jump between industries or business problems.

Ad Hoc Analytics Analyst

As the value of the analytics team is increasingly understood by the broader organization, demands on team members' time often increase substantially. The role of the Ad Hoc Analytics Analyst is to answer questions from the business.

Typically, many of these requests do not require the creation of new models but instead are simply applications of reporting, ad hoc analysis, and sometimes relatively simple forms of advanced analytics (such as correlations, basic regressions, or one-off clustering exercises).

As these insights are more often than not generated without any intention of being deployed as repeatable processes, the focus is more on quick and accurate response rather than achieving model robustness and repeatable process design. The requests tend to be very ad hoc and, although there is often some degree of commonality against existing assets, the process of getting to the answer can vary with every request.

Most organizations have high levels of demand for insight. Because of this, explicitly managing this function is critical—in the absence of this management, analysts within the team can easily get totally consumed responding to ad hoc insight requests from the business.

The role of Ad Hoc Analytics Analysts is to ensure that:

- Ad hoc questions from the business are answered as required
- External stakeholders are getting the insight they need from the team
- The time taken to answer ad hoc requests is as short as possible

Their core capabilities often include:

- Strong data literacy
- Detailed familiarity with advanced forms of reporting and exploratory data analysis

- A strong focus on customer service and rapid delivery
- Strong communication skills

The background of Ad Hoc Analytics Analysts tends to be heavily focused on reporting and exploratory analysis. Similar to Advanced Analytics Modelers, their ability to communicate complex results in a comprehensible way is a critical skill. Unlike Advanced Analytics Modelers, however, they may not come from a mathematical background; instead, it is far more important that they be comfortable with technology and have a strong passion for finding answers in data.

Good Ad Hoc Analytics Analysts come from a variety of locations but are commonly involved in existing reporting and analysis initiatives. Due to the requirement for rapid response, it is often the case that they already have a strong familiarity with the industry or business problem. While it is not essential that they come from within the industry or organization, having the right background does tend to make them more effective in a shorter period of time.

Domain Expert

Analytics without context is next to useless; the role of the Domain Expert is to provide that business context. These individuals fill an essential knowledge gap within most teams by providing deep domain expertise, assisting by ensuring the analytics is relevant, useful, and achieves target business outcomes. Specifically, they frequently:

- Provide insight into how the industry and the organization operate
- Sanity-check outcomes and outputs for business relevancy and value creation
- Assist with interpreting business measures and the meaning of data

Domain Experts provide subject-matter expertise within the team and may or may not have a deep understanding of how to do analytics at a practical level. Their primary focus is on making sure the team is using information correctly, creating outputs that are of value to the business, and reducing the odds of the team making industry-related mistakes. It is common for teams without this support to focus on the wrong metrics.

A good example lies in optimizing inventory levels in the newspaper industry. It is reasonable to assume that the best outcome would be one where sales profits are balanced against holding costs, maximizing sales while also taking into account wastage costs. In practice, this is not the case; as revenues are primarily driven by advertising, increasing exposure is far more important than minimizing wastage costs. Because of this, the preferred position is to ensure that every outlet has at least one paper left over at the end of every day, regardless of how that impacts wastage. By taking this approach, the organization can ensure that it has achieved the maximum exposure possible.

Having access to a Domain Expert can greatly reduce the mistakes made by a team due to a lack of understanding around business models and industry-specific characteristics. Although the ideal situation would be that existing team members would also have this experience, it is rare for this to occur in practice. Developing this level of industry understanding often takes years; because the application of analytics is a relatively portable skill, it is more common for analytics specialists to have relatively shallow experience across a number of different business applications and industries.

Although it is useful to have Domain Experts within the team proper, it is not essential. Many teams leverage people within other business units to provide this expertise, working as part of a virtual team.

The role of Domain Experts is to:

- Ensure that the team is creating results that are relevant and useful to the organization
- Validate that the team is using information in an appropriate way
- Increase the value of analytical results by helping avoid known industry pitfalls

Their core capabilities often include:

- A deep understanding of the industry they operate in
- Good exposure across a significant portion of the organization's business processes
- A background in a field other than analytics

Their background tends to be focused on one or more areas of the business, often focusing on planning or operational aspects of the organization. Having a detailed understanding of analytics is rarely a key requirement; often, their lack of knowledge actually acts as a benefit, as they provide an internal litmus test of how comprehensible the team actually is. If they cannot understand the value the team is creating, it is unlikely that anyone else in the organization will.

Though there is no direct requirement that they have a long history within the organization, it would be unusual if they did not have a long history within the *industry*. Often, they may have worked across multiple areas of the organization, covering roles as diverse as pricing, management, and possibly even marketing. Good Domain Experts can come from anywhere—what is important is their level of business knowledge.

Data Steward

Most analysts spend the majority of their time managing data, not modeling. Given the need for clean, well-formatted data, this is not surprising. The role of the Data Steward is to reduce as much of this time as possible.

If there is one analyst on the team, spending a significant amount of time managing data is simply inevitable. However, where there is more than one analyst on the team, the risk of each analyst doing redundant data manipulation increases. Every analyst on the team may need to know how recently customers have bought something, how frequently they shop, and how much they spend (also known as *recency, frequency, and monetary analysis,* or RFM). If these processes are not standardized, each analyst will create the same datasets using potentially different assumptions and rules.

These different processes create inefficiencies and potentially confusing outcomes. Different counting rules may be used and processes will be repeated. A better approach involves consolidating the extraction, transformation, and cleansing activities into a series of standard processes, each of which can be automated and managed. However, without identifying a clear owner to monitor these data creation and usage routines, the default behavior of most teams is to gravitate back toward individually defined data management processes.

The role of Data Stewards is to ensure that:

- The amount of redundant data within the team is minimized
- Data extraction and transformation processes are standardized and automated
- Data is cleansed and corrected (as appropriate) before hitting the common data repository
- Data definitions are established and a data dictionary is created

Their core capabilities often include:

- Data warehousing knowledge
- Experience with operational data management and transformation processes
- Experience with data quality and cleansing activities

The background of Data Stewards tends to be very data- and detail-focused, often involving designing or working with data warehouses or similar information technology (IT)–based initiatives. In contrast to other roles, a detailed understanding of analytics is not a requirement for Data Stewards; what is more important is their ability to interface with the team, provide some governance over its operational data management activities, and constantly look for efficiency improvements. However, a basic understanding of data manipulation is key; often, their responsibilities will include providing the first level of validation that various aggregations and data transformations appear correct.

Good Data Stewards often come from an IT or computer science background and, although it is not essential, they may have worked with architecting and delivering various datamarts or data warehouses.

A detailed understanding of industry or organizational data structures is less important than good data architecture capabilities; in practice, much of their data will be dictated by the analysts. Their focus is to make sure this data is as clean as it can be as well as determining the most efficient mechanisms for storage, extraction, and delivery, taking into account the highly dynamic requirements of most teams.

Analytics Process Designer

Good business analytics is built around repeatable processes. The role of the Analytics Process Designer is to ensure consistency across processes.

Although the insight generation and model creation may be bespoke for each new application, the overall process of data extraction, model deployment, and ongoing scoring should be standardized to a point where new processes can be easily integrated. Additionally, these processes should be well understood, subject to appropriate levels of governance, and fully transparent.

Analytics Process Designers must create and manage these processes as efficiently as possible. Although their activities may seem to overlap with other roles (such as that of Data Steward), their focus is more on the entirety of the process rather than the specifics of any particular activity. They may not be responsible for creating the implemented extraction routines themselves, but they are responsible for ensuring that they are subject to appropriate security controls, well documented, and understood by everyone.

The role of Analytics Process Designers is to ensure that:

- Processes are documented and standardized
- The team is always identifying and implementing efficiency gains
- There exist clear handover points between the various roles within the team

Their core capabilities often include:

- Process mapping
- Systems design and integration
- Requirements analysis

The background of Analytics Process Designers tends to be very process focused and not necessarily analytics focused. Their ability to investigate and translate often abstract activities into representative processes is critical; due to the high degree of ad hoc and unique activity within most analytics teams, this is no small challenge. While it is essential that they be comfortable with extending their knowledge of how analytics works in practice, their value comes from their ability to profile, model, and improve processes.

Good Analytics Process Designers often come from consultancy and advisory organizations that are focused on answering general business problems or doing systems integration work. They often help create the low-level transformation road map within a project, and are responsible for identifying all involved stakeholders, their roles and responsibilities within the overall process, and an ideal "to-be" end-state process. As with Data Stewards, their knowledge of business analytics is less important than their ability to look at the process as a value-creation activity and constantly seek out efficiency improvements.

Monitoring/Validation Analyst

Models, like every asset, depreciate over time. Their accuracy decreases and, as it does so, their value to the organization falls. This could be a decrease in the model's ability to discriminate between customers interested in buying and those uninterested, or it could be an inability to discriminate between good and bad credit risks. The role of the Monitoring/Validation Analyst is to ensure that a common measurement framework is used to measure both value and speed of depreciation.

An important part of any effective analytics team is its ability to quantify the value it is bringing to the organization as well as ensuring that this value assessment and monitoring process is being done in a standardized way. The role of Monitoring/Validation Analysts is to ensure these two activities are being done robustly and with repeatability.

While it is not their responsibility to monitor individual models for decreases in accuracy, it *is* their responsibility to ensure that a common workflow, monitoring framework, and value measurement process is being used across the team as a whole. For comparison, while Advanced Analytics Modelers may be responsible for their own models, Monitoring/Validation Analysts are responsible for ensuring everyone is working to a common measurement framework.

When it comes time to quantify the total real value being delivered to the organization through the application of analytics, these are the individuals who have the ability to measure, track, and report on it.

The role of Monitoring/Validation Analysts is to ensure that:

- Standard model development and life-cycle-management processes are used
- Standard model-monitoring processes are used and all models are being appropriately monitored by their owners
- Value creation is being measured and tracked on a regular schedule

Their core capabilities often include:

- A strong understanding of predictive and classification models
- Financial modeling capabilities and business case development experience
- Process design and potentially team-mentoring experience

The background of Monitoring/Validation Analysts tends to span both analytics and value identification, with experience both in developing models and in building various business cases to support investment in these initiatives. Whereas they likely have the ability to develop models themselves, their focus in this role is often more on financial and governance. It is often a growth path for existing analytics team members interested in expanding their skills and capabilities.

Good Monitoring/Validation Analysts often come from pricing and profitability backgrounds, primarily due to a higher probability of involvement with business cases and other financial measures. Although definitely not limited to a given background, they may have worked with modeling price elasticities and other financially driven analytical tools. Their understanding of the technicalities of modeling is critical, and so is their capacity to model the economic return from the team's analytical initiatives in a standardized way.

Deployment Specialist

Models are worthless unless put into action; although they may provide excellent predictions when tested in a sandbox, it is not until they are used in the field that their value becomes real. Complications usually arise, however, when an organization follows good practice and establishes separate discovery and operational environments. When this happens, scoring processes need to be migrated and results validated, and data management processes need to be made enterprise-grade and robust. The role of the Deployment Specialist is to minimize the time it takes to action a model.

Deployment Specialists must manage this transition from the discovery platform into the operational platform where it will be used to score real-world data on an ongoing basis. It is their responsibility to minimize the amount of time it takes to get models into production without compromising on bulletproof levels of process repeatability. As they are dealing with operational processes, it is absolutely critical that processes do not fail.

The role of Deployment Specialists is to ensure that:

- Models are migrated into production as quickly as possible without sacrificing accuracy or process robustness
- The broader operational stakeholder community is aware of these processes and takes them into account when re-architecting core systems
- A flexible framework is delivered that will allow multiple core systems to take advantage of the insights being generated by the team

Their core capabilities often include:

- Enterprise architectural experience
- Data management and process design skills

The background of Deployment Specialists is often in data management processes. A good understanding of analytical modeling is desirable but not essential; more important is a good understanding of systems integration and enterprise architecture principles. Whether they are dealing with an on-demand operational analytics environment or in-database deployment processes, a solid background in enterprise architecture is critical.

Good Deployment Specialists frequently come from an IT background, having often worked with a variety of data warehousing systems. They often have some experience as business analysts and appreciate the importance of fast time-to-market. They act as the interface between the analytics team and operational IT, so it is critical that they have the ability to speak both languages.

CHALLENGES OF APPLYING BUSINESS ANALYTICS

Thus far we have covered the core intent of a business analytics team, the types of outputs it creates, the things it works with, and the core set of roles it needs to cover. However, this is obviously a very introspective view of the team; to understand the requirements for success, we also need to understand its context in the broader organization as well as the challenges it often faces.

Every business analytics team operates within a larger organization, regardless of whether the team is simply part of a large functional group or a center of excellence in its own right. The team itself faces a wide variety of complexities that present daily challenges. In turn, the organization faces a variety of competitive and regulatory challenges, many of which must be overcome in order for the organization to be successful.

Complicating matters somewhat is that often the business analytics team does not have ownership over the execution process. While the assets the team creates can be a critical input into the efficiency of these processes, it is often beyond the team's control to act on the insights it creates.

Challenges to the team come from two locations:

1. *Exogenous sources*, such as the environment within which the team operates
2. *Endogenous sources*, such as the skills and capabilities of the team

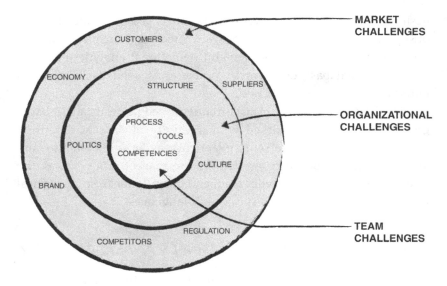

Figure 3.5 Sources of Challenges

The relationship between these and the business analytics team is shown in Figure 3.5.

The exogenously driven challenges can be further divided into two categories: organizational challenges and market challenges.

These have been well covered within the wider literature; as discussed in the previous chapter, a significant part of strategic planning is focused on understanding the influence environmental factors have on strategic direction. Such considerations may include:

- The level of management commitment to the application of analytics
- A cultural willingness to accept change
- The degree to which fact-based decision making is favored
- The level of technology platform support

From the perspective of a person with the mandate and power to enact organizational change, these may be key leverage points to focus on in order to transform the organization into an analytical competitor.

The key qualifier is that although transforming an organization is a lofty and worthy goal, many of these changes are outside the ability of a business analytics manager to directly control. Given that the vast majority of business analytics teams are still functionally aligned, their primary focus and control operates at a functional level.

These overarching strategic objectives are still critical. One of the roles of effective business analytics managers is to influence business strategy to leverage and value better decision-making processes. However, regardless of how good their vision is, they still need to deliver on a daily basis. And so, their primary focus almost inevitably falls to identifying and managing endogenous factors, such as the team's competencies, the tools they are using, and the processes they have defined. Through gaining control over these endogenous sources of challenge, they can leverage their newly developed competencies to minimize or mitigate entirely various exogenous challenges.

FINDING THE PATH TO PROFITABILITY

Unfortunately, navigating this path is rarely easy. There are excellent materials that provide guidance around the role of business analytics as a corporate-level differentiator; however, trying to effect total organizational change without explicit management sanction is often frustrating at best and career limiting at worst. Strategic change at an organizational level can take years—a horizon that is not normally available to the average business analytics manager.

Selling the value of analytics on a tactical basis instead requires focusing on what *can* be changed. It requires the manager to persuade, influence, and achieve incremental efficiency improvements to a point where the value of business analytics is so well recognized that it gets explicit sanction at the most senior levels of the organization.

Sadly, there is relatively little guiding material for a business analytics manager interested in getting a better understanding of how planning, delivery, and communication frameworks can be optimized to deliver these incremental political and delivery improvements. This relative lack of guidance is especially challenging because managers are often unsure about how to best leverage that first critical step in creating a grassroots-led transformation: a successful project.

Having a plan is an essential part of transformation, and that first step is an even more critical part. Without having successfully convinced the organization of the value of that first project, successfully completed it, and successfully convinced the organization of the benefits realized, the best road maps in the world are useless.

As stated earlier, the key is in these endogenous elements: Because they are under the direct control of the business analytics manager, they are also the most flexible when it comes to transformation. Considerations such as role focus, communication strategies, and value estimation can all be modified relatively easily. And by effectively modifying these directly controllable factors, business analytics managers can create incremental improvements. These in turn help persuade, convince, and influence sources of exogenous challenges, helping deliver transformational strategies.

SELLING THE VALUE OF ANALYTICS

An interesting experiment is to ask a relatively large crowd of business analytics practitioners how many are in sales. Most will describe how they support sales activities through the application of analytics. This fundamental misunderstanding of the importance of sales in business analytics is one of the biggest blockers of success.

The reality is very different, even if it is not always understood: Being able to *sell* what one is doing is a critical aspect of success. Business analytics is not well understood, trusted, or often even communicated. Surprisingly, there is still a somewhat pervasive belief that outside of direct sales, selling is not that important. After all, the facts, when presented to stakeholders, should speak for themselves, shouldn't they?

History shows fairly conclusively that in most organizations, the facts *do not* speak for themselves. Decisions are often made for political or subjective reasons, and relationships deliver a significant proportion of internal support.

In an ideal world, business analytics is easy. As a leader, you have:

- The right people on your team
- Well-defined business problems and staged initiatives

- Sufficient resources to deliver everything
- CEO-level commitment to your initiatives

Alas, we do not live in an ideal world. The more common reality for most of us is that:

- The business does not understand business analytics and cannot tell you what it needs.
- Your management team is unsure whether there is anything in this "analytics" thing people keep talking about (let alone what it actually means!).
- You have inherited a team with significant skill gaps.
- You are already running at full capacity and need at least two additional heads to do everything you need done, neither of whom is likely to get funding approval.

While some organizations do actually have the level of commitment described in the first set of points, they tend to be few and far between. For the vast majority of teams, it is within the second context that they need to continue to deliver value while also advancing the use of business analytics within an organization—and it is challenging.

Analytics managers need to play the role of "change agent," convincing the organization to change. Business analytics has the potential to deliver tactical returns, create sustainable competitive advantage, and differentiate an organization in the market. Fundamentally, this means doing things differently, and this inevitably means selling the value of business analytics. Without a good reason, nothing will change. It means being able to explain *why* the change is important and *how* the change will occur. It means being able to explain *what* the change will deliver.

Selling Your Way to Success

It is for this reason that effective, persuasive communication is critical. For the average analytics team, success involves selling:

- Its vision
- Its competencies

- The value it will be providing
- Its approach

In some organizations, this means selling in the literal sense; cross-charging or running an internal consultancy are well-established organizational structures. In others, it means persuading, influencing, and encouraging other teams to change their processes to leverage the outputs of the business analytics team.

Regardless of the structural models used, attracting investment and convincing stakeholders to operate differently requires the business analytics managers to:

- Communicate their vision and approach effectively and with clarity
- Persuade naysayers and build allies
- Influence the organization to do things differently
- Evangelize analytics and champion change

Simply put, success requires three things: Effectively communicating the value of analytics, effectively balancing priorities, and understanding how to deliver "tactical revolutions" through iterative improvement and explicit measurement.

Over the remainder of the chapter, we will delve a little deeper into the main challenges encountered when trying to convince stakeholders of the value of business analytics. We will also provide a broad framework on how to communicate the value of business analytics.

Why Teams Fail

Selling one's vision is a critical competency within an effective business analytics team. However, establishing what will be sold is only the first step. Working out the pitch is equally important and it is here that a number of common problems start to appear.

It is not normally overly challenging to convince people of the importance of using information to make better decisions. Exceptions do exist, but in the main, people will typically agree that it is better to be informed than not. At first glance, that looks like instant support for business analytics. If that is the case, though, why is it so hard for teams to convince stakeholders of the importance of business analytics?

There are many reasons, but four stand out above all others:

1. Teams do not identify the value.
2. Teams fail to communicate effectively.
3. Teams never actually deliver.
4. Teams cannot prove they had success.

It is often hard for stakeholders to get a good understanding of what the initiative will actually deliver. Sure, it will create a number of models, but what does that actually mean to a neophyte? The likely value of these assets at the end of the project is extremely opaque to anyone not well-versed in the technical detail, and far too often the team does not adequately communicate the value of what it has created in a context that makes sense.

Equally, communicating effectively with clarity is challenging— anyone who has sat through a few days of PowerPoint Hell knows the importance of targeted communication! There is significant value in communicating effectively, but communicating effectively is far more than just making sure there is a limited amount of information presented and no more than three bullet points per slide. Many business analytics teams, despite their best efforts, struggle to translate the technical detail of their activities into something the business will understand; given that analytics is a technical field with a broad lack of understanding about what is involved, this challenge is relatively unsurprising.

Compounding this is the sad reality of many business analytics teams: Their vision is greater than their ability to deliver. Nothing kills trust faster than a lack of clarity around delivery except a total failure to deliver.

Finally, assuming that the initiative is completed successfully, demonstrating that success can be a challenge. A large number of assets were created, significant amounts of time were invested, and processes were changed, but what level of impact did it have? In many situations, quantifying the value created by these changes to any level of confidence is difficult, creating hesitation for further change.

MEETING AND OVERCOMING THESE CHALLENGES

These are all very real challenges, faced by many teams on a daily basis. Unsolved, they create barriers that prevent the creation of competitive advantage. However, that is not to say that they cannot be resolved.

To successfully communicate the value of business analytics, you must remember four things:

1. *Money talks.* Not linking what you are doing back to tangible returns will lead to a lack of interest.
2. *Everyone is different.* Not tailoring your messages will lead to a lack of understanding.
3. *Ideas are a dime a dozen.* Not delivering will lead to a lack of trust.
4. *Prove it or it is not real.* Not measuring your success will lead to a lack of future commitment.

In Chapter 4, we will review what *value* means and various ways of measuring it. We will look at the core elements of building a business case around business analytics, methods for getting buy-in into a business case, and the balance between strategic and tactical value.

In Chapter 5, we will review a number of strategies to improve the efficiency and effectiveness of communicating the value of business analytics. We will look at communication preferences, cultural considerations, and ways of creating a desire for change.

In Chapter 6, we will review the importance of developing an execution plan. We will look at ways to manage uncertainty, approaches to dealing with insufficient resource coverage, and the role of road maps in consistent value delivery through business analytics.

In Chapter 7, we will review the importance of developing a measurement framework. We will look at the importance of up-front planning, the criticality of measurement in ensuring future growth, and the role of automation in value measurement.

Within each of these chapters, we will also review some practical case studies and some examples of what happens when they are not considered, and provide a checklist for execution.

Money Talks

"Value" is obviously important, but what does it mean? We will look into a variety of ways of measuring and defining it in Chapter 4, but for now we can define *value* as any outcome that has a real and measurable positive impact on an individual or the organization more broadly. The most important concepts in that definition are the measurability of the value provided and the realization of that value; it is a subtle distinction but an important one.

For example, an improvement in the accuracy of a predictive model may be a positive outcome, but unless it changes something for the organization in a measurable way, it has not yet actually delivered any value.

Why is this so important? The reality of the organization as an economically driven entity is that:

- Economic scarcity is real and projects needs to be prioritized.
- Tangible benefits are prioritized over intangible benefits.
- Measurability and accountability are often the litmus test for funding approval.

Every organization, regardless of how well funded it is, has a limited budget. The use of that budget needs to be prioritized to provide maximum return. For many organizations, this involves a fairly detailed planning process that can take upwards of a few months. At one extreme, an organization I worked with never actually left the budgeting stage—its processes were so complicated that by the time management had finished allocating budgets for the current year, they had already started their planning for their next financial year!

By necessity, this prioritization process needs some measures to help identify which projects should get funding ahead of other projects. Typically, this is decided through a variety of factors, including:

- Economic return estimation (often in the form of a business case)
- Political relationships (often in the form of a senior sponsor)
- Exogenous influences (often in the form of competitive movements)

Without some form of value definition and measurement, most analytics projects are dead before they have even been presented. In the absence of any comparable measures, heavyweight senior sponsors, or severe market threats, the analytics projects will inevitably lose out to other projects that have quantified their value.

While value is often a subjective measure, one thing is constant: Tangible returns are almost always given financial priority over intangible returns. Regardless of what position you take, a key role of private sector firms is to make a return. Equally, public sector organizations exist to deliver stated policy objectives at a minimum of cost. In both, demonstrating return on investment is often a key measure in decision making, regardless of whether it is in the form of profitability or social welfare/net economic utility gain. All the greatest intentions in the world will fall to the wayside if you cannot convince investors of a positive (and measurable) return in some form.

Identifying those tangible returns is a good starting point. Equally important is having a strategy to measure them after execution. There are two reasons for this:

1. It provides proof of the success of the project.
2. It provides a justification for further investment in business analytics.

Unless you understand how your projects are being compared, you identify the tangible returns, and you put in place a strategy to measure those returns, you will probably struggle to get a project off the ground in the first place.

Everyone Is Different

The next thing to remember is that we are all different. That may seem obvious, but it is probably the single biggest reason why organizations fail to invest in analytics in the first place: They literally cannot understand it. Put simply:

- People look for different things when they communicate and have substantially different thinking preferences.

- The perception of what value entails will vary from person to person.
- Levels of understanding vary significantly based on backgrounds and areas of specialization.

We often talk about organizations as entities in their own right with dominant cultures and standardized processes. This is misleading at best; businesses are pluralistic entities populated by individuals with their own views, agendas, and opinions. As anyone who has ever argued over how many customers a company has will probably agree, truth is highly subjective and dependent on your point of view.

This subjectivity is obvious and important, but it is too easily forgotten. It affects how people interpret what is put in front of them; different people process information differently. Correspondingly, we need to present information differently to different people to make sure it has the greatest and most effective impact. Failure to do so will at best limit the impact, at worst completely confuse.

Even if you overcome the initial communication hurdles, there is no guarantee that people will agree with you. The concept of value is both objective and subjective: Though most people within an organization will agree in principle with broad measures (such as profitability, revenue, and so on), they will not necessarily agree that those measures are accurate or with the calculations used. Additionally, those measures may comprise a subset of everything they consider valuable—often, their own comfort levels are equally important. Focusing on personally irrelevant or subjectively incorrect measures does little to win allies.

Also important is that most ideas involve enacting change in some form. It may be a small change or it may be significant; either way, it implicitly requires individuals to work differently. Organizational psychology demonstrates that change is often threatening. Without some form of strategy to manage that change, the odds of organizational resistance increase significantly.

Finally, the importance of recognizing varying levels of understanding cannot be overstated. Not everyone is a statistician—in fact, most people are not. Depending on whom you are talking to, explaining the hairy details may or may not be important; pitching at the wrong level runs the risk of losing the audience.

The key thing to remember is that if you do not tailor your message to your audience's preferred communication style, make it relevant to their own value constructs, and provide the right level of detail (no more and no less), you are probably talking to deaf ears and wasting everybody's time.

Ideas Are a Dime a Dozen

Having ideas is easy; doing something with them is hard. Without action, ideas are just a series of great intentions. Ideation, the process of creating new ideas within an organization, is a frequently misunderstood process. While the ideas themselves are essential, they're only part of the picture (and not always the most important part!).

The reality of formalized ideation is somewhat more complex:

- Having too many ideas without any form of prioritization can actually make things worse.
- Value is created through execution, not ideation.
- Every idea requires change, something that's often scary.

It seems counterintuitive, but in isolation, having too many ideas can actually be a hindrance. The driver for this is similar to the reason why too much multitasking tends to decrease productivity: By spreading ourselves too thin, we achieve less than we otherwise could have. While it is tempting to consider the job done once the ideas have been documented, having the ideas is only the first step. Establishing some form of prioritization for these potential opportunities is the only way to avoid "analysis paralysis."

The often-overlooked harsh truth is that the ideas themselves are worthless—it is the execution of the idea that creates value. Business analytics is exactly the same: The greatest of intentions are not worth anything if they never eventuate. Regardless of whether you are dealing with reducing customer churn or optimizing post-presentation medical follow-ups to reduce emergency room returns, the value materializes only when you have done something. No execution means *no* value.

Remember that unless you prioritize, until you execute, and until you can convince the rest of the organization to change, all you have is hot air and good intentions.

Prove It or It Is Not Real

There is an Internet meme that is invoked when someone makes an outrageous statement: "Pics or it didn't happen!" Without some form of proof, it is easy to doubt outrageous statements. Delivering a business initiative is much the same; unless the returns are tracked and the benefits measured, someone will inevitably challenge it. At best, it will delay any further investment until political consensus can be achieved. At worst, it will derail an entire analytics program of work.

The reasons why measurement is so critical are fairly straightforward:

- Credibility comes through a demonstrable history.
- Perception is reality in the short term.
- Success breeds success.

Building trust takes time. And we trust more the things that we know were successful; things we know are "safer" than things we do not know. Measuring success in an agreed structure is the most direct path to building this credibility. If everyone agrees on the measures and the measures have improved, people will be more willing to take on further change. However, if everyone has just gone through a significant amount of change-related stress and there is nothing to show for it, do not expect future support.

Unfortunately, for many business analytics groups starting out, a demonstrated history of success is a luxury that they simply do not have. A vision, no matter how inspiring, by itself is not enough. One of the hardest things to accept in this situation is that *perception is reality*. It does not matter what the business analytics team believes— the views held by the stakeholders the team is engaging with are the reality they need to deal with. If other teams believe that every other organization is different and that advanced forms of analytics simply will not work in their context, that is their reality. Trying to rely on case studies as a mechanism for encouraging cultural change simply will not work, no matter how hard you try. Making business analytics contextually relevant is one of the most critical things a potentially successful team needs to do.

Finally, the fastest path to ongoing investment in business analytics is success: A project that has demonstrated measurable financial return in a commonly agreed structure will almost inevitably attract additional investment for future expansion. The caveat is that unless the rest of the organization knows about this success, it did not happen. Communicating successes achieved through the application of business analytics is almost as important as getting the project approved in the first place.

Remember that the results need to be measurable, they need to be contextually relevant, and they need to be sold on successful completion, regardless of what that is. If you do not believe they can be measured, you need to go back to the drawing board. If you are not evangelizing your successes, you are making your job harder.

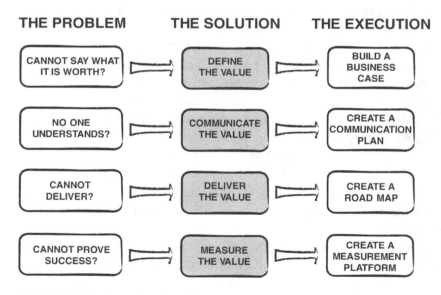

Figure 3.6 Selling the Value of Analytics

THE FOUR-STEP FRAMEWORK

The remainder of this book focuses in more detail on a four-step framework for *defining*, *communicating*, *delivering*, and *measuring* the value of business analytics. As with most things, the process itself is quite simple; the challenge is in the execution. Selling the value of analytics breaks down to four major steps, described in Figure 3.6.

In upcoming chapters we will investigate each of these in turn, exploring some of the most important concepts behind them and providing a number of practical examples of how things work and what to expect when they do not work. To make execution easier, we will also provide in each chapter a checklist of items to consider when developing your management strategies.

NOTE

1. T. H. Davenport and J. G. Harris, *Competing on Analytics* (Boston: Harvard Business School Press, 2007).

CHAPTER 4

Defining the Value of Business Analytics

INTRODUCTION

Organizations exist to create value, an abstract concept often considered to be the worth of various goods and services as identified by the market. They do this through a variety of activities, one of which is the application of business analytics. As discussed in Chapters 2 and 3, business analytics is unique in that it leverages a number of competencies and assets that can typically be applied to multiple discrete value-creating activities within an organization.

Although this value takes different forms depending on the objectives, context, and culture of the organization, the importance of value-addition as an outcome of an activity is constant. This commonality is both a strength and a weakness.

On one hand, it provides a common starting point to consider, compare, and contrast different activities; activities that add more value should be prioritized over activities that do not. On the other hand, this commonality means that it cannot provide guidance around what form the specific measures should take; what is considered value-adding in a government department may be significantly different from what is considered value-adding in the private sector.

Whereas business analytics acts as an important enabler for competitive advantage and organizational differentiation, the application of analytics in isolation does not normally create value. Value is created only when *action is taken*, not when insight is generated. Often, this requires changing existing operational activities to integrate the results of analytics.

Because this normally impacts multiple teams within an organization, enacting these changes requires the analytics team to provide sufficient reasons to justify the change. Defining the value created is therefore a critical component of successful organizational transformation. Without this:

- The organization will often be reluctant to invest in change.
- Other teams will be reluctant to change their processes.

In this chapter we review the two major classes of value: tangible and intangible benefits. We will pay close attention to different levels of value capture: organizational and personal. We will then review some common measures and approaches to identifying and measuring these sources of value within a business analytics context. Finally, we will look at some more advanced considerations as well as some practical examples of measuring value within a business analytics project.

WHY YOU NEED TO DEFINE THE VALUE

Too often, teams do not get past the planning stage. They are full of great ideas but when it comes to actually executing, things somehow fall apart. Some of the most common reasons are because they:

- Try to do too much
- Do not prioritize
- Get blocked by other stakeholders

The Good Idea That Never Got Off the Ground

A great example I was once involved with had to do with a team tasked with "doing things differently." The organization in question had quite a conservative culture but recognized the need to be more competitive. Unlike many teams, this one was explicitly established to identify potential sources of competitive advantage, find ways of doing things smarter, and assist the organization in making the necessary changes. Although the scope of its remit was extremely large, business analytics formed a key competency in its toolkit.

The team launched with great internal fanfare, high morale, and a great deal of enthusiasm. Unfortunately, despite a great start, it had not managed to progress much in the months following its creation. Making the situation even more confusing, the team had all the right prerequisites:

- A cross-functional group of extremely skilled people
- A supporting set of tools and technologies
- Explicit management sanction to "do things differently"

My involvement came through trying to help the team members clarify why they were not achieving the progress they had expected and to come up with a solution.

Detailed investigation drew out a number of unexpected challenges stemming from their approach. First, their broad set of competencies was actively working against them. Given the team members' broad focus, their high intelligence, and the number of internal sources of opportunity many organizations have, their potential list of problems to solve was enormous. When tallied, there were over 200 unique initiatives a team of roughly 10 people was working on! In short, the team was trying to do too much.

Second, the team had no understanding of which of these initiatives was most valuable to either the organization *or* individuals within the organization. While every single initiative was solving a legitimate business problem, there had not been any research into either the objective or subjective value delivered by each initiative. This lack of visibility of the potential value its initiatives were creating meant that the team had no way of prioritizing its activities.

Finally, because they had not explicitly considered the value being created by each of their initiatives, the team members also had not identified where this value would flow. Instead, they had jumped straight from problem to solution without communicating the benefits of their new approach, putting a variety of internal stakeholders offsides in the process. By not mapping where the value would flow, they struggled to build internal support for their proposed changes.

Once this was understood, the solution was fairly straightforward. It involved:

- Estimating the tangible and intangible value being delivered by each initiative
- Ranking the initiatives based on their potential tangible value
- Adjusting the ranking based on the degree to which intangible value would increase internal support
- Limiting their focus to their top-ranked activities based on available resourcing
- Establishing a communication strategy to promote the value they had identified

Going through this process was fairly straightforward and only took a matter of days. However, by understanding the value they were creating, the team members managed to break free of their inertia, start delivering, and increase support provided by internal stakeholders. Without understanding the value they were creating for the business, it had been impossible for them to:

- Prioritize their own activities
- Communicate their value
- Persuade stakeholders to support their initiatives

In a Nutshell: What You Need at a Minimum and How to Do It

Defining the value of business analytics comes down to understanding the benefits delivered and costs required by a given business analytics initiative. Doing this effectively helps:

- Build internal support and gain access to funding
- Eliminate bias and minimize counterarguments
- Increase focus and the probability of successful delivery

Much of this is reliant on clearly identifying the tangible and intangible benefits the initiative will deliver. It also requires identifying who will receive these benefits, either at an organizational or personal level.

Counterbalancing this is an understanding of the investment required by the initiative. By combining the two, the organization can consider the net value of the initiative, often a key requirement for financial release.

The three measures of most interest are normally the financial return, the rate of return, and the time to return. Most organizations use a variety of standardized measures to simplify this value definition process. Some of the most common measures include:

- Total cost of ownership (TCO)
- Return on investment (ROI)
- Payback
- Net present value (NPV)
- Internal rate of return (IRR)

By understanding and applying these, it is possible to translate the relative complexity of business analytics into an outcomes-based language that the rest of the organization can relate to. Additionally, by applying advanced techniques such as scenario analysis and simulation, it is also possible to provide insight into not only what the most likely outcome is but also the range of possible outcomes.

Successfully *defining the value* comes from:

- Incorporating this information into a comprehensive business case
- Socializing this information with stakeholders and decision makers to solicit agreement that the data is correct and the outcomes realistic

DIFFERENT TYPES OF VALUE

As discussed in Chapter 2, the value from business analytics stems from the outcomes achieved, not the analysis. This is an important distinction: By definition, *without action there is no value.*

Understanding this value plays an important role in creating internal commitment to change. Business analytics has a key role in creating competitive advantage, but for the vast majority of teams, a wide variety of internal challenges exist that form barriers against successfully leveraging business analytics. One of the biggest of these barriers is change itself. Doing things smarter often means doing things differently, and for many organizations, this goes directly against an inherent cultural aversion to change.

Convincing people to do things differently is not easy; we are creatures of habit, and trying to get us to change is notoriously difficult. It follows that if you want people to change, you need to give them a good reason.

Change management is a complex topic in its own right. Within this chapter, we will focus on one of the ways of encouraging this initial change: providing specific evidence on *why* the change is necessary or a good thing. Doing so requires that the *value* of the change be defined; without explaining how the change will make the organization or individual better off, it can be exceedingly difficult to convince people to do things differently.

An extremely important qualification is that while defining the value creates a *reason* to change, it *does not actually create any value*. For the value to be made real, the team needs to execute. Until that happens, it is only *planned* value.

It is a simple concept, but the execution is often complex. *Value* means different things to different people. It helps to consider that there are two dimensions in which the benefits of a business analytics project can be placed:

1. *Tangible* versus *intangible* benefits
2. *Organizational* versus *personal* benefits

Not for Money or Love: Tangible versus Intangible Value

By definition, any well-defined business analytics project is well aligned to at least one specific business outcome. These outcomes will vary by industry and organization but they will inevitably have one thing in common: They should create measurable value for the organization in some form.

Though the measures will change, what will not change is the measurability. As with any good investment, the project needs to improve things in a measurable way. If it does not, the hard truth is that regardless of how well executed the work was, it is hard to demonstrate what value has been added.

These *tangible* (or *economic*) benefits form the core of what is often considered "value." They are often the minimum criteria for getting a project approved and funding released. Common examples may include:

- Improving revenue or profitability
- Reducing rates of risk exposure
- Decreasing fraudulent lodgments and associated losses

While these benefits are often essential, they are often not the entirety of benefits delivered by a business analytics project. Many projects will also deliver various benefits that, although difficult or impossible to measure, are still real and of value.

The project may also:

- Increase retention rates through providing improved career paths
- Create higher levels of job satisfaction and improved productivity
- Lead to better decisions through having access to better information

The positive outcomes stemming from these are often still measurable, but tracing the direct relationship back to the project can be quite challenging. There is no doubt that these benefits are real and of value to the organization. They are often, however, extremely difficult to measure.

These *intangible benefits* are also of value to the organization but are less likely to justify investment or support for a project. Although still considered "value," their lack of measurability limits their ability to support an argument for investment.

Most well-defined business analytics projects will deliver both tangible *and* intangible benefits. However, a key mistake some teams make is to consider them of equal importance or even substitutable. For the vast majority of organizations, tangible benefits form a necessary condition for financial release. Equally, though, intangible benefits can often create internal political support—if the outcomes are good, it can help paint the project as being "the right thing to do."

Without being able to identify the specific (and measurable) positive outcomes delivered by the project, it is unlikely that it will obtain funding. Intangible benefits, however, often help strengthen the political case for investment. The next few sections will investigate these in greater detail, identifying common measures and sources of tangible and intangible value.

What's in It for Me: Personal versus Organizational Value

Another important dimension of value lies in where the value is accrued. Organizations are complex entities made up large numbers of individuals working to a common goal. In theory, decisions are made to further the organization's goals. In practice, however, decisions are also made based on a variety of political and personal factors.

A well-defined business analytics project will create value. Often, this value will flow to a variety of locations, ranging from the organization itself to the individuals within the organization.

The classic view of measuring value involves identifying the value created for the organization itself. In theory, the organization makes objective decisions using perfect information on how to allocate limited resources based on what will maximize the value-creating abilities of the organization.

In practice, the process is often more complex. Decisions are often made:

- With high levels of internal and external uncertainty
- Within limited time frames
- Based on the impact they will have at a personal level

The creation of organizational value is often a critical deciding factor in whether to invest in a business analytics project. However, the value that flows to individuals can often tip the scales sufficiently to change the outcome of the decision-making process.

For example, an organization may need to prioritize between two projects. Whereas the second project may deliver greater levels of organizational value, the first may help reduce a key decision maker's day-to-day frustrations through providing more immediate access to high-quality information.

Even though it is not directly measurable, this personal value may be enough to build stronger political support for the first project, despite its delivering less organizational value than the second project! Having an excellent understanding of where the value will flow is a critical part of building internal support for a business analytics project.

Value Identification as a Technique to Build Support

Together, these two different ways of looking at value provide a framework to help consider all the sources of value a business analytics project may create, as shown in Figure 4.1.

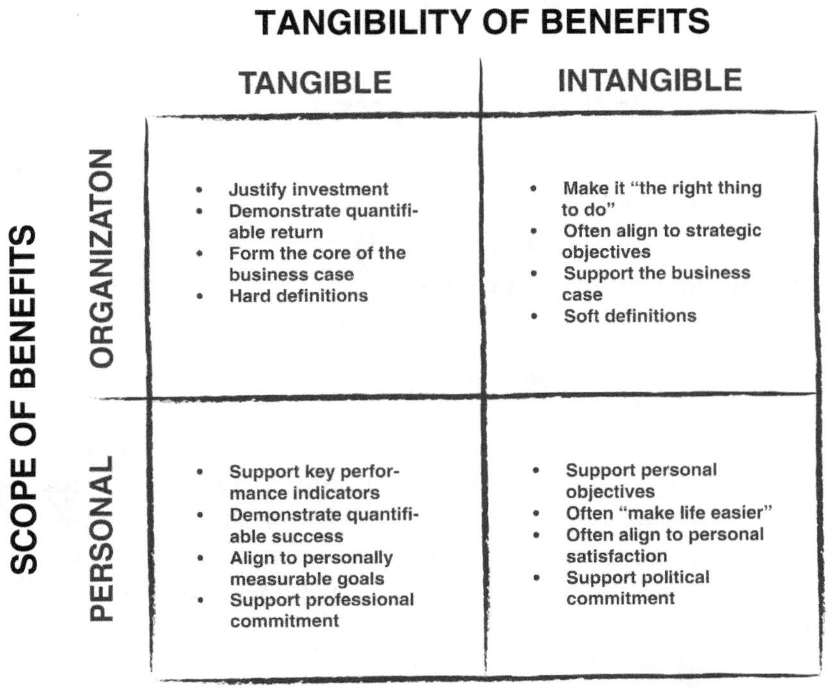

TANGIBILITY OF BENEFITS

	TANGIBLE	INTANGIBLE
ORGANIZATON	• Justify investment • Demonstrate quantifi-able return • Form the core of the business case • Hard definitions	• Make it "the right thing to do" • Often align to strategic objectives • Support the business case • Soft definitions
PERSONAL	• Support key performance indicators • Demonstrate quantifi-able success • Align to personally measurable goals • Support professional commitment	• Support personal objectives • Often "make life easier" • Often align to personal satisfaction • Support political commitment

SCOPE OF BENEFITS

Figure 4.1 Value Matrix

By explicitly considering each of these four quadrants, a business analytics manager can build a comprehensive picture of how both the organization and the individuals within the organization will be better off once the project has been completed. Without understanding the value to be delivered, a manager will often undermine the organization's overall communication strategy.

More specifically, understanding the value is important for two reasons:

1. Organizations will not invest unless there is a return.
2. People will not commit unless they benefit somehow.

The tool most commonly used to quantify and articulate the value created from a business analytics project is a business case. A well-balanced business case often acts as a critical component within an overall communication strategy; it persuades and convinces using broadly agreed-upon facts. Importantly, it will often cover both tangible and intangible benefits.

The focus of the next few sections is on a number of concepts critical to measuring the value of business analytics. It is the minimum of what is important, namely:

- The role of the business case
- Techniques to measure tangible value
- Techniques to identify intangible value

ROLE OF THE BUSINESS CASE

Why build a business case? This is not such a silly question—creating a good business case requires work, ingenuity, and a good understanding of the fundamentals of financial modeling. And, in certain circumstances, the business case is not even necessary; given sufficient political support, the reasons to justify investment will almost inevitably be found.

Unfortunately, such situations are rare and, depending on the scale of change involved, often nonexistent. It is one thing to convince an organization to make small changes with relatively minor investment. It is another to convince an organization to rebuild its approach to risk and fraud management with an accompanying seven-figure investment.

Developing a comprehensive business case is a complex topic, worthy of an entire book in its own right. This chapter focuses on only the core of what is important in justifying an investment in business analytics. Creating a business case is an essential part of communicating the value of business analytics in that it:

- Justifies to decision makers the reasons for releasing funding
- Minimizes bias through establishing a series of objective statements
- Clarifies and targets focus on specific outcomes

The first is the commonly understood reason for creating a financial model describing the benefits from any given business analytics project; simply, it is a formal argument that the returns from doing something will be greater than the investment made in doing it. It is more than that, though—the reality is that every project is being compared against other potential projects. Because of this, a business case also acts as tool to compare the relative benefits of various projects with totally different outcomes in an objective way. By formalizing the logic behind and outcomes from a project, highly discrete projects can be compared with relative confidence.

The objectivity of this process is critical; if everything were totally subjective, comparisons would be difficult if not impossible. Complicating things is the fact that there exists extensive research demonstrating that we suffer from natural and ingrained biases, not only in terms of interest but also in terms of psychology. By formalizing the process and creating a methodological approach to measuring economic value, we help minimize not only our own biases, but also the biases of the people we are dealing with.

Finally, one of the biggest advantages (and weaknesses) of business analytics is that it has the potential for such significant benefit. Any given project could have a multitude of potential benefits. Often, the challenge is not in identifying them; instead, it is in delivering them. By focusing too broadly and on too many benefits, the risk is that the project will be consumed by scope creep, failing to deliver anything at all.

By clarifying focus and identifying the specific outcomes that will be achieved within a project, the business case acts as a tool to limit the scope of activities and provide a barrier against scope creep. After all, if additional benefits exist that cannot be delivered within the scope of a positive business case, they are prime targets for subsequent improvements.

A Necessary Requirement for Financial Release

Whether the money is yours or someone else's, someone always cares about how it is being used. Finance is, for anyone who is not a central bank, a finite resource; implicit in any investment is an expectation of return in some form. For most private sector organizations, this expectation is typically a financial one. For many public sector organizations, it is an expectation that a given outcome will be achieved, whether it is an increase in economic welfare, reduced levels of harm, or any one of a multitude of other public benefits. If this expectation is not met, the investment leads to a loss. For obvious reasons, ensuring that investments give a positive return is a major focus of the people controlling access to money.

However, as important as the absolute return is, there is more than just that. The opportunity cost of an investment can be high; even if a project is successful, it is possible that the money could have been used elsewhere for greater return. For example, the opportunity cost of investing in a term deposit may be high if the stock market is going through an extremely bullish growth cycle; had the same money been invested in the stock market during the same period, it probably would have given a far better return. Project investments are no different; although a project may give a positive return, there might have been other projects that, had they been invested in, might have given a far better return.

It is within this context that the business case acts as a tool to convince the people with the money to release it for investment. An effective business case communicates three things:

1. It identifies the expected return.
2. It quantifies the investment required.
3. It describes the timing and limits on the return.

The core of the business case is the expected tangible and intangible return; it allows the financial controllers to make an objective comparison between a given initiative and other potential initiatives. Typically, this quantification takes the form of a dollar value simply because measuring intangibles is frequently challenging. Without this, the financial controllers have little more than persuasive argument to base their investment decisions on. For example, a project aimed at reducing the level of churn in an organization's customer base might lead to a revenue increase of $10 million per annum. In isolation, this seems like a no-brainer. Unfortunately, reality is often more complex.

The absolute return is only one dimension of consideration; equally important is the level of investment required to achieve the identified returns. If the project requires a $20 million upgrade to the organization's customer relationship management (CRM) systems, the $10 million return suddenly does not look as attractive any more. However, if the project simply requires a $500,000 project investment and process changes involving another estimated cost of $500,000, that $10 million return starts looking pretty good again. Quantifying the total level of investment required is an essential component of evaluating the true benefit of a project.

At face value, it seems that is all that is needed. However, there is an important dimension that is still missing: the timing of the investment and return. It may seem that in the long run the timing is irrelevant—a project will eventually deliver a certain amount of value. However, as Keynes rightly pointed out, "In the long run, we are all dead"! What happens in the short term often has a far greater impact on us.

The timing of investment and return is critical for two reasons:

1. Money needs to be allocated within budgeting processes.
2. Other options may offer return sooner, allowing for a greater total return through reinvestment.

For a project to be approved, the necessary funding needs to be available. Without understanding the timing of the investment required, it is impossible to ensure that appropriate funds will be available and liquid.

Equally, that ever-important specter of opportunity cost raises its head once again. While a project may offer a $10 million return, there may be better options if that return is realized only after a 10-year wait. By factoring in a concept known as the "time cost of money," this timing can be incorporated into comparisons made between projects in an objective sense.

In a nutshell, if you cannot identify what your return is, the investment you need, and what your expected payoff timing looks like, it will be an uphill battle to organize support and direct investment.

A Way of Minimizing Bias

Creating organizational change is a challenging prospect; extensive research has shown that in the vast majority of situations, we tend to resist change. And, the application of business analytics is almost always a change agent—becoming smarter, more efficient, and more agile almost inevitably means change in some form.

However, being human means being subjective; our reality is defined by our perceptions. Everyone is familiar with the way optical illusions play with the way we see the world. What is not always as well recognized is that we suffer similar biases when it comes to predicting future events, assessing relative probabilities, and making comparisons.

Some of the types of psychological bias we suffer from include:

- Subjective biases
- Historical anchoring
- A preference toward specifics over trends

One of the most common sources of bias is our own context. Because we favor situations that benefit us personally, proposed changes will often be blocked simply because they involve change. By qualifying this with the expected *returns* from the change, it becomes harder to argue against the change for personal reasons.

We also have a tendency to base our predictions on what we have experienced most recently. This is often also known as the "business as usual" problem. By definition, using business analytics often means doing things differently. However, because many stakeholders in an organization are buried in business as usual, the belief that doing things differently will not really change things is seductive. Again, quantifying the value created by applying and executing business analytics helps break down these anchoring biases.

Another common bias is our natural tendency to ignore trends in favor of specific measures. This is also known as *base rate bias* and is especially problematic in situations where business analytics has been unsuccessfully applied in an organization previously. There may be a multitude of reasons why a previous project failed, often for one or more of the reasons described in Chapter 2. Unfortunately, because of this bias, people will often discount another business analytics project "because we tried that last time," even if it is in a totally new area of the business or relies on a completely different competency.

Understanding and overcoming these biases is important—they cloud our own and other people's judgment. If not appropriately managed, these biases can easily block value creation for the wrong reasons.

A business case is a useful tool to help mitigate these biases for three reasons:

1. It provides quantitative (and not subjective) measures.

2. It uses a standardized and transparent process.

3. It requires explicit documentation of the assumptions used to quantify returns.

Moving from a subjective opinion to a series of objective (and quantifiable) statements ensures that anyone who is interested in debating the detail can have access to it. And, it helps provide reasons to move away from subjective opinions; quantifying the benefits from a project encourages decision makers and investors to focus on more than the execution and to instead consider the project as a return-generating activity.

A Way of Creating Focus

As mentioned earlier, one challenge of business analytics is that, because of its generalizability, it is tempting to try to solve every problem at once. In theory, this leads to the creation of significant organizational value. In practice, however, it also creates a tremendously unwieldy project that will take years to deliver, if it can be delivered at all.

For example, a team may start out considering building a series of retention models. This in itself may provide millions of dollars of return. However, by extending the application of its core competencies, the team might also be able to deliver a series of cross-sell and up-sell models. And, by developing and applying some segmentation modes, it may also be able to improve the accuracy of its retention and cross-sell/up-sell models by tailoring predictions to common sets of customers, increasing accuracy and return.

Unfortunately, measuring the value of this framework is difficult without providing some sort of dashboard or reporting structure. So, the team may also decide to incorporate the creation of an entire management reporting framework, slightly reducing the return on investment but significantly increasing the intangible value of its activities by giving management visibility over its activities.

After thinking about it a bit more, the team may also decide that the value of the reporting framework could be substantially increased by also allowing management access to various workflow-triggering functions, giving them the ability to action specific campaigns or market responses based on operational performance.

Although everything in the team's approach is valid and would probably increase value significantly, the complexity of such a large project with a single deliverable date:

- Increases risk and the odds of failure
- Lengthens the time until value is realized
- Broadens the focus of organizational transformation, requiring significantly more consensus and support within the organization

It is within this context that a business case can act as a clarifying force. Restricting the focus of activities to those that provide the most significant return prevents the business analytics team from taking on more than is possible to deliver. Forcing the inclusion of time frames and various standardized measures of return creates a focus on delivering returns sooner rather than later.

Through constructing a business case, the team may find that the first stage justifies sufficient investment to deliver the project in a reasonable time frame, creating value for the organization while also minimizing the organizational change necessary. Each subsequent activity would then form a business case in its own right, thereby phasing organizational change while regularly delivering real value.

IDENTIFYING TANGIBLE VALUE

Tangible benefits are returns that can be directly mapped to some form of economic return. The most common examples are revenue increases and cost reductions, but they are not necessarily limited to those two supergroups. Other examples include:

- Profitability improvements
- Capital investment reductions (such as through decreased inventory stock levels)
- Improved liquidity (and the corresponding reinvestment potential)
- Decreased bad and doubtful debts
- Deferred investments

One of the biggest reasons why these are so critical in any tactical project is that when defined and measured accurately, they are often indisputable. A good example of the difference this can make is in the creation of a customer satisfaction insight process.

Most organizations care about what their customers think; it is tremendously easier (and cheaper) to sell to a happy customer than it is to either sell to an unhappy customer or acquire a new customer.

Getting some insight into customer satisfaction level and the reasons behind customer dissatisfaction therefore seems like a logical application of analytics. And, for many organizations, it becomes a project for the business analytics team.

Where the difficulties emerge is in the value the insight brings to the business. Inevitably, getting an understanding of customer satisfaction levels is a challenging (and time-consuming) process. Not only do customers need to be accurately and representatively surveyed, their answers need to be analyzed. And, given that the best insight often comes from what was not included in the survey, this analysis will often involve both structured and unstructured (text) data. If that were not enough, the process typically needs to be made repeatable (often on a quarterly or annual basis) and the results regularly summarized and reported on.

Such a process often brings great insight to the organization. It might find out that its customers are exceedingly happy or that its customers do not like the color purple. Everyone agrees that the information is highly valuable and should be gathered on a regular basis. After much celebration and back-patting, the business analytics team, stressed out from all this extra work on top of its existing workload, goes to the financial controller to ask for more resources to support its analysis. And, surprisingly to the team, its request gets knocked back or significantly reduced—despite all the insight, there are often more important investments that need to occur first. So, the business analytics team becomes further under-resourced, generates more work for itself through demonstrating value, and limits its own future growth.

The problem does not stem from a lack of value from the analysis; it stems from a disconnect between the insight and the action. Ideally, the insight provided from the analysis is eventually used within a variety of outbound campaigns, including:

- Direct customer contact for retention and satisfaction improvement
- Product redesign
- Creation of new markets
- Market message tailoring and refinement

The issue is that whereas these outcomes each have tangible economic returns that can be associated with them, the analytics process itself is not yet linked to that value. In isolation, no economic returns can be booked against the business analytics project. This challenge is not only associated with customer satisfaction; given that most business analytics teams are not tasked with the actual execution of their findings, this disconnect occurs more often than not. In practice, I have seen it manifest with customer retention, outbound direct marketing, reduction of bad and doubtful debt, and risk modeling, just to name a few different applications.

The solution to this dilemma involves shifting the measurement to involve the entire value chain, not just the delivery of the analytical outcomes. This is challenging in its own right; it means that the business analytics team is heavily dependent on other teams if it is to demonstrate economic value. Typically, this means forming a mutually beneficial partnership with other groups within the organization. For an analytical marketing team, it means aligning closely with the operational marketing team. For a risk modeling team, it means aligning closely with the debt recovery and product lines of business. And, for a customer loyalty team within a retailer, it means aligning closely with buyers and planners.

Common Financial Measures

Communicating the economic value of an investment seems relatively straightforward. It is simply a measure of how much a given investment will return. However, the complication lies in the detail; as is relatively well-known, there are many ways to look at return.

The simplest measure is just the dollar value of return. So, if a move to analytically based pricing increases revenues by $1 million, the return is $1 million. Obviously, this ignores the investment made in enabling technology. So, any and all associated investments need to be subtracted from that $1 million return to paint a fairer picture of return.

Before we get into the specifics behind a number of common measures, it is helpful to identify the single biggest reason for using them: They are a common vocabulary. There is a great deal of debate over whether they really have the ability to discriminate between good and bad projects, but regardless, because they are commonly used they are also well understood.

Much like statistics, they also provide a number of clarifying views based on a series of simplifications. Using different measures helps provide different ways of looking at what type and how much value is being created by a given project. Although individually no measure accurately represents the totality of a project, when used appropriately common measures can still be extremely useful.

This ability to discriminate between investments is a key driver behind the use of commonly calculated measures. Because they are calculated using a standard formula, they are an ideal way to simplify normally highly complex business cases into some key directly comparable measures.

Unfortunately, although the measures are directly comparable, the returns rarely are. Projects vary significantly, and it is extremely difficult to provide any recommendations around what would be expected for a given project; the reality is that indicative ranges are likely to vary according to industry, relative starting point, and business problem. For example, it would be unreasonable to expect an equivalent return from two marketing analytics projects if one was in a retail-focused organization while the other was in a business-to-business–focused organization. Ignoring any potential differences in relatively analytical maturity, because the two organizations are dealing with fundamentally different marketing approaches, customer bases, and product offerings, it is highly unlikely that their levels of expected return would be the same.

Most measures deal with three primary factors:

1. Money
2. Time
3. Rate of return

When investing money into a new venture, the amount of money returned is obviously of key interest. At a minimum, we hope we will have more money after the investment than we had before. However, time is also a critical consideration; if it takes 100 years to get paid, it may not be as attractive an investment as another that gives a smaller return in 10 years. And, when comparing projects, it helps to understand the relative rate at which each will create a return.

Calculating these measures is fairly straightforward. Because there are already a wide variety of sources that provide this information, we will refrain from running through their practical application in detail. It is more important within the context of this book to be aware of some common measures and the role they play in identifying tangible value. The core measures we will examine are:

- Total cost of ownership
- Return on investment
- Payback
- Net present value
- Internal rate of return

Total Cost of Ownership

Total cost of ownership (TCO) is the simplest and, in most situations, the least enlightening. It simply involves adding up all direct costs incurred by the investment over the expected life of the investment.

Calculating TCO is a relatively straightforward process. Most business analytics projects involve various forms of technology investment, process change, data sourcing, and potentially headcount increases. Each of these has a number of associated costs; for example, the technology investment will often include software licensing fees in the first year, potentially support in the first year, and renewals or ongoing support in subsequent years, not to mention various hardware purchasing or leasing costs. Each of these costs over the life of the investment is identified and included in the calculation, ideally capturing all direct costs incurred.

TCO is a popular measure in information technology, but because it fails to include any measures of return, it has a number of significant disadvantages. In its favor, it:

- Ensures all costs are captured, not just the obvious ones
- Is simple to calculate and communicate

However, its disadvantages include:

- Discouraging investment in high-cost/high-return projects and biasing investment toward low-cost projects
- Encouraging a culture of cost-cutting over profit seeking

Because of these disadvantages, TCO tends to be a poor measure to put forward as a key indicator, especially in situations of high economic return, such as business analytics.

Return on Investment

Return on investment (ROI) takes this a step further by including return as a measure. ROI is an often-used and -misused term. Depending on the context, it can mean either of the following:

- A simple calculation to represent the simple return from an investment
- A class of measures that provide different perspectives on investment return

Neither is more correct than the other, but it is important to understand the distinction.

The simplest measure of ROI is the total return from the investment less the total cost of the investment. It generally uses TCO as an input, subtracting it from all the tangible returns delivered by the investment.

Much like TCO, ROI has a number of advantages and disadvantages. In its favor, it captures both returns and cost in a single measure and is simple to calculate and communicate.

Its primary disadvantage is that it treats investments that have a long payoff time the same as investments that pay off immediately. This may not seem like an important qualification, but it is; to see why, assume that someone offers to pay you $1,000 at the end of the week if you will loan her $100 today. Now, assume the same person offers to pay you $1,000 at the end of 10 years if you loan her $100 today.

The return on investment is the same in each situation, but there is obviously something that makes the second far less attractive than the first. That something is the time cost of money; money today is valued more than money tomorrow. There are many reasons for this, but the simplest is that we can do more with money today than we can with money tomorrow.

Given access to capital immediately, we can invest in a variety of other investments that will at a minimum match (and hopefully beat) inflation; the most common measure is the target rate, set by various central banks. For money in the future to be worth the same amount as money today, it needs to include this underlying rate of return available elsewhere. In practice, the longer the period until return, the less the money is worth.

Payback

Before we move on to dealing with this time cost of money, it is worth considering one final calculation: *payback*. Simply, payback is the time needed to cover the cost of the investment. So, if a project returns $1,000 a month and the investment had a total cost of ownership of $6,000, the payback period is six months.

The biggest advantages of this measure are:

- It provides insight into the ability of the investment to cover its costs.
- It is simple to calculate and understand.

Its disadvantages include:

- Not considering any acceleration in the rate of return in the post-payback period
- Not taking into account the greater value of money delivered sooner
- Failing to represent potentially large returns in the post-payback period

Payback is a useful measure only in situations where cash flow is a critical consideration. Given that it ignores the actual return from the project in favor of how long it takes for the project to cover its costs, it obviously provides a very limited view on the tangible value created from a project.

Net Present Value

Net present value (NPV) represents a slightly more complex measure, one that attempts to take into account the time value of money. As briefly discussed when covering ROI, money today is worth more than money tomorrow. Inflation, comparative rates of return through other investments, and other factors decrease the value of money in the future relative to having money today.

The key elements of calculating NPV are to:

- Define the life of the investment
- Understand the cost and return schedule over the life of the investment
- Identify the discount rate to be used

Every investment has a limited lifespan. For many business analytics projects, this is often three to five years. Anything outside of this horizon is likely to be replaced due to depreciation or technological advancement. The value accrued from the project must therefore be captured within this time frame.

Equally, the tangible value being created requires economic investment. This investment will normally occur before the value can be captured. Because money in the future is worth less than money today, calculating NPV requires the analyst to understand when these investments and returns are occurring.

Finally, the analyst must also define how much less money in the future is worth when compared against money today. Once defined, this discount rate is overlaid against the investment and return schedule and the total value of the project over its expected lifetime can be calculated.

NPV is described in direct financial return. As this represents a direct economic valuation of the project over a given time frame, projects can be directly compared against each other to see which will deliver the greatest value to the organization. This direct comparability is a significant advantage of using NPV as a valuation mechanism; even if the projects are fundamentally different, decision makers can still make an objective decision about which to invest in.

In its favor, it:

- Provides a directly comparable measure between projects
- Articulates the net economic value of a project, taking into account the time value of money

Its disadvantages include:

- Requiring a certain level of financial acumen to understand and apply
- An inability to deal with strategic and long-lifespan investments

Because NPV increasingly discounts the benefit of returns the further they are in the future, projects that involve very long horizons can be penalized when compared against shorter-term investments, even if the longer-term investments actually make more strategic and financial sense.

For example, some manufacturing or capital infrastructure projects deal with horizons of 16 to 50 years. Using purely NPV to compare projects, these projects will almost inevitably lose out to projects with shorter delivery time frames, even if they create less financial value in the long term. Considering the strategic value of a project is also an important consideration, especially when dealing with projects that may span decades.

Internal Rate of Return

A final measure of value creation is the *internal rate of return* (IRR). Unlike net present value (which focuses on the *magnitude* of return), IRR measures the project's *rate* of return. In technical terms, IRR is equal to the interest rate needed to make the net present value of future cash flows equal to zero. A simpler way of looking at it is as a comparison measure between projects to identify which generates higher average rates of return. In principle, a project with a high IRR estimate should generate greater growth than a project with lower estimated IRR.

Where NPV is represented as financial return, IRR is represented as a percentage. Like NPV, IRR is in principle comparable across projects. IRR can be useful as a measure to help prioritize projects that deliver greater growth.

However, also like NPV, IRR provides only one perspective of the value created by a project. Given limited availability of capital, it might be more advantageous for an organization to select a project with a lower IRR if it delivers greater NPV in a reasonable time frame.

For example, when considered over a two-year return period, one investment might have an IRR of 35 percent with the second having an IRR of 25 percent. If the organization has the resources to execute only one of these two projects, the first may appear the logical choice. However, if the NPV of the second project is $350 million and the NPV of the first project is only $100 million, it may make more sense for the organization to focus on the second initiative, despite its having a lower IRR.

Do Not Put Numbers in People's Mouths

Identifying the numbers is one thing. Getting people to agree to those numbers is another matter. The best returns in the world are not real unless the people that will own them agree with them.

As discussed earlier, the business analytics team often does not directly own the outcomes. It is a key enabler in the value chain, but it is not normally responsible for execution. The forecasting team may be responsible for identifying underlying demand, but actual fulfillment and ordering may be the responsibility of buyers and planners in a retail organization. The analytical marketing team may be responsible for identifying who is and is not a good target for cross-sell, but the actual execution may be the responsibility of the direct marketing team.

Because of this, it is critical that the team responsible for execution agrees with the tangible returns identified through the business case. The team may or may not become the primary party responsible for delivering the returns, but it will inevitably be expected to support the numbers. Nothing undermines a business case faster than internal disagreement.

Sources of Tangible Value

Economic value comes from many areas. The most obvious are associated revenue increases, but creating an effective business case typically requires identifying more than one source of economic value. The logic behind this is simple: The greater the coverage of value sources, the less likely it is the business case can be undermined through critics challenging one aspect of it.

Consider a business case that is built primarily on improving customer retention rates. The business case may be built to support investment in new recruits, additional technology, hardware and support arrangements, and process change. The project owner, after identifying $10 million of incremental revenue through better churn identification, puts forward a case for $1 million total investment, confident that her case will be quickly approved.

Unfortunately, when the case goes up for approval, one of the key decision makers questions the applicability of predictive modeling in their particular field. As it is a legitimate question, the project owner is prepared; she explains that they have done extensive testing using a robust holdout process to test the predictions against situations where the outcome was known. With a knowing smile, the stakeholder sits back in his chair and says that while it is important to make sure they are using a good process, the only real test is in the market. So, before the company can commit to this kind of investment, it really needs to test it in-market first.

Stuck without a response, the project owner can do nothing but agree; after all, given the focus of the business case, a failure in the in-market performance eliminates all value accrued from the project. And so, the project owner goes off for another six months, conducting extensive in-market testing that will in all likelihood match the out-of-sample tests conducted during the model development process.

On one hand, this validation was a critical component of demonstrating real economic return. On the other hand, it also introduced months of delay, each of which was creating real economic losses through needlessly high churn rates. Stuck between these two equally compelling arguments, what is a project owner to do?

The answer is simple: A good business case should identify multiple sources of value, each of which in isolation provides an attractive (if not necessarily sufficient) level of return. In the case of this hypothetical project, it may be that if the project owner had investigated further, she might have discovered that the organization was already using various forms of outsourced analytics services in the form of relatively expensive consultancies with each contract focusing on addressing an ad hoc request from the business.

Internalizing these capabilities might have led to $300,000 worth of cost avoidance through canceled consultancies, accrued each year and worth $1.2 million over the four-year life of the investment. Additionally, by moving to a largely automated system of target selection and campaign execution, the organization's capacity to deal with increased campaign volumes might have also increased, delaying the hiring of a new marketing analyst on a different team by two years. This cost deferral, when overheads have been fully allocated, might have been worth another $200,000 per annum, or $400,000 total.

In addition, investigation might also have uncovered:

- $150,000 savings through software license consolidation, accrued each year for a total value of $600,000 over the life of the investment
- $200,000 savings through internalizing the creation and updates of the organization's customer segmentation model, accrued each year for a total value of $800,000 over the life of the investment
- $50,000 of transfer-pricing cost avoidance involved in getting the IT department to recode models, accrued each year for a total value of $200,000 over the life of the investment.

While the churn retention models will provide a direct return of $10 million on their own, when aggregated these other benefits have the potential to provide another $3.2 million of incremental return. Critically, by balancing the business across each of these additional sources of economic value, the project owner could have increased the overall strength of the business case. If anyone had disagreed with a specific aspect of the business case, there still would have been another set of elements that in isolation would justify investment in an alternative process.

Economic benefits can be sourced from a wide variety of locations. Some good starting points for investigation are:

- Revenue and profitability improvements
- Productivity improvements

- Cost deferrals
- Risk mitigation

Revenue and Profitability Improvements

Revenue increases are typically the most obvious starting point, if not always the easiest to prove. Common examples include getting existing customers to buy more of what they are already purchasing (share of wallet), buy more expensive (up-sell) products in substitution, or buy additional alternative products (cross-sell). Other potential economic benefits could come through improving profitability by migrating customers to more profitable services or optimizing supply-chain or marketing activities to reduce cost of delivery or communication.

Productivity Improvements

Another source of economic value often considered is the creation of productivity improvements. A good example lies in the delivery of improved model development and deployment activities; by streamlining processes and leveraging technology, it is not unheard of for teams to decrease the time they spend managing data by an order of magnitude. Assuming there are five analysts on a team and assuming they spend two days a week simply managing data, process improvement could deliver a conservative reduction in time spent of 4 hours per person per week, translating to 20 hours per week for the whole team. If the average cost of a team member (including overhead) is approximately $200,000 per year, this translates to a potential savings of approximately $70,000 per annum, or more than $250,000 over a four-year investment period.

At first glance, this seems like an attractive position to put forward; the improvements are real, the returns are significant, and when combined with other economic benefits, the business case should become even stronger, right? Unfortunately, most financial controllers are reluctant to book economic savings unless those savings are actually realized. So, in this situation, although the team overall has definitely become more productive, the only way the economic benefits can actually materialize is if one of the team is let go. As their salaries are a fixed cost, productivity improvements are hard to account for.

The only way to demonstrate a financial return in this situation is to reduce current operational costs by reducing headcount, something few teams are interested in doing if their strategy relies on growing value, not reducing costs.

Cost Deferrals

Productivity gains do offer a potential economic benefit that is not always recognized on first analysis: the ability to defer costs for a period into the future. If the team's productivity is increased by 20 percent, it might defer the hiring of an additional team member for another two years. If this increase in headcount has already been budgeted for, this deferral of cost is a real economic return. The organization no longer needs to spend the money. So, although there may be an increase in cost through investing in the project, the savings gained through deferring the cost of hiring another individual may actually outweigh the investment made in the project.

This obviously does not apply only to headcount; one of the best examples I have worked with involved a project that was focused on inventory management. By improving forecast accuracy, this particular retailer believed it would be able to reduce inventory holding costs through its distribution centers by approximately 5 to 8 percent. In practice, this amounted to millions of dollars of savings. In isolation, this was quite attractive. As part of building a comprehensive case though, we jointly investigated a bit further and discovered that the retailer had plans to invest in another distribution center, bringing its total count to 21 centers.

Given a 5 percent reduction in inventory, we realized that over the retailer's existing 20 distribution centers this improvement was roughly equal to the contents of an entire distribution center in its own right. By achieving this reduction and then populating the newly empty space with additional inventory, the retailer could defer the construction of another distribution center for another six months based on the company's current growth rates.

Six months may not sound like a significant period of time, but the key was in the cost of a new distribution center. The retailer's best estimates had the cost of a new distribution center at approximately $140 million. By deferring its investment, the organization would suddenly have an extra $140 million to invest temporarily in other initiatives or markets. Using the prevailing interest rate at the time as a benchmark of the minimum return it would be able to achieve, we realized that this increase in liquidity was actually worth over $5 million in direct return, a value roughly equivalent to the returns accrued from the inventory reduction in the first place. By simply recognizing the impact that the inventory reductions would have on the organization's liquidity, we doubled its estimated return.

Another often overlooked element of cost deferral (and potentially total reduction) is in contractors; no matter the organization, significant amounts of money are often spent on using contractors or consultants. Often, by internalizing and sometimes slightly extending the focus of the business analytics project, these ongoing costs can be limited or sometimes eliminated. As these are budgeted items that cost real money, they are also very real tangible returns if this is achieved.

Risk Mitigation

A final common category of economic return is risk mitigation. Risk may seem like an abstract concept, but when that risk is being realized on a daily basis, it is a very real cost. A good example is in the management of bad and doubtful debts. Given the prevalence of credit cards and home loans, it is not surprising that every financial organization out there has a budget for losses associated with giving the wrong people money. The well-acknowledged reality is that not everyone who is given a loan will pay it back; models help limit exposure through preventing clearly insolvent individuals from getting access to credit, but statistics and fraud being what they are, it is inevitable that some people will default after being given access to credit. As some of these losses will be unrecoverable, it is critical that the organization budget for them. Otherwise, it will be spending more money that it really has.

What may be a bit more surprising is that this problem is also faced in any industry that provides post-payment facilities. Utilities, despite being in a totally different industry, face many similar challenges: They provide services on credit, they deal with a small set of customers who either are unable to pay or have no intention of paying, and they need to budget for these losses if they do not want to experience a sudden shortfall in liquidity.

It is within this context that better risk management can have many accruable economic returns. Better risk identification models can limit the number of individuals being inappropriately offered access to credit. Better recovery models can decrease the amount of bad and doubtful debt recovered. And better recovery classification models can reduce the amount of recoverable debt sold to third-party recovery agencies. Although each of these actually limits losses, these losses are often budgeted for. Any reduction achieved, therefore, can be claimed as a tangible return and included within the business case.

However, it is especially important to consider the overall environment in these situations. Unlike marketing activities where (broadly speaking) what is considered successful does not change, risk is understood to be a position taken, not an absolute outcome; risk is fundamentally a trade-off and not necessarily something to be avoided. Because of this, it is possible for better risk management and risk identification processes to not actually achieve any economic returns in the short-term.

For example, better risk identification models are useless if the organization has a strategic objective of growing market share in the short term. Even though the risk will be accurately identified, the organization will likely become less risk averse in the interests of growing market share. As it increases the number of loans that are made to higher-risk individuals, it will naturally see an increase in its rate of bad and doubtful debts. The better risk models in this case will fail to achieve any reduction in the bad and doubtful debt budget, putting the project owner at risk of failure.

A prime example lies in many electrical utilities. In many countries, electrical retailers are heavily regulated, not only in terms of structure and operation but also in terms of pricing. Because of this, competitive innovation can vary significantly. Interestingly, although not a major problem, fraud is a very real issue. It typically occurs on two levels:

1. Individuals acting fraudulently on application
2. Individuals fraudulently using other people's interconnections as their own

The first generally occurs when individuals have failed to pay their debts previously; due to a poor credit record, they are often unable to have their premises connected using the standard connection process. If they are unwilling to pay a sometimes rather significant deposit, they might resort to identity theft or credit theft to bypass standard risk management processes.

The second, although not necessarily frequent, generally occurs when an individual either modifies the meter on the premises or bypasses it entirely. One highly dangerous approach involves splicing the individual's circuit post–meter into his neighbor's circuit, transferring his consumption onto his neighbor's meter. Apart from the obvious savings this method implies, it is often used to temporarily mask illegal activities that are highly dependent on high energy consumption, such as drug production.

For some electrical utilities, these are simply the costs of doing business. For others, these are seen as sources of "free money"—by targeting them, the company can deliver real tangible returns.

IDENTIFYING INTANGIBLE VALUE

Tangible benefits are important, but they are not the whole picture; people make decisions based on more than just economic return. Strategic, personal, and general benefits may not be sufficient to get a business case over the line, but they should help win internal support for a given project.

Business analytics projects often deliver substantial intangible returns. These could include:

- Personal time savings and improved productivity
- Strategically valuable insight
- Reductions in uncertainty
- Faster and better decision making
- More trustworthy data

Observant readers will note that each of these indirectly delivers economic return; the challenge is that the economic return is often difficult to capitalize or measure. A good example is improved productivity/time savings. While it is true that increased amounts of available time offer the opportunity to either redeploy resources or increase activity coverage, the reality is that most organizations are hesitant to book economic returns from productivity improvements unless headcount is reduced. As this is often counterproductive to the objectives set by the business analytics team, it commonly means that the organization is unable to book the associated benefits in any meaningful way.

However, the importance of these benefits in gaining internal support cannot be understated. Although the organization may not be willing to book the economic returns associated with time savings, a manager within another group will probably personally value his ability to get home on time during the week to see his kids. That might not be enough to get a business case over the line, but it would do wonders in creating an ally for changing process!

Everyone Cares, but Not Enough to Give You Money

The key limitation of intangible benefits is that although they are often a significant source of personal value, they are also normally hard to map against organizational value (let alone measure). So, while they may make life easier for a variety of stakeholders within the organization, by definition they are not specific enough to demonstrate an economic return.

A common misconception stemming from this is that because intangible benefits cannot be related to direct economic returns, they are somehow of little or no importance in a business case. Viewing them this way undermines the strength of a business case for a very real reason: These benefits have the ability to build political strength.

Because of the personal value they create, they are an excellent way of building support. Whether it is helping to reduce someone's workload, making it easier for her to make decisions, or helping her build her industry credibility through success, the role of identifying and communicating intangible value cannot be understated. Successful execution of business analytics often requires working across multiple teams. While tangible returns may justify the release of funding, it is often the intangible returns that help build the political support necessary to galvanize a cross-functional group into a common team.

Intangible returns should be seen as a complementary component of a balanced business case, fleshing out the personal value side of the equation. The role that career growth, personal interest, and strategic vision can play in decision-making processes can in the right circumstances outweigh the role of measurable organizational economic return.

Sources of Intangible Benefits

Intangible benefits are in some ways easier to deal with than tangible benefits. The subjective nature of intangible benefits often means that it is enough that someone agrees that he or the organization will be better off by changing processes. One way of looking at intangible benefits is to view them as an answer to the "What's in it for me?" question often faced by business analytics managers.

Here are a few sources of intangible benefits worth considering:

- Strategic value
- Time savings
- Insight and ease of decision making
- Career growth

Applications of business analytics can create significant strategic value. Improved customer engagement can improve branding and positive association. Developing competencies can create competitive advantage. Improving supplier relationships through better demand forecasting and planning can create significant goodwill. These are notoriously hard to quantify but, if delivered, are often considered of significant organizational value.

On a more personal level, business analytics often creates more efficient processes through automation and operational analytical processes. These efficiencies generally reduce the workload of the execution team members, making it easier for them to do their jobs. As discussed earlier, these time savings are more often than not ignored within the economic side of the business case. As the only way to realize these benefits is to reduce headcount, most teams are reluctant to book these savings. However, freeing up time allows the team to focus on areas of higher importance, creating new value indirectly through improved productivity or expansion into new areas.

Similarly, access to better information commonly makes the team's decision-making processes easier. Less time needs to be spent managing data, giving the team more time to make better decisions. For many stakeholders, this is a very real benefit—it provides them with more certainty around their decision-making processes.

Being aligned to a successful, innovative, or interesting project often leads to additional career opportunities. Presenting key stakeholders with an opportunity to do things better may create support by providing them with an avenue for career advancement.

SIMULATING BUSINESS CASES

One of the more interesting extensions to a standard business case involves the use of simulation to conduct sensitivity analysis and financial stress-testing. And, given the focus on business analytics within this book, it is also a nice demonstration of the power of analytics in improving insight.

A key challenge with most financial modeling processes is they are by their very nature a static representation of potential outcomes. They take a series of fixed inputs, apply a variety of deterministic calculations to them, and provide a number of immutable outputs. This is a great abstraction of reality, but it is also a very blunt tool.

Reality is nowhere near as deterministic as a classic business allows. The assumptions used within most business cases are deliberately severely constrained, not because that is what reflects reality but because that is what a business case allows. Inputs such as the percentage reduction in churn expected to be achieved by the initiative, the degree of contagious churn quarantined through using social network analysis, or the expected aggregate rate of default are normally fixed to a single value and used to calculate a single set of outputs. At best, the business case may involve rerunning the calculations a few more times to accommodate low and high potential outcomes.

To give a better understanding of potential best-case, most-likely, and worst-case scenarios, the same business case is sometimes run three times, each with different values for all inputs corresponding to the best, most likely, and worst possible outcomes. Due to time constraints, these are often modeled using three sets of inputs, with each vector of inputs treated as a static list of fixed values. The results of this analysis are then attached to the overall business case to provide a level of comfort around possible outcomes; if the worst-case scenario still shows a positive return, it may relieve investors' fears.

As with most things done due to ease of calculation, these simplifications have a number of advantages and disadvantages. In their favor, they are easy to:

- *Compute:* Most outputs in a standard business case are relatively simple arithmetic calculations.
- *Trace:* Because only a small set of calculations are needed, validating a business case is generally a fairly simple affair.
- *Understand:* Because such a small set of inputs are used, getting a holistic understanding of the business case is relatively simple.

However, simplifying to such a high degree also carries a variety of disadvantages. These include:

- *A disconnect with reality.* The use of fixed inputs within a business case implies a level of certainty of outcomes that typically does not really exist.
- *An overly static view of the world.* Outputs such as NPV are likely to vary up or down due to the real-world variability of inputs.
- *A lack of awareness around sensitivities.* Although there are multiple inputs within any business case, computing a static business case does not normally identify or rank the key inputs that have the greatest influence on outcomes.
- *A complete disregard for interactions between inputs.* Specific inputs may be varied as part of a scenario-testing process, but it is extremely time consuming to vary all inputs.

The simplest (and probably most extreme) example is one of a start-up offering a new service that is as yet untested in the market. Based on its estimates, the firm may have concluded that due to its competitive differentiation, it is expecting to achieve a 15 percent market share within an existing segment. From this, the company can then calculate the number of transactions processed, the average profit per transaction, and in turn its overall NPV over a five-year horizon. Thus far, everything seems to fit well within a classic business case.

However, being a start-up, the organization has a number of other complications. Although they are expecting to achieve a 15 percent market share, management also believes that the company's services are so differentiated from the competition that they may actually grow the market by attracting new entrants as well as achieving a 30 percent market share within the investment period, equivalent to a 50 percent market share in the current market. All is not rosy though; management is also concerned that due to significant research and development investment being made by the incumbents, the company may lose its first-mover advantage sooner than expected, capping its expected market share capture to 10 percent of the current market. Making things even worse, this is only one of a set of about 20 different inputs about which management has similar levels of uncertainty.

If that were not enough, the firm also needs to justify its return on investment to potential angel investors. Given that it is not operating with existing capital, it must go to the market to get it. And, the market being what it is, the potential venture capitalists are extremely interested in understanding the likelihood of their making their money back as well as the likelihood of their making a substantial return.

Communicating all this through a standard business is extremely difficult, if not impossible. With a single business case, management will end up with one set of measures of return. At best, they will end up with a few; although it is possible to rerun the business case across a variety of scenarios, their fear would be that doing so would likely confuse potential investors with pages of numbers without any context.

One potential solution to this dilemma is actually the application of advanced analytics to the business case itself. In practice, simulating the business case with the aid of Monte Carlo sampling can act as a major enabler toward communicating this high level of complexity in a relatively simple manner.

Monte Carlo sampling is, in technical terminology, a process by which samples are repeatedly taken from a predefined probabilistic distribution and used as inputs into a function, and the results stored for future use. In simpler terms, it involves repeatedly feeding a variety of values into every input within the business case and storing key values for further analysis. The biggest advantage of this approach is that it not only gives a point estimate of a prediction—it will also give the *range* of possible outcomes.

For a practical example, consider the potential market share the management of the start-up described previously might believe they will achieve. Their estimates could be represented by the distribution described in Figure 4.2.

This is an extremely common distribution within most business cases. It represents the simple best-case, most-likely-case, and worst-case approach to describing potential results. This is often known as a *triangular distribution*, so called for its shape. There is nothing wrong with this; business cases deal with uncertainty, and for many factors within a business case, it is hard to identify a more representative distribution with any level of confidence or certainty.

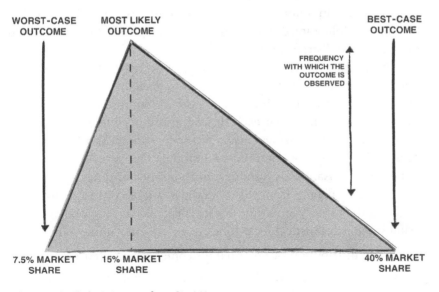

Figure 4.2 Likely Outcomes for a Start-Up

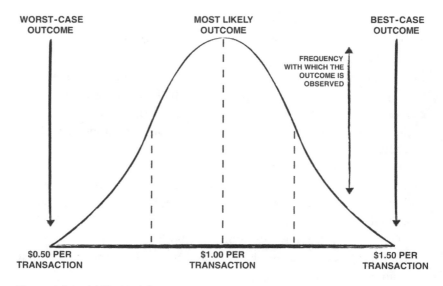

Figure 4.3 Variability Modeling

Another factor management of the start-up may be considering is their estimated cost per transaction (necessary to calculate profitability). In this situation, they may be pretty confident that they have estimated it correctly, but they are also aware that in practice it may vary by a certain amount. So, they decide to describe this variability through the following distribution, shown in Figure 4.3 (often referred to as a *normal* distribution).

Every input is given a distribution that describes it; each distribution takes the form that best represents management's knowledge at that point in time (including fixed values, if appropriate). A random value is then pulled from each distribution independently and used as an input into the business case. Calculations for NPV, IRR, and other values of interest are captured and stored. The process is repeated hundreds, thousands, or hundreds of thousands of times.

The net outcome from this analysis is a table of results for NPV, IRR, and the other values of interest. This table can then be analyzed using standard statistical techniques to get a better understanding of:

■ The distribution of potential outcomes given what is known

■ The upper and lower limits of what is possible given the interaction effects of these variable inputs

■ The probability of achieving a particular outcome given what is known (such as achieving an IRR above 60 percent)

Before we delve further into each of these, it is critically important to identify a core limitation of this approach. As the process is extremely dependent on the assumptions used for the input distributions, the results need to be tempered with an understanding that it represents a way of communicating the uncertainty around a business case, not a series of definite outcomes. As the input distributions typically represent a best guess based on the knowledge held at the time, it is impossible for them to carry any true level of certainty. By its very nature, a business case represents a particular view of the future, one designed to communicate a variety of assumptions and beliefs in as concise a manner as possible.

Should these assumptions or beliefs turn out to be invalid, the entire business case is invalid. However, as this applies equally to a statically calculated business case, applying simulation methods to a business case simply adds clarity around the level of uncertainty inherent in the business case.

Once the results have been collected, assessing the distribution of potential outcomes given what is known is a simple process. These values are simply aggregated into a histogram, as shown in Figure 4.4.

On the left-hand axis is the number of simulations that led to the NPV estimated on the lower axis. Another way to interpret this histogram is that given the assumptions, 25 percent of simulations led to an NPV of less than $950,000. The lowest NPV observed was $600,000 and the highest NPV observed was $2.6 million. On the optimistic side, 25 percent of simulations led to an NPV of greater than $1.55 million.

Of key interest is that this distribution may not be (and in all likelihood, is not) normally distributed. As many inputs are triangular to represent the degree of uncertainty inherent in any business case, these will inevitably introduce skew into the final distributions. This skew is interesting from two perspectives:

1. It indicates that the potential to make less than the most likely outcome is bounded relatively close to the median value.

2. It suggests that if the stars align, there is the potential for extremely high return.

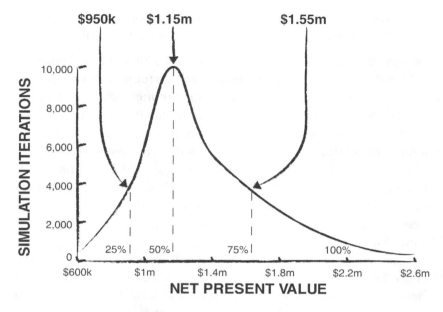

Figure 4.4 Outcome Distribution

Finally, by transforming this distribution into a cumulative distribution, the start-up can also identify the probability (based on what is known and the assumptions inherent in the business case) of its business achieving greater certain value of NPV, IRR, or any other measure. This is shown in Figure 4.5.

To investors, this information can be extremely valuable—it allows them to objectively consider the likelihood of return above a certain threshold given a particular level of investment.

PRACTICAL EXAMPLE: REDUCING CHURN IN TELECOMMUNICATIONS

Reducing churn in telecommunications serves well as a general example; it typically has all of the core characteristics that require a fairly multidimensional business case. The problem is easily understood: The term *churn* is generically used to describe a current subscriber or customer going to another provider. Postpaid telecommunications services are often a key target for reducing levels of

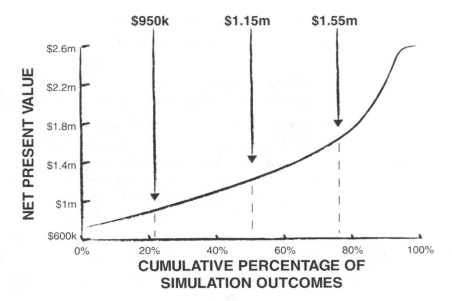

Figure 4.5 Cumulative Distribution View of Return

churn. Customers who use these services pay for their usage on a typical monthly subscription plan. In the retail consumer space, home phones, Internet, and mobile contracts are the most common examples. Their key characteristic is that unlike prepaid services, customers pay for their usage *after* they consume data or minutes.

While the logic is slightly different, churn is also a target for improvement when a rolling contract does not exist. For example, churn in a prepaid mobile situation (where customers pay for credit and then use it at their leisure) might mean the migration of customers to another prepaid service provider. Often, a distinction is made between those who actually go to another provider and those who simply never use their phone again.

Within postpaid telecommunications services, multiple elements can be considered within a business case. Although there is a direct and real financial cost to the business every time a customer cancels his or her contract, that cost only represents one element within a good business case. It is an important one, but it is not the only one.

The most obvious financial considerations include:

▪ The direct reduction in revenue associated with a service cancellation

▪ The loss in second-round cross-sell and up-sell service provision (as some customers later go on to purchase additional services)

However, there is more than that. Although the models themselves might assist in making the identification process more accurate, the business analytics team often does not own the actual campaign execution. This responsibility often falls to the direct marketing or retention teams, each of which has its own challenges and pains. Some of the benefits that these teams may also accrue include:

▪ The reduction in contact costs associated with more accurate identification

▪ An increase in marketing opportunities due to the reduction in inaccurate customer touchpoints

By applying what we have covered in this chapter, the business analytics team might follow the process and identify the following benefits:

▪ $14 million of retained revenue due to lower cancellations

▪ $4 million of incremental revenue due to additional cross-sell and up-sell

▪ 8 percent increase in *average revenue per user* (ARPU)

▪ $600,000 savings in outbound marketing costs

▪ 15 percent increase in total outbound campaign volume

These tangible benefits are critical, but the team can do more to help build internal support. Building a balanced business case requires an understanding of the intangible value being delivered to these groups. Other things that might be worth considering within a comprehensive, meaningful business case could include:

▪ Greater trust and credibility through assisting other teams in hitting their targets

▪ A reduction in stress across the two teams through increased automation and standardization

- An increase in internal and external visibility and the associated career prospects this may create

We will cover building an effective communication strategy in the next chapter, but for now suffice it to say that this value needs to be communicated to the business. At a minimum, a good communication strategy might include:

- A financial estimation of the direct economic return brought through predictive modeling
- An overview of the proposed process alteration and how it differs from the current one (including any reduction in steps or time)
- An overview of the strategic and market-based reasons driving the change in process
- A "what's in it for me" for each involved party, targeting their key concerns

SUMMARY

Defining the value being created by a business analytics initiative is a critical task of a successful team. Without this level of clarity, teams often find it difficult to:

- Build political support
- Establish objective comparisons between projects
- Overcome personal and organizational biases
- Prioritize activities
- Justify organizational investment in business analytics

By understanding the *tangible and intangible benefits* a business analytics initiative will create, the business analytics team can overcome these common pitfalls. By understanding *where the value will accrue*, the business analytics team can increase the relevancy of its communication strategy. And, by using a common measurement framework, the team can make it easier to compare and contrast various projects.

Defining the value forms one part of a comprehensive strategy to achieve success through business analytics. Equally important, however, are:

- Communicating the value
- Committing to it
- Measuring the benefits

In the next chapter, we will investigate how to create an effective communication strategy, review the importance of tailoring your message based on stakeholder-specific considerations, and look into how organizational culture can have a significant impact on a communication strategy.

THE CHECKLIST: DEFINING THE VALUE OF BUSINESS ANALYTICS

Key Considerations

Creating Value

What nonfinancial measurable outcomes will the initiative deliver?

What immeasurable outcomes will the initiative deliver?

For each of these outcomes, who will primarily benefit from them?

How do these projected benefits align with the strategic goals of the organization?

How do these projected benefits align with the tactical goals of other departments?

Measuring Tangible Benefits

What impact will these outcomes have on revenue?

What impact will these outcomes have on profitability?

Given successful completion of the initiative, what existing investments will be able to be deferred?

What impact will these outcomes have on risk?

Measuring Intangible Benefits

How will the initiative make other people's jobs simpler?

How will the initiative make other people more effective?

How will the initiative improve people's career prospects?

Identifying Costs

What technology investment will be required?

What additional roles will be required?

What training will be required?

What will be the cost of process change?

What will be the cost of additional data and storage processes?

Defining the Value

Has a comprehensive business case been built?

Has this business case been socialized with stakeholders and key decision makers?

Do they understand the measures used and do they agree that the data is correct?

Do they agree with the projected benefits and outcomes?

CHAPTER 5

Communicating the Value Proposition

INTRODUCTION

Change is challenging. Because a significant component of business analytics revolves around encouraging an organization to change existing practices, it is important to consider how change can be encouraged.

In practice, there are three main ways of encouraging an individual to change:

1. Control
2. Persuasion
3. Influence

Even though control is sometimes a direct means of encouraging change, more often than not the scope of control is limited to the person doing the controlling. It is extremely difficult (and often futile) to tell someone to change without the person's agreement.

Most change is enacted through applying persuasion and influence. People need to be persuaded that a change will be beneficial. Equally, people can be influenced to go along with a change even if they do not necessarily agree with it.

Persuasion and influence both require an *understanding* of what the change entails. They also require *reasons* why the change is worthwhile. And finally, these reasons must also be *relevant* and *comprehensible*. If they are not, they will be ignored.

Communicating the value proposition from business analytics involves taking the objective measures identified in Chapter 4 and translating them into a contextually relevant and comprehensible framework within an organization. An ideal communication strategy makes the information *personally relevant*, provides motivation, and acknowledges tacit cultural factors that aid in decision making.

When personal relevancy is missing, stakeholders often:

- Form misconceptions about the initiative
- Fall prey to fear, uncertainty, and doubt (FUD)
- Ignore the initiative entirely

In this chapter we will review the key elements that go into an effective communication strategy. We will examine how communication occurs and how this affects message creation. We will investigate how to create a common understanding in situations where awareness of analytics is low. We will also consider the impact that culture and conceptualization preferences have on decision making. Finally, we will review and provide an example of how to develop an effective communication strategy.

WHY YOU NEED TO PLAN YOUR COMMUNICATION STRATEGY

Although business analytics typically revolves around doing things smarter, implicit in any business analytics project is a need for change. The business analytics team rarely owns the processes that will execute on the insights it creates. Because of this, other stakeholders within the organization will almost inevitably need to work differently if the value is to be realized. Effective communication therefore requires the business analytics manager to:

- Convince others of the need for change
- Achieve consensus in how this change will be delivered
- Generate commitment to this change

A big part of a successful business analytics project is therefore identifying sufficient reasons for change. And, a major factor in this convincing process is typically the additional value that will be created by doing things differently. Building a comprehensive business case is a critical step in building support for a business analytics project. Without this business case, it is hard to identify specific examples of how the organization will be better off after the project is completed.

As discussed in Chapter 4, there are many ways of defining the value created from business analytics. A project may create a variety of tangible benefits including:

- An increase in average revenue per customer
- Growth in customer acquisition
- Reductions in customer churns

The same project may also create a number of intangible benefits for a variety of stakeholders within the organization. These might include:

- A reduction in effort required to deliver outcomes
- Better insight and improved decision-making ability
- Reduced uncertainty and improved confidence

In an ideal world, defining and committing to these would be sufficient to get internal support. They are highly quantitative, they are typically well defined, and there is explicit ownership over the outcomes.

Unfortunately, as with most things, reality is more complex. No matter how apparently self-explanatory the business case and the reasons for change are, they still need to be communicated to decision makers and key stakeholders.

Sometimes, this communication is easy. When this happens, it is as if the business analytics manager and the person she is communicating with are on the same wavelength. Communication is painless, both parties are often in full agreement, and little time is actually spent explaining the detail of the business case. In these situations, it is almost as if the need for change is self-evident.

In other situations, however, this communication process can be challenging. The two parties cannot even understand each other, let alone agree on an outcome. Instead of communicating *with* each other, they often spend time talking *at* each other. And, no matter how many times they repeat themselves, the other party "just doesn't get it."

If managed inappropriately, this breakdown in communication can derail the entire project. It does not matter how much value the project will create; if the team cannot convince stakeholders and decision makers of the value that *will* be created, it is impossible to deliver the changes that are needed. A good example of the impact communication can have on a team's ability to encourage change involves a project I worked on with a marketing group.

Breakdown in Communication over Modeling in Marketing

The marketing group's primary focus was on developing campaigns and driving sales. As with many similar groups, the team was filled with people mainly from a creative background—very intelligent, very holistic, and very focused on message. Unfortunately, although their execution was excellent, their targeting was not as good as it could have been. There was a common belief that the group as a whole was spending more than it needed to on direct marketing. These people were not failing; there was just an unstated belief that they were underperforming compared to their competitors.

This belief was also held by the marketing director, but he was not entirely sure how to fix it. My involvement stemmed from trying to help the analytics group, a parallel team within the organization, improve the perceived value of analytics to the organization. In the months leading up to my engagement, the analytics team had unsuccessfully tried to get the marketing team to adopt a more model-driven approach to target identification.

For context, it is useful to contrast the different approaches employed by the two groups. As the marketing team came from a longstanding background of generally quite successful qualitative analysis and experience-based decision making, its identification of potential targets was based on a rules-based segmentation approach where personas were identified through high-level usage analysis and focus groups. These segments were then defined based on sociodemographic assumptions (e.g., individuals below a certain age with a certain minimum spend) and identified through a series of business rules. Marketing campaigns were then targeted at these individual segments.

The analytics team, on the other hand, made no a priori assumptions about who would be interested in what. Instead, it followed a classic analytical approach and identified all individuals who purchased a similar product when offered as well as those who did not. The team members then collected all available information about these people and built a series of predictive models to help classify all remaining customers into those who would be likely to buy versus those who would not. In practice, they found a particular algorithm known as a neural network outperformed all their other algorithms. When tested against a random sample where the outcome was already known, they found that their model was over 40 percent more accurate at identifying the people who would buy versus those who would not when compared against the organization's existing targeting processes.

When I became involved, tensions between the two groups were already quite high. When I spoke to the marketing director, he explained in great detail how the analytics team simply did not understand the market. And when I spoke to the analytics director, he complained about how the marketing director refused to acknowledge the facts of the situation, as explained by the data.

In reality, they were both right; the issue was a simple breakdown in communication between the two teams. At the most basic level, both groups were interested in improving their overall marketing effectiveness, as measured by sales conversions on offers. However, beyond that, the two groups had a very significant difference in where they looked to identify the benefits from a process.

As the marketing group was heavily linked to the creation of the creative message, its perception of value was based on the group's ability to communicate effectively with its targets. So, understanding its customer demographics was critical to that group; without that insight, it was impossible for the group to create a value proposition.

The analytics group, on the other hand, was more concerned about its ability to identify the right people to market to. How they were identified or what their personal details were was less important than finding them as efficiently as possible. As it had no involvement in developing the value proposition and communication, these simply were not important to the analytics group.

One of the limitations of a neural network is that it is exceedingly hard to deconstruct what the dominant influencers are within a model. So, while the model itself used income, age, and a variety of behavioral patterns as inputs, the analytics team had absolutely no way of profiling which inputs were having the greatest level of influence or what the relationship was between the inputs and the likelihood of someone purchasing. With a divide like that, it is no wonder the two teams were barely on speaking terms by the time I got involved!

The solution was fairly simple. Once each team could understand the bigger picture and stop focusing purely on its own small part of the picture, they became more willing to try a slightly different approach. For its part, the marketing team agreed to try a different approach in a classic champion/challenger test against its existing selection strategies. And in return, the analytics team retrofitted a decision tree over the neural network to get a better understanding of what some of the reasons for the model's patterns could be.

In the end they found that by partnering, looking at the bigger picture together, and making that small change to their processes, they were able to reduce their marketing costs by over 15 percent and increase conversions by approximately 10 percent. And, probably more importantly, it laid the groundwork for a much more positive and ongoing relationship between the two groups.

In a Nutshell: What You Need at a Minimum and How to Do It

Everyone communicates differently. Because of this, effective communication often does not occur naturally—instead, it requires a plan.

At a personal level, our understanding and frame of reference varies based on our background. Getting over this hurdle often requires establishing a common starting point that others can relate to. By doing this, it becomes easier to relate the information they are considering to their conceptual frame of reference.

Communication preferences need to be considered at two levels: environmental and personal. At an environmental level, organizations and cultures exhibit distinct preferences when it comes to how timeliness and implicit understanding/explicit communication are treated. Failure to factor these into how things are communicated inevitably causes discomfort and frustration.

At a personal level, individuals tend to approach interpreting new information from one or more of four perspectives:

1. The analytical perspective
2. The process perspective
3. The personal perspective
4. The strategic perspective

By understanding how individuals prefer to approach interpreting information, you can more easily:

- Tailor communication the value of business analytics to a given audience
- Create holistic communication that is more likely to be accepted by a broad audience
- Link key messages to personal motivations

These, in aggregate, help the factors that are likely to influence the formal and informal decision-making processes within an organization.

Successfully *communicating the value* involves:

- Identifying the formal and informal decision-making processes
- Mapping and profiling and decision makers within that process to understand their roles and communication preferences
- Developing a holistic communication strategy to increase the effectiveness of the team's ability to communicate the value of business analytics

NEED FOR A COMMUNICATION STRATEGY

Considering most of us spend the vast majority of our time interacting with others, it is sometimes surprising how challenging it can be to successfully communicate an idea. Even at the best of times, everyone comes across people with whom they find it difficult to communicate.

Because business analytics requires creating organizational change, failing to effectively communicate an imperative for change is a death knell for the project. Regardless of how significant the intended value is, if people do not buy into that value, nothing will change. Critically, though, effective communication is far more than just simplifying and clarifying the message; it requires *an understanding of whom you are communicating with*. Failing to have this understanding can only make bad situations worse.

The reasons for this are simple. Everyone:

- Has a different level of understanding and is being driven by different things
- Fits within his or her own cultural context
- Has different communication preferences

Analytics is a complex field and it is rare that any given audience will necessarily have the right background to implicitly understand everything that is being communicated. Translation, by necessity, often falls to the analytics manager. Although some people are lucky enough to be innately effective communicators and persuaders, the vast majority of us benefit from applying a more structured approach to make sure that what is being communicated:

- Is *interpreted* correctly
- Is made as *relevant* as possible
- Creates the desired *outcome*

A communication strategy helps through explicitly considering the *differences* in our backgrounds and thinking patterns, thereby assisting the business analytics manager in tailoring his or her communications for maximum impact. When effectively created and executed, it helps:

- Minimize misunderstandings between stakeholders
- Persuade and convince stakeholders of the need for organizational change
- Improve linkages between the analytics team and execution channels

Defining the Communication Process

Understanding effective communication requires first considering *why* we have breakdowns in communication. Figure 5.1 describes a typical interaction between two individuals.

Our reality is created through our perceptions; we form opinions and understanding based on external influences and the internal mental framework we develop over our lives. When something is said to us, the first thing we need to do is decode that message into something that makes sense to us.

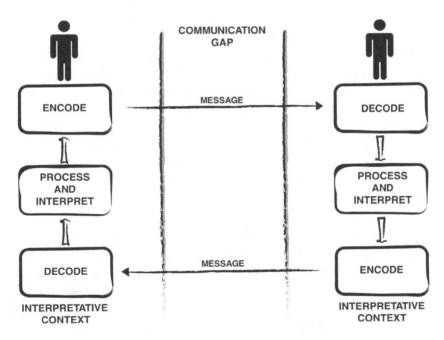

Figure 5.1 The Communication Process

That may seem like a simple process, but in reality we often do significant mental gymnastics to get to that point. Simply, *if the message is not delivered effectively, it is likely to be lost.*

If we are conversing in a language we are not fluent in, we need to spend a significant amount of mental effort translating what is being said into something that makes sense. Importantly, this does not only apply to languages such as English or French; an often missed subtlety is that *technical vocabularies form a language in their own right.* Disciplines develop jargon for a variety of reasons, including brevity of communication and specificity of definition. However, this technical language can act as a significant barrier to outsiders. Depending on our language skills, we may accidentally misinterpret what is said, introducing varying amounts of inaccuracy into our understanding of what is being said.

This is especially true in analytics; over time, the discipline has developed an entire vocabulary to help describe a variety of relatively complex concepts. Terms such as *lift, gains chart, Type I error,* and *independent variables* may be second nature to an analyst but are often incomprehensible to an outsider.

The medium of the message also has a significant impact on our ability to decode the original intent of what is being said. It is estimated that over 50 percent of our communication takes place through visual characteristics, something that is immediately lost if communication takes place in written form. Roughly another 40 percent of communication takes place through vocal characteristics such as pitch, timbre, tone, and pacing. Depending on what medium is used for communication and how well aligned the two individuals are in their communication styles, this decoding process has the potential to introduce significant misunderstandings. Because of this, *overcoming the limitations of the medium while meeting the other party's communications preferences is an essential step in communicating effectively.*

Many analysts have a strong preference for written communication over verbal communication. It is easier to achieve a high level of specificity when writing than it is when speaking. Unfortunately, doing so may be counterproductive if the audience is a highly verbal person. Because of this, it is important to remember that the audience should dictate the medium, not the other way around.

Once the message has been decoded, it needs to be *processed* and *interpreted*. To do this, we need to rely on our experiences and understanding of the world through applying our own interpretive context; this interpretation leads to our final reaction to the message. We may be supportive or we may disagree. Or, we may not understand the message or even care about it. Whatever our reaction, we encode a reply using our own interpretative context and communicate it back to the other party, closing the loop.

Within this loop, there are two potential sources of disconnect between the intent and the interpretation of a message:

- *External breakdowns*, where the message is incorrectly encoded
- *Internal breakdowns*, where our interpretative framework leads us to the wrong conclusions

Correctly encoding a message in a technical sense is beyond the scope of this book. Typically, it requires a good understanding of:

- Persuasion, negotiation, and influencing techniques
- Presentation skills
- The role of body language (or lack thereof) in communication

Although these are essential skills, there is little about them that is unique to communicating the value of business analytics. Of more interest is an understanding of the reasons behind *why* people sometimes misunderstand or ignore the value of a business analytics project.

There are a multitude of factors that define our own personal psychology. Three of the most interesting within the context of selling the value of business analytics are our:

1. Understanding of what is being communicated and our ability to create *information relevancy*
2. Personal context and *cultural factors*
3. Communication preferences and *conceptual relevancy*

Structure Helps Create Focus

Understanding the influence these factors have on various stakeholders and their relevancy to the initiative of interest is only half of the picture; much like advanced analytics, it merely helps to create insight. Arguably more important is translating this insight into a practical execution plan.

This can be difficult without structure. An effective business analytics manager presents information in a way that is:

- Understandable

- Persuasive

- Relevant

Effective communication requires maintaining a focus on ensuring the message is communicated as efficiently as possible. Trying to communicate too much in too many ways may move outside of the recipient's interpretative context. Trying to communicate too little in too few ways may leave the audience with unresolved questions.

Equally, communicating with the *right* people is more important than convincing *everyone*. Persuasion and evangelism take time and, although their importance cannot be understated as a driver for change, an effective strategy requires just the right amount of communication effort (and no more). Targeting too many people will create a drain on the manager's time, hurting other activities. And, targeting too few people will often delay the launch and delivery of an initiative.

By applying a structured approach to planning communication, the business analytics manager can:

- Identify those who should be targeted within the strategy

- Understand their likely drivers and interpretative context

- Map out an appropriately tailored communication strategy

AWARENESS AND INFORMATION RELEVANCY

Assuming a message is appropriately delivered at a technical level, the next most important thing is to ensure that it contains a high level of informational relevancy. The audience needs to be able to understand it within their personal interpretative context; if they do not, at best they will be confused. This message needs to be aligned to their motivators; otherwise they will not be interested in even considering it. To explain what this means in practice, let's revisit the example from earlier in this chapter.

Fundamentally, the analytics team was interested in encouraging the marketing team to change its processes. The analytics team had built a model that had a high level of accuracy and, by embedding it within the marketing team's operational processes, the team expected to see a substantial improvement in targeting efficiency.

Both teams had high motivational alignment; each was being benchmarked on the accuracy of its marketing efforts. Despite this, the two teams had been unable to get past each other's apparent ignorance. The critical thing they were missing was the ability to relate the activities of the two groups to each other.

If someone cannot make the information he has received relevant to his personal context, he is unlikely to pay any attention to it. Our two most important considerations are normally whether:

1. We can *comprehend* what is being said or *relate* it to our context

2. It aligns to our *personal motivations*

Successful *understanding* requires the first, successful *motivation* the second. Technical fields such as business analytics often face higher-than-normal communication challenges. As there is a certain minimum level of comprehension that is needed in order to understand the detail, trying to explain the *reasons* behind something may actually be counterproductive if the audience does not have sufficient grounding. At best, the people interpreting the message will be bored; at worst, they will become actively doubtful.

Analytics managers are responsible for creating this informational relevancy in the minds of their audience. Without it, they will be ignored or misunderstood. Often, it comes down to trying to understand the background of the audience they are speaking to and creating appropriate analogies and conceptual mappings. For example, talking about models to a marketing group may be counterproductive. However, if they already compare the efficiency of different processes as part of their daily business, describing it as a challenger customer-acquisition process using different techniques may be far more familiar.

Once the message has been understood correctly, our willingness to even start considering it depends on how well it aligns with our personal motivations. These do not necessarily have to be mercurial: Relational considerations, philanthropic concerns, or appeals "to the greater good" may also be motivational. However, unless there is something in the message that aligns against the audience's personal motivations, it is unlikely that they will do anything differently.

Comprehension and Relevancy

Business analytics is a complex field. It spans from the strategic level to an operational level, ranging from high-level business issues to low-level technical challenges. Because it aims to improve business outcomes, business analytics requires a good understanding of the business, its model of operation, and the environment within which it operates. Equally, because it leverages various forms of analytics, it also requires at an operational level a solid grounding in mathematics, information technology, data management, and even sometimes hardware platforms.

Business analytics is not unique in this sense; every reasonably complex discipline has this level of depth, whether it is accounting, engineering, or marketing. However, what *does* make business analytics relatively unique is its relative immaturity when compared against other disciplines.

Few organizations have a firmly entrenched analytical culture. This is important because while a manager might have sufficient knowledge to explain the detail behind the most commonly applied areas of analytics such as segmentation and predictive modeling, *it is unlikely that anyone else in the organization will have the necessary level of comprehension to understand what is being explained to them.*

Unlike many other disciplines, few people have a solid understanding of the technicalities of business analytics. While many university courses provide an overview of other competencies such as accounting or economics, they do not do the same for business analytics. This lack of foundational knowledge often makes it difficult for stakeholders to "trust" the results of business analytics. This is not because they are incapable of understanding it, but merely because they do not have the right background.

When presented with this lack of foundational knowledge, many managers try to educate. Sometimes this is an appropriate strategy, especially if that is what their audience is looking for. However, it *is not* always the *right* strategy. Rather than focus on the message, it is often better to reexamine the reason behind the message.

Remember that the point of communicating the value of business analytics is not to turn other stakeholders into analysts. Instead, it is to:

- Convince others of the need for change
- Achieve consensus in how this change will be delivered
- Generate commitment to this change

A key focus of an effective manager of business analytics is to identify the shortest path to value creation within ethical and legal boundaries. Educating the entire organization on the low-level details of analytics is rarely the shortest path. Often, all that is required is identifying a common frame of reference.

Returning to the example from earlier in this chapter, the marketing team had an excellent grounding in the creative and execution side of marketing. Equally, the analytics team had an excellent understanding of the technicalities of model development. Unfortunately, the level of commonality between these two activities was relatively low, preventing each team from understanding what was important to the other.

In presenting the technical detail of the models it had developed, the analytics team had moved well outside of the marketing team's interpretative context. Because the marketers were unable to relate the model to anything they were familiar with, they could not understand it. And because they could not understand it, they refused to buy into it.

Our knowledge does not exist in a vacuum; the fastest way to understand new things is by linking them to things we already understand. We use analogies, metaphors, and extensions to existing ideas to simplify this process; by building on what we already know, we find it easier to grasp new concepts. The alternative is to develop an understanding from first principles, a bottom-up approach that takes significant time investment. It is an approach that is often necessary when venturing into fundamentally new territory, but as nice as it would be to educate every stakeholder in an organization, it is rarely a feasible strategy.

Finding a common starting point is one of the keys to effectively communicating the value of business analytics. For the marketing team, it involved the creation of a model that, although analytically based, had outputs that were similar to existing processes. Once these outputs could be analyzed, it was a relatively small step to explain how the analytical approach differed from a rules-based approach. And, once this was understood, the marketing team could apply its newfound understanding to suggest ways the model could be tweaked to better fit the team's requirements. From that point, it was a small step to convince the team to benchmark the two approaches against each other, another activity it was familiar with.

By making a small amount of extra effort to translate its model into something that had higher informational relevancy, the analytics team moved past incomprehension and into consideration. It was only after this happened that a real dialogue could begin.

Motivational Understanding

Providing informational relevancy will ensure only that the message is understood. Whether members of the audience decide to consider it further depends heavily on how well the message broadly aligns to their personal motivations. If there is nothing in the broader message that aids this alignment, it is unlikely that they will either consider it or act on it.

Lest this should sound like a terribly cynical and downright Hobbesian view of the world, it is important to clarify that in practice many different motivational factors exist. Direct value, including tangible and intangible benefits, is often a significant consideration. However, it is not always the strongest. Other motivators may include:

- Respect for the individual making the request
- Political or relational considerations

- Interest in the work and the resultant self-actualization
- Involvement in a broader team
- Philosophical considerations
- Goal setting and self-determination
- Career development

The value delivered through the business analytics initiative may provide sufficient motivators in isolation to encourage further consideration by the audience. However, considering these broader motivators can go beyond merely strengthening alignment; if successfully identified, they can directly counteract other demotivators.

One example I was involved in revolved around an individual who was frustrated with repeated organizational failures to deliver change. He was passionate about making his team more effective but, because of burnout, was reluctant to commit to executing on the insight. No amount of persuasion on the expected value of the change was sufficient to convince him to participate in the program.

The breakthrough came from demonstrating that we had a detailed plan for change *as well as* strong internal commitment to try to do things differently. We demonstrated that we had already:

- Successfully demonstrated that the problem could be solved
- Attained internal management signoff on the project
- Created a detailed implementation plan and sourced the appropriate resources

Once he understood that we had a real chance of successful delivery, his desire for organizational improvement outweighed his reluctance caused by his bad experiences. Importantly, though, it was only after I had reconsidered what motivated *him personally* that I was able to identify a successful strategy to get him to move past understanding to consideration.

ORGANIZATIONAL AND SOCIETAL CULTURAL CONSIDERATIONS

Understanding is important. However, if the delivery of a message violates a contextual taboo, ignores accepted practices, or bypasses important individuals, it may be discarded out of hand. Having an understanding of the broader cultural context within which the organization and the individuals within it operate is an essential component of crafting an effective message.

Culture plays a significant role in modifying our *resistance* or *acceptance* of a given message. If a message contradicts either our own or the organization's values or norms, it is likely to meet significant resistance. Some of the most important factors that influence our level of message acceptance include:

- Our *historical experiences*
- The *delivery* of the message
- The degree to which *implicit understanding* of political, relational, and organizational knowledge is expected

As discussed in Chapter 4, we suffer from a variety of biases, one of which is our innate preference to interpret things based on what we have most recently experienced. For individuals or organizations that have had previous negative experiences with business analytics, this can be a major factor in creating resistance against even considering any communication about business analytics. Acknowledging these negative experiences up front and explaining why things are or are not different along with how these problems can be avoided this time may be an effective strategy for overcoming this cultural bias.

Equally, the delivery of the message can be a critical factor in individuals' willingness to receive a message. This goes beyond structural elements; if the communication pattern does not align with their cultural and contextual expectations, they can be made so uncomfortable as to be unable to even consider the message. For a highly numerical person, glossing over the detail may create resistance. Equally, for a numerically illiterate person, going into extreme amounts of detail on the functional form of the models being used may push him well outside of his comfort zone.

Finally, having an understanding of how much implicit knowledge is expected when communicating is critical. Organizations have wildly different cultures; in some, decisions are made entirely through common implicit understandings. Failing to plan around this subtext inevitably means creating significant resistance and limits the effectiveness of any communication.

Historical Influences: Background and Experiences

One of the biggest contextual limiters is our own experience. When we start from a blank slate, we are more often than not willing to consider a proposal on its merits. Unfortunately, it is extremely rare that this is the case; because we try to create informational relevancy whenever we are presented with something we have no experience with, we inevitably carry some baggage into our evaluation, positive or negative. Business analytics is no different. If an organization has had some experience with business analytics in some form, it will often carry its experiences into any future business analytics projects.

This has advantages and disadvantages. In its favor, it is one of the most effective ways of building ongoing support for business analytics. A single, demonstrably successful project is often sufficient to grow the use of business analytics within an organization. However, a single unsuccessful project is often enough to create significant internal biases against attempting a new project.

This is not unique to business analytics; given the high rate of failure of IT projects, it is a dilemma often experienced by information technology professionals. Because of this, it is essential to understand what has and has not been successful previously in an organization, regardless of how directly applicable other projects have been.

A good example lies in another organization that had recently experienced a failed business intelligence platform project. Although the technology had been more than up to the task, the project team had failed to adequately define where the value would be coming from or how it would be measured. So, although the implementation had been successful, the broader organization had not migrated to the platform. In isolation this would not have been of concern, were it not for the extremely large investment the organization had made into an "insight platform" that no one was using.

The analytics team had recently been put under the direction of a new manager. His first order of business was to identify a variety of viable projects but, in failing to understand the organization's historical influences, he walked directly into a series of landmines. Being a good corporate citizen, he had tried to direct his team's projects to leverage the existing (unused) business intelligence platform IT had delivered. However, recognizing that the platform lacked any advanced analytics capabilities, he had also called out for additional investment into an analytics platform.

His first meeting with management went less than successfully. Despite having well-defined benefits and a clearly defined execution plan, he was rapidly shut down and told to focus on business as usual. He left confused and later came to me for a second opinion.

On further investigation, it turned out that he had failed to take two things into account. First, by describing his project as an "insight" project, he had used the same language as the previous project, creating an unfortunate association with the previous project that *had not* delivered any returns. Because the prior project was not perceived as having delivered any value, there was a significant tacit concern that because this project was apparently similar, it would be running a similar risk of non-return.

Second, by discussing his use of the existing platform first, he had hit a raw nerve with the executives he had been talking with. Unbeknownst to him, they had approved the initial project and were under pressure to demonstrate success. While his using the platform was definitely seen as a good thing, their belief was that the existing investment should be sufficient to cover *any* new insight project, even one that involved advanced analytics. Even though the platform did not have any advanced analytics capabilities, the investment had been sufficiently large that there was concern about further investment in *any* apparently similar capabilities.

Unfortunately, by this point the damage had been done. My colleague was forced to go back to the drawing-board and focus on business as usual until he could develop a plan for an alternative initiative that had sufficient historical separation to get management buy-in. This took him approximately six months, but had he considered the broader organization's historical context, he might well have avoided this delay and focused on his highest-value project first.

Message Delivery: Proxemic Factors and Time Sense

Just as organizational history influences our perceptions, so does our own personal development. We exist in a wide variety of cultural contexts; although organizational culture has an influence on our perceptions, it is not the only influence. Our formative years, the broader culture in which we live, and our social network also influence our perceptions and preferences.

Organizations often have a dominant culture, but it is important to remember that individuals also have their own cultural preferences. And, because of this, making assumptions based on one particular culture without any further thought can be dangerous, especially for multinational organizations establishing analytical global centers of excellence.

Two of the most relevant broader cultural influences are our nonverbal communication preferences (also known as *proxemic* factors) and the way we perceive time (also known as *time sense*). These are often heavily influenced by our broader context and may be common across organizations.

Proxemic Considerations and Global Operations

Because the vast majority of communication takes place outside of language, it is not surprising that body language and spatial characteristics have a strong influence on our communication. In most situations, this happens entirely outside the realm of our conscious thought; when we are communicating with individuals who share our cultural context, this spatial understanding takes place intuitively. We naturally gravitate toward a distance and posture that matches our emotion. If we are close to those with whom we are communicating, we will naturally gravitate closer to them. If we are distant or hostile, we will step away.

In our context, this occurs naturally. However, when one is dealing across cultural or geographic boundaries, it is very easy to mistakenly breach etiquette and unknowingly make the conversation uncomfortable. At the simplest level, it is easy to encroach on your audience's personal space if you are from an urban background and your audience is from a rural background. Similarly, constantly backing away from someone from a high-density background can make everyone uncomfortable.

This often has minimal impact at a national level, but it is a critical consideration for business analytics teams operating at a regional level.

Some multinational organizations have regional or even global centers of excellence, providing support and advice to offices across the world. Because a significant component of business analytics is actually focused on change management, a failure to appreciate these cultural differences creates real frictions, often preventing the team from delivering success.

For a team operating across cultural boundaries, maintaining an open mind and observing these differences is a critical component of success. Equally, understanding how space and body language can influence comfort levels is critical. Understanding the impact of volume, tonality, and eye contact is also important. Appreciating these differences and deliberately working within them can sometimes be the differentiating element between a successful team and a team that fails to transform the organization.

Time Sense and Delivery Expectations

Just as spatial and physical characteristics have an influence on communication, so does our preferred perception of time. Broadly speaking, people can perceive time in two ways:

1. A continuous stream, where events flow into each other (also known as *polychronicity*)

2. A discrete measurement, where events occur sequentially and are separate (also known as *monochronicity*)

To someone who sees time as continuous, working on multiple things is normal, as everything will eventually be completed anyway. Time management is a foreign concept to many polychrons: Mood, interest, and enthusiasm often dictate focus. And, because of the flowing nature of time, setting aside specific time to discuss topics is rarely important; relationships and a willingness to speak often lead to an immediate conversation when needed.

To someone who sees time as a discrete measure, time is something to be explicitly managed. Work is often conducted in a very sequential nature with a high degree of scheduling and order. Deadlines are taken very seriously and detail is appreciated. Conversations often need to be scheduled well in advance to ensure they do not impact any existing commitments. And being late is an extreme offense.

Note that neither is a better perspective than the other: They are simply two different ways of viewing the world. Because they represent polar opposites, individuals often appear somewhere between the two extremes.

Cultures can exhibit broad preferences toward time sense. In many Western cultures, including the United States, Northern Europe, and Australia, monochronicity is the norm. Alternatively, Latin America and sub-Saharan Africa tend to exhibit polychronic preferences.

Just as with proxemics considerations, these preferences are almost invisible to someone who is accustomed to them. However, they can cause great offense if they are not followed, largely due to cultural dissonance. For a business analytics team providing support across a broad geographical region, understanding the impact of time sense on creating commitments is critical.

For example, consider a predominantly Western team providing EMEA (Europe, Middle East, and Africa) support from Singapore. Its coverage may extend from Australia to Kenya, and using the same strategies to solicit commitment will most likely lead to significant frustration.

Because of the team's cultural background, getting commitment on delivery time frames in Australia may be fairly simple. A plan will be agreed on, the steps to getting there negotiated, and a date set. Progress reports will likely be implemented, and the project will be tracked across multiple milestones. Interaction will often be limited to the project and further communication only necessary if the project is starting to drift.

Unfortunately, using the same strategy in Kenya may lead to discomfort on both sides. Although it is still critical that the project be delivered at an agreed-on date, the project reporting structure may be considered overly formal and impersonal. The lack of personal contact may create friction. Milestones may shift regularly as other initiatives rise and fall in importance. And, progress reports may be late, early, or never arrive at all.

Managing a global center of excellence requires an awareness of the impact time sense has on business relations. It requires managers to tailor their communication strategies to suit the individuals they are dealing with. And it requires enough flexibility to work outside of one's cultural comfort zone without losing track of the importance of delivery.

Implicit Understanding: High and Low Context

A final important cultural consideration is the level of implicit understanding that is expected within interactions. It can sometimes feel as if there is more that is unsaid than is said. For someone who is not attuned to these largely tacit information flows, trying to get consensus can be extremely frustrating. Ideas will fail to gain traction, previously unknown issues will continually crop up, and often relationships, not facts, will drive decision-making processes. However, someone who is used to a highly relationally driven decision-making framework can often find it frustrating to continually have to explain everything in great detail.

Edward Hall, in his book *Beyond Culture*, described these two situations as *high-context* and *low-context* cultures.[1] High-context cultures tend to be characterized by:

- More relationally driven decision making
- Situational and personal knowledge
- A higher level of implicit (or internalized) understanding of taboos, knowledge, and acceptable behavior
- Greater use of nonverbal and indirect communication
- A need for consensus and a preference for team-based problem solving
- A focus on accuracy and deductive thinking

By contrast, low-context cultures tend to be characterized by:

- More rule-based and process-driven decision making
- Public and transferable knowledge
- Explicit identification of acceptable behavior and common activities
- Greater use of written and formal communication
- A belief in personal ownership and independent execution
- A focus on speed and inductive thinking

Culture is not static. Messages and communication exist on a continuum. Because of this, it is important not to view any given cultural context as being static or stereotypical. Cultures overlap and it is possible for a series of interactions and messages to individually vary along the continuum. Not only that, but many contexts exhibit both high and low characteristics, often defined by how central any given individual is within that context. However, it is an extremely useful framework for better understanding how to communicate and sell the value of business analytics.

For a manager looking at transforming an organization, adapting to the organization's dominant cultural preferences is essential. For example, an organization that exhibits low-context characteristics may emphasize outcomes when assessing investment options. Decision makers may favor a detailed explanation on how the outcomes will be achieved. They may also look for debate, defense, and justification as part of the decision-making processes. Often, a single person will own the final decision of whether to proceed.

Alternatively, an organization that exhibits high-context characteristics may emphasize agreement that "it is the right thing to do" when assessing investment options. Decision makers may favor trust and strength of relationship as a consideration of concern. Execution may be delayed until concerns are resolved and explicit disagreement may be avoided. Often, a variety of people will be consulted when the decision of whether to proceed is made.

Failing to fit into a given context inevitably leads to frustration and discomfort for everyone involved. For someone from a high-context culture interacting in a low-context culture, it can feel extremely frustrating having to explain everything. If things are not explained, the individual can even seem irrational, making decisions for no apparent visible reason. The person may also spend significant amounts of time seeking consensus from stakeholders who have no real influence on the final decision, creating broader frustration in the organization because of the slow speed of delivery.

Equally, someone from a low-context culture interacting in a high-context culture can accidentally create dissonance. This person will often fail to talk to the "right" people, even though these people may not be identified in the organizational chart. The low-context individual may be seen as a "loose cannon," operating independently from the organization. This person will often be seen as an outsider, oblivious to "the way things work here."

CONCEPTUAL RELEVANCY

We do not all view the world the same way. Although we can choose to view the world in any way we want (given enough effort), we all have preferred ways of thinking. And, if the message being delivered does not align with our thinking preferences, *it is likely to be ignored*.

Once a message has been understood and accepted, we need to process it within our personal conceptual framework. Making information *conceptually relevant* is critical—failing to do this can lead to an impasse where one party simply ignores the other. Effective communication requires the person doing the communicating to have an understanding of how the other person prefers to understand things and, in so doing, tailor his communication style to suit.

This involves moving beyond technical understanding and into conceptual understanding. Although we are all different, it is useful to consider some common perspectives within most organizations and use those as a starting point to try and frame a message. Effective communication often involves "getting in the other person's shoes" so as to provide greater conceptual relevancy.

Regardless of whether one or multiple approaches are used to frame communication, identifying the value created from the initiative is a common feature. Although it will primarily appeal to people who prefer to conceptualize analytically or sequentially, it is a generally accepted minimum criterion for acceptance. It will not always be the most important factor, but it usually will be a necessary one.

By applying a relevant conceptual framework, the person interpreting the message can find it easier to relate to what is being discussed. A useful model is to consider four perspectives:

1. The *analytical* perspective
2. The *process* perspective
3. The *personal* perspective
4. The *strategic* perspective

By considering each of these, building a message that covers all four conceptualization preferences, and emphasizing different elements where appropriate, the business analytics manager can reduce the probability of stakeholders switching off.

The Analytical Perspective

One approach is to focus on the facts. Often, this is the default perspective taken by an analytics team. It relies on logic, rigor, and rationality. For someone who operates in this conceptual space, focusing on value and outcome is often a key consideration. The person may be interested in first understanding how a business analytics initiative will create economic value, deliver a new competency, or improve overall performance.

Communicating with people who prefer this mode of conceptualization often involves explaining *how the initiative will work*. While more formalized methods of communication are often preferred, it is also important that an individual with a preference toward the analytical perspective be able to engage in a dialogue to support critical evaluation. They frequently will be interested in understanding the detail behind the outcomes, including:

- The amount and types of value being created
- Numerical measures
- How the value is defined and will be measured
- The types of models used and the assumptions underpinning those models
- What other approaches were considered and why they were not as effective
- What evidence supported the particular course of action that had been selected
- Examples of other organizations or projects that followed a similar approach and were successful

Establishing logical relationships and structured explanations is often important to people who prefer to conceptualize in this space.

For a manager interested in communicating in this way, a useful structure is to explain through a formal presentation:

- The *tangible and intangible value that will be created*
- The *evidence that demonstrates success* will be achieved—for example, this may be the results of a proof of concept
- An explanation of *how the evidence was collected*, such as the approach used within the proof of concept
- The *next steps* that need to be taken to realize the value
- The *expected delivery time frames*

The Process Perspective

Another approach is to focus on what needs to be executed. This often involves identifying the changes that will need to be made to existing processes in order to realize the defined value. For people who operate within this conceptual space, focusing on quality, governance, and process is often important. They may be interested in first understanding how things will need to change to support value creation.

Communicating with someone who prefers this mode of conceptualization often involves explaining *what needs to be done*. More formalized methods of communication are often preferred, such as structured presentations with defined outcomes. These individuals will frequently be interested in understanding the structure behind the execution and how risk will be adequately managed. Some of the things they may be interested in knowing include:

- The processes that will be impacted
- Process diagrams and time frames
- How the changes will lead to improved quality, governance, or transparency
- The detailed sequence of steps that will need to be taken in order to deliver the project
- How project delivery will be managed
- Specific examples of how efficiency will be improved
- Hard measures around execution times/outcomes and how the changed process will change these

Establishing order of execution and referring to specific details is often important to people who prefer to conceptualize in this space. For a manager interested in communicating this way, a useful structure is to explain through a formal presentation:

- The *tangible value that will be created.*
- The *current process and outcomes being achieved.* This could include the time needed for various forms of analysis, the number of people who can be contacted, offer-acceptance rates, or the amount of time wasted due to poor information. Unlike the business-level measures, these are often operational statistics.
- The *proposed process and outcomes that will be achieved.*
- The *changes that will need to be made.*
- *Whom these changes will impact.*
- A detailed explanation of *how these changes will be implemented.*

The Personal Perspective

Another approach is to focus on how the initiative will impact stakeholders within the organization. This often involves specifically identifying the intangible value that the initiative will create and how it will create better cross-functional relationships. For someone who operates in this conceptual space, establishing trust and ensuring a positive impact on stakeholders is often important. These individuals may be interested in first understanding how the initiative will impact the people they manage.

Communicating with those who prefer this mode of conceptualization often involves explaining *how it will make people better off.* Less formalized methods of communication are often preferred, whether it be over a meal or through a simple discussion. Often, these people will be interested in talking things through to get to a common understanding and possibly contribute supporting ideas. They will frequently be interested in understanding whom the changes will impact and whether the changes will support their team's interests and career development preferences. Some of the things they may be interested in knowing include:

- How the changes will improve their team's quality of working experience
- The emotional impact the changes may have
- The opportunities to work together as a broader team
- The ways in which the initiative will support their team's career and personal development
- How they will be able to support the initiative

Thinking about things in terms of people and relationships is often important to people who prefer to conceptualize in this space. For a manager interested in communicating this way, a useful structure is to explain through a more informal context:

- What the *initiative is trying to achieve.*
- The *intangible value that will be created.*
- The business-level measures of *tangible value that will be created.*
- The *people who will be involved in the initiative.*
- An overview of *how the teams will work together.*
- An explanation of *how the teams will extend their responsibilities.*
- An overview of *how these responsibilities will help the teams.* This may be by reference to internal strategic objectives, reference to admired industry participants exhibiting these characteristics, or specific career development plans.

The Strategic Perspective

A final approach is to focus on the holistic impact of the initiative. This often involves identifying the competitive differentiators being developed, the strategic advantage created by the initiative, or the innovations the initiative will deliver. For someone who operates in this conceptual space, being visionary, doing new things, and seeing the bigger picture are often important. These individuals may be interested in first understanding the strategic implications of the initiative.

Communicating with someone who prefers this mode of conceptualization often involves explaining *how it will make the organization better off*. Less structured methods of communication are often preferred (including rapid cycling of ideas) although they often need to be supported by conceptual diagrams and open discussion. People who conceptualize in this space may be interested in contributing to the ideas and trying to make them better. They will frequently be interested in understanding the conceptual linkages within the initiative as well as how the initiative will change the organization's participation in the market. Some of the things they may be interested in knowing include:

- Current best practice in the market
- Diagrammatic descriptions of what is being proposed
- The competencies that the initiative will develop
- The competitive differentiators to be created
- How the initiative aligns with strategic imperatives
- The sources of innovation being created
- How things will be different

Thinking about the holistic view and synthesizing concepts is often important to people who conceptualize in this space. For a manager interested in communicating this way, a useful structure is to explain through a more informal context:

- The *tangible and intangible value that will be created*
- How the initiative *aligns with strategic goals*
- A *comparison against industry best practice*
- A *conceptual view of how the initiative maps into the organization*
- The *new competencies and innovations being developed*

Structuring Holistic Communication

In practice, the vast majority of people are able to operate across multiple conceptual spaces. When dealing with specific individuals, it is often simply a case of considering their most likely perspectives and tailoring the delivery method to suit. However, when dealing with a group of individuals, it is quite easy to have a range of different preferences in the room at one time.

Crafting effective communication therefore often involves balancing all four perspectives within the same presentation. Focusing on a single conceptualization space runs the risk of alienating or boring certain members of the audience.

THE PATH TO PERSUASION

Thus far we have covered:

- The importance of informational relevancy
- Being aware of and managing cultural considerations
- Framing a message within a variety of conceptual spaces

In terms of communicating with an individual, these are critical considerations. However, they are also tactically focused, aimed at convincing an individual or group. Although essential, they do not help with *identifying a strategy to persuade and convince*.

The first step in developing an effective communication strategy is to understand what is being communicated and how to communicate it most effectively in a given context. However, that is not enough. It is equally important to explicitly consider:

- How decisions are made within the organization
- Who owns and who will influence the final decision
- How to most effectively overcome objections and provide coverage

These things need to be specifically considered because if unmanaged, communication can be a significant drain on resources. Understanding what roles people have in the decision-making process is critical if information is to be appropriately communicated and framed in a relevant way. Equally, explicitly considering conceptualization preferences prevents the manager from introducing delays by presenting material in an inappropriate way. And explicitly allocating time and effort to communication helps ensure that it will happen. Depending on the manager's conceptualization preferences, this framework may not be one that she is comfortable operating in.

Understanding the Decision-Making Process

It is an obvious requirement, but it is essential that a business analytics manager be fully aware of how the organization makes decisions to invest. Typically, understanding how decisions are made in practice requires a good understanding of two processes: the formal process and the informal process.

Depending on the organization's culture and whether it is high or low context, these may have equal or disproportionate importance. One common trend, however, is that the greater the level of investment being sought, the more likely it is that the formal process will need to be followed.

The Formal Process

Almost every organization has a formally defined process that is used to evaluate investments and make decisions. This process typically has defined roles, owners, milestones, and information requirements. One commonly applied approach involves using a gated process to:

- Identify an opportunity and determine whether it is possible to deliver a solution
- Evaluate potential solution offerings and scope the range of costs for the project
- Select a solution and conduct a detailed scoping
- Deliver the changes and realize the return

Each of these activities requires access to proportionally higher levels of capital. Because this process is centrally managed, decision makers in principle have the ability to evaluate alternative investments based on their expected return, risk, and delivery time frames.

Understanding this process is critical for obvious reasons. However, unless it is explicitly investigated and understood, it can sometimes catch a new manager unawares. One manager I worked with thought he had a good understanding of his organization's capital-release process right up to the point where he found out that he was still only in the feasibility stage, not the release stage. He was naturally rather discouraged when he discovered that instead of delivering within the next few months as originally expected, he was probably looking at up to a year's internal justification before capital would be granted.

The Informal Process

Most organizations also have a variety of informal processes that are used to make decisions. These often revolve around key decision makers, political relationships, and access to already-allocated funding. Although the formal process may require submission to an investment board, it is often the case that group-level capital can be reallocated within an existing budget to support a good idea.

The challenge is that by definition, these processes are not defined. They tend to represent a manifestation of the organization's informal structure where power bases are not necessarily aligned with the formal organization chart. Decision makers will often consult with key influencers when decisions are being made on whether access to capital should be granted.

One approach to getting a better understanding of how the informal process works in practice is to investigate how previous projects were approved. By talking to other project sponsors within the same functional arm, it is sometimes possible to identify the relative importance of the informal process in decision making as well as who the key decision makers are.

Mapping Stakeholders and Decision Makers

Once the formal and informal decision-making processes are understood, the next step is to identify the key stakeholders involved in the initiative. Generally speaking, of key interest are:

- Decision makers
- Key influencers
- Potential supporters
- Anyone else being impacted by the changes

Decision makers are the people who have the power to approve or to veto the project. They will normally be fairly senior and will often be primarily interested in understanding the outcomes from the project and understanding the cost and risk implications. For obvious reasons, convincing the decision makers of the value of the change is of key concern. However, their decisions will rarely be made in isolation: Often, they will rely on a variety of other stakeholders to provide advice and recommendations.

Key influencers are often subject-matter experts or advisors who work closely with the decision makers. Although they do not always have direct control over the decision, decision makers will often rely heavily on their opinions when making decisions. To facilitate a favorable decision, the business analytics manager must make a concerted effort to convince these influencers of the value of the initiative.

Often, the initiative will benefit multiple individuals within an organization. By identifying these individuals and gaining their support, the business analytics manager can create broad-based internal pressure for change. Identifying potential supporters and building cross-sectional support for the initiative can greatly assist in getting funding released.

Finally, it is critical that the business analytics manager identify everyone else who may be impacted by the changes. Without their understanding and visibility of the project, it is highly likely that the initiative will be put on hold for further consideration as soon as they raise their objections. Their support is not always guaranteed—change is challenging and sometimes it is impossible to get them over the line. However, disagreement or resistance does not necessarily mean that the initiative will be put on indefinite hold—if appropriately managed and correctly sold to decision makers and key influencers, the project will often be considered on its merits.

Tailoring a Communication Strategy

Once everything covered thus far has been considered, the communication strategy must be defined. After taking into account organizational culture, at a minimum this needs to identify:

- Who needs to be contacted
- The core message that needs to be delivered to each person

- The best starting point for each person to create informational relevancy
- Their likely motivational factors
- Their likely preferred conceptual models
- The desired outcome

It is not essential for this strategy to be documented, although many managers find it useful to do so. The point of the tailoring is to make information relevant and comprehensible to a wide variety of people within the organization. Explicitly considering these in turn ensures that:

- No one is missing who *should* have been contacted.
- Information is presented in the most readily comprehensible manner.
- The desired outcomes from these meetings are defined ahead of time.

The most effective strategies view communication as a holistic, multifaceted activity, one that covers a variety of different communication styles. *Visualization* often forms a key part of this, summarizing detailed information in a way that is interesting, accessible, and most importantly, tangible. Although it is only one dimension of communication, it is often a highly effective one—compelling visualizations can sometimes spur others to action.

Once the communication strategy has been defined, all that remains is to execute on it.

PRACTICAL EXAMPLE: A FORECASTING MODEL FOR PLANNING

One of the best examples I have dealt with that highlighted the importance of a communication strategy involved a project to develop a planning framework for a government department. In the interests of building some quantitative measures by which different policies could be objectively compared, the project sponsor was keen to develop a *what-if* model that would allow policymakers to change various parameters under different assumptions and consider the resulting outcomes. Although it would have been impossible for the model to provide accurate predictions, the intention was to create a model flexible and broad enough to stimulate discussion under a common framework.

Despite these good intentions, it had all the hallmarks of a complex and high-risk project. There was a:

- Lack of clarity around objectives or success criteria
- Low level of understanding around the value of analytics generally
- General lack of visibility in the broader department of the project and its intentions

However, despite these challenges, there was a clear desire by the department to be more structured and considered in their approach to policy. By effectively developing and executing a broad-based communication strategy and communicating the value of the project to a wide variety of stakeholders, we successfully achieved buy-in into "doing things differently."

Our first objective was to separate the model development activities from the communication plan and execute them in parallel. Because of the general lack of visibility of the project and the low level of existing understanding of the value of analytics, a key starting point was to identify key representatives from every functional group that would either contribute to or be impacted by the policy planning process. The level of implicit knowledge within the department was extremely high; many individuals had been with the organization for over a decade. Because of this, we were extremely aware that we would be perceived as outsiders and that there was no way we would be able to build the required knowledge to be properly accepted within our required delivery time frames.

To support contact and ensure we would be at least listened to, we decided to leverage one of the most central individuals within the high-context culture and sought the support of the department secretary. We understood through talking to the project sponsor that he favored logical explanation combined with a strategic point of view.

To fit with his conceptual preferences, we built the presentation around the importance of being able to deal with innovation and changing conditions within policymaking processes. We then used a variety of innovative examples to demonstrate how analytics can create insight within planning processes, stepping him through a small selection of detail to demonstrate how models could give the ability to be creative without losing track of the bigger picture. After giving a briefing on the project's objectives, he gave us his full support and agreed to ensure that we would be able to meet with all of the different functional lines within the department.

Given that the model was intended to change the way the department did their planning, it was critical that everyone involved in the planning process agree with the approach. To achieve their commitment to the project, we identified that the model would deliver the following intangible benefits:

- Commonality of process
- Improved cross-functional planning
- Holistic, not functional, consideration of policy impacts
- Fact-based decision making

Given that what-if modeling was unlikely to deliver direct tangible returns, we decided to focus on building political and consensus-based support for the initiative. To achieve broad support, we focused on making sure that the model included specific contributions from each department. Though the model itself was analytically based and therefore had little room for direct modification, we recognized that the structure of the model was open to interpretation.

To achieve this buy-in, we conducted a process-mapping activity, supported by the secretary, giving every functional unit the opportunity to contribute to the structure of the model. Prior to meetings with each stakeholder, we considered their major motivational drivers and likely conceptualization preferences. By ensuring that everyone had contributed their major activities to the model, we ensured it represented their current processes. Because it represented the way they did business, even the most doubtful individuals found it difficult to find reasons not to support it.

Although her reasons were never made entirely clear, one individual refused to participate in the program. Rather than fight this, we accepted it and moved on; because we had the support of the secretary and broad consensus on the initiative, her refusal to partici-pate created cultural dissonance when we later presented our findings and recommendations. But because we had accurately profiled the internal culture of the department, she subsequently voluntarily joined the program and became one of the strongest supporters.

By mapping all the key stakeholders, understanding their concep-tualization preferences, and getting their buy-in through getting them to contribute to the model, we successfully delivered the model *and* achieved departmental commitment to using it.

SUMMARY

Creating a structured communication strategy is a critical part of suc-cessfully selling the value of business analytics. It is not enough for the manager to understand the value; if the rest of the organization does not understand or agree with the value identified, it will be impossible to encourage organizational change.

Critical within this strategy is an understanding of:

- The organization's culture
- The key stakeholders who need to be persuaded or influenced
- The most effective way to build understanding for each of these stakeholders
- The motivators that will persuade stakeholders that change is worthwhile
- Each stakeholder's preferred conceptualization patterns

When this strategy is missing, teams often:

- Find it difficult to establish consensus
- Struggle to have management sanction their initiatives
- Unintentionally create a variety of cultural tensions within the organization
- Become frustrated at their inability to convince the organization of the value offered by business analytics

By understanding *who is important* and *how they think*, the business analytics team can greatly simplify its efforts to convince the organization of the value of business analytics. And *working within the organization's culture* will reduce the number of misunderstandings created and focus attention where it is most worthwhile.

Establishing a communication strategy forms one part of a comprehensive strategy to achieve success through business analytics. Typically, *defining the value* is a necessary prerequisite. Equally important, however, are committing to it and measuring the benefits.

In the next chapter, we will investigate the importance of establishing an execution strategy, review the challenge of balancing business as usual against value-creating initiatives, and look into some practical strategies to create value when resources are tight.

 ## THE CHECKLIST: COMMUNICATING THE VALUE

Key Considerations

Understanding the Decision-Making Process

What is the formal process for making investment decisions?

Who is responsible for releasing funding?

What do these individuals consider when prioritizing between initiatives?

What other initiatives are currently under consideration?

What is the informal process for making investment decisions?

Who influences the decision-making process?

What background do they have with any related or similar projects?

Understanding the Environment and Culture

What proxemic characteristics does the organization exhibit?

What time sense does the organization exhibit?

What level of implicit understanding does the organization expect (high or low context)?

How will this affect the communication strategy?

Understanding Communication Preferences

How well does each stakeholder understand business analytics and the initiative?

What common starting point will be used to give stakeholders an understanding and start the persuasion/influencing process?

What motivates them?

How do they prefer to interpret new information?

How will this affect each of their individual communication strategies?

Communicating the Value

What does the stakeholder map look like?

What role does each person play within the stakeholder map (e.g., decision maker, influencer, etc.)?

How will stakeholders' decisions be influenced?

What is the communication plan?

NOTE

1. E. Hall, *Beyond Culture* (New York: Anchor Books, 1976).

CHAPTER 6

Creating the Execution Plan and Delivering Value

INTRODUCTION

Most organizations have at least one analytics team. Many have more, each functionally aligned to a specific area of the business. Despite the best of intentions, though, many teams struggle to deliver sustained growth or create substantive value. This is not through lack of enthusiasm—often, it is because of the challenges associated with translating a good idea into practice.

Quantifying the value and convincing the organization to invest resources are absolutely essential steps on the path to success. However, they do not create value in and of themselves. All they do is establish consensus and contextual relevancy. Creating value requires the team to deliver the project it has identified. This often proves challenging for a variety of reasons.

Possibly the biggest of these reasons is a general lack of under-standing about what constitutes best practice in business analytics. Teams use a variety of different approaches and some are more effec-tive than others; it merely takes a comparison between the best teams and average teams to highlight the difference. And, for relative newcomers charged with reinventing an existing team (or creating one from scratch), it is often extremely difficult to find guidance.

This uncertainty stems from the relative immaturity of the discipline; compared to other fields such as engineering, accounting, or economics, business analytics is a positive toddler. That is not to say other disciplines inevitably come to better conclusions. As recent economic turmoil shows, the most developed of professions are not immune to making bad decisions.

Comparatively, though, there is a limited common understanding on how to best deliver business analytics projects. Although best practice varies by application and domain, best-practice delivery characteristics do exist. By applying these characteristics, teams can:

- Meet business as usual requirements
- Consistently deliver more with less
- Find new applications for the use of business analytics
- Deliver regular incremental value to the organization

In this chapter we will review the importance of planning before executing. We will establish a structured approach to tactical delivery, focusing on the types of initiatives a team can deliver. By applying this framework, teams can explicitly balance evolution against innovation, giving them the ability to map tactical value creation into creating strategic competitive advantage. Wrapping up the chapter, we will spend some time discussing the most important things to plan for as well as how to turn small improvements into true revolutions, helping cut through the resource constraints faced by most teams.

WHY YOU NEED AN EXECUTION PLAN

Planning is an essential component of successful delivery. Although the "draw-shoot-aim" school of delivery might be exciting, it is nowhere near as successful or efficient as having a well-structured plan *before* the project is executed.

Inevitably, teams that fail to plan experience a wide variety of challenges when trying to deliver tactical initiatives. They:

- Often experience significant delays because of unforeseen issues
- Constantly fight against scope creep due to badly defined project objectives
- Struggle to maintain the value they have created
- Face significant and constant resource constraints
- Create internal friction by failing to give other stakeholders sufficient notice of their required input

As if these issues were not bad enough, failing to plan also creates a variety of strategic issues. While business analytics has the potential to create competitive advantage, it is rare that an organization is able to realize this goal without understanding the path it will need to take to get there. When team members are missing this road map, they not only usually fail to create any real competitive advantage; they often struggle to simply prioritize their tactical activities. They will often try to do everything and, more often than not, deliver nothing.

The Analytics Team That Never Delivered

One memorable experience involved a fairly detailed discussion with an analytics team in a midsized organization. I had met with the team members to try to help identify ways they could add value. It was clear that they wanted my help, but when prompted, it seemed like they already had all the answers.

To kick things off, I had organized a half-day workshop with the entire team to profile where they wanted to be, where they were, do a gap analysis against their current capabilities, and prioritize their potential activities to create a mid-to-long-term road map. Although the team members were quite enthusiastic, things fell apart shortly after we started the first session.

When asked about the things they could think of that they were not already doing that would add value to the business, the room went silent. After a pregnant pause, I suggested a few ideas: improving the number of models they had in production, reengineering their analytics datamart to deliver greater efficiencies, extending their segmentation model to provide greater granularity, and so on. With a smile on his face, their manager nodded and said they were already doing all of those.

Surprised, I suggested some more advanced concepts: the creation of an analytics center of excellence, creating a "fail early, fail often" model for rapid innovation, extending their applications into detecting internal fraud, and embedding design of experiments into their standard marketing test processes to deliver greater campaign efficiency. With an even bigger smile on his face, he nodded again and said those (or something similar) were already in progress.

Flummoxed, I looked around the room at the five people included in the meeting and asked, "Where's the rest of your team?" With a slightly confused look on his face, he responded, "They're all here!"

After a bit more investigation, it turned out that even though the team members had done an excellent job of brainstorming everything they could be doing, they had never gone through a prioritization process to limit their focus on delivering regular blocks of value to the business. Although the team had a road map, there were so many interdependencies and so many big jobs that the team's first real deliverables were not expected for another two years! Despite having existed for over a year, the team had not actually produced anything the rest of the business could recognize as being of value. Needless to say, the team's credibility was seriously under threat within the business, all because its vision was bigger than its ability to execute.

In a Nutshell: What You Need at a Minimum and How to Do It

Delivering value through business analytics requires an understanding of how strategic outcomes can be linked to tactical activity. Doing this effectively requires managers to balance value maintenance against growth, creating innovations while delivering regular evolutionary improvements.

The starting point is having an understanding around how different types of initiatives create value, their potential for outsourcing, and the outcomes they normally produce. These initiatives include:

- Growth initiatives
- Operational activities

- Research initiatives
- Enabling initiatives

In isolation, these create or maintain value for either the team or the broader organization. However, competitive advantage stems from creating a road map around these initiatives, progressively developing differentiators and new competencies while still delivering regular value.

This roadmapping process normally involves four activities:

1. Scanning for opportunities
2. Prioritizing these opportunities
3. Mapping these opportunities into a series of sequentially delivered initiatives
4. Analyzing gaps in current assets and capabilities and establishing enabling initiatives to close these gaps

The road map acts as a tool to maintain focus, share the team's vision with the broader organization, and provide a sanity check that value is being created on a regular basis.

Delivering to this road map often requires greater resources than the vast majority of teams have available. Creating the necessary resourcing usually involves delivering a series of "tactical revolutions," where small incremental efficiencies are rolled up into increasingly large time savings. This newfound freedom allows teams to demonstrate return through additional initiatives and, by doing so, justify the headcount they need to sustain future growth.

Managers can also increase their odds of successful delivery by avoiding common pitfalls. Chief among these is explicitly planning for uncertainty. Many initiatives involve creating new competencies or applying existing competencies in new ways. By planning for this uncertainty, managers can monitor slippages and establish early warning systems for projects that are going off-track. This usually involves planning for the eventual transition of analytics into an operational context, an activity that is often difficult to execute when approached in an ad hoc or unplanned manner.

Finally, establishing clear ownership and reward structures helps clarify focus and reduce uncertainty. This ownership needs to cover both internal and external stakeholders, clearly identifying roles and responsibilities across the entire, often cross-functional team.

ROLE OF THE EXECUTION PLAN

Effective teams balance the need for immediate value against the creation of competitive advantage. Critically, this usually needs to occur within a context of constrained resources. Most managers not only need to deliver, they also need to work out ways of increasing their team's productivity levels.

A good execution plan helps the team do a few things. It:

- Defines the direction being taken
- Communicates this direction in practical terms to the broader organization
- Prioritizes activity and establishes how value will be maintained
- Identifies how tactical initiatives will translate into competitive advantage
- Balances organizational value creation against productivity improvements, allowing the team to scale

Creating a competitive advantage is not easy; if it were, it would not be a competitive advantage. Importantly, though, it is not impossible: It simply requires an understanding of where this advantage will come from, how it aligns to the organization's business model, and a plan to get there. Defining this longer-term plan does two things. First, it allows managers to identify the sequence of steps necessary to create competitive advantage. Second, it allows them to socialize this direction with the rest of the organization and achieve internal commitment to that path.

Once this direction has been established, the individual steps need to be executed. This requires a series of tactical delivery plans that identify the resources needed, the approach that will be used, and how success will be measured. These provide a business analytics manager with visibility and control over delivery, increasing the odds of success when appropriately managed.

Finally, once the initiative has been completed and the identified value created, this value needs to be maintained. Part of the execution plan includes identifying how this value will be managed in such a way as to ensure it continues to exist after the initiative has been completed.

Over the next few sections we will investigate each of these in turn, focusing on some of the major factors that managers must consider if they are to effectively deliver success.

ESTABLISHING DIRECTION

Business analytics managers face a variety of delivery challenges. Above all else, they need to:

- Create and maintain value in the short term
- Demonstrate their ability to innovate and create organizational competitive advantage

When initiatives are treated in isolation, they run the risk of creating conflicting management priorities. For example, focusing purely on short-term value often results in firefighting, preventing the organization from developing and reusing a true competency. Although the team may deliver regular value, it will often fail to take advantage of the efficiencies involved with reusing existing competencies.

Equally, when a team focuses purely on creating competitive advantage, it is easy for project timelines to slip from months to years. Although the team may eventually realize its target competitive advantage, the risk is that turnover or an internal restructuring may prematurely halt the project, rendering the team's significant investment in time and effort worthless.

Balancing these requires a good understanding of how short-term value creation will map into creating competitive advantage. Doing this involves an understanding of:

- What types of initiatives a team can deliver
- The different types of value these initiatives usually create
- How these initiatives can be structured into a strategic road map

Defining Tactical Initiatives

Viewed from the outside, a business analytics team is involved in a variety of activities, some of which deliver value to the organization and some of which deliver value (and productivity enhancements) to the team. Although these activities create organizational value in various forms, *how* that value is created is often irrelevant—what is important is just that value is delivered.

From the inside, though, being able to understand what is working and what is not forms a critical part of prioritizing activities. Managers need to be concerned with allocating often very limited resources for maximum benefit. Equally, deciding whether to insource or outsource work is also an important consideration. For many resource-constrained managers, leveraging consultants or outsourcers may be an attractive proposition.

Because of this, managers need to monitor activities. The most effective way of getting this visibility is to directly relate value creation to specific activities. By viewing activities as value-creating processes, managers can get an understanding of whether the team's time is being used effectively and whether external groups should be leveraged.

Complicating things somewhat is that while business analytics shares characteristics with service-based industries such as consulting, it also exhibits similarities with operational reporting and management disciplines. Teams may be involved in:

- Ongoing activities with no defined starting or ending point or short delivery time frames
- One-off activities with clearly defined starting and ending points involving longer delivery time frames

Common examples of the first are creating reports for the business, providing ad hoc insight into specific business issues, or monitoring the effectiveness of models currently in production. Often, each report or insight will take a relatively short period of time to create. Many will be produced on a regular basis.

By contrast, a good example of the second type of activity is the creation of a predictive model to aid in the identification of fraud. This project might take a number of weeks or months to complete and, once the model has been built and deployed, the team will move on to a new project.

These activities are fundamentally different, and have different success criteria and different efficiency measures. Having a framework to consider the various types of projects a team is executing makes it easier for a manager to understand where things are or are not working. By creating a standardized way of measuring the characteristics of different initiatives, managers can make objective comparisons. It also makes it easier to decide whether to use external groups as supporting resources.

Broadly speaking, there are four main types of activities a business analytics team will normally be involved in:

1. Growth initiatives
2. Operational activities
3. Research initiatives
4. Enabling initiatives

Growth Initiatives

Almost every business analytics–derived benefit started out as a growth initiative. Someone within the organization saw an opportunity to create value and, by convincing the organization to invest in an initiative, realized that value. Classic examples include the use of retention models to aid in reducing customer churn, propensity models to improve marketing targeting, or credit models to reduce the rate of defaults.

These projects tend to have fairly well-defined deliverables and fixed time frames with expected end dates, and involve the creation of new assets and processes. In the case of a retention model, a project might involve:

- Establishing the definition of churn along with current churn rates
- Consolidating the data required to create a leading indicator of likelihood of churn

- Developing and testing a series of models to aid in the prediction of churn
- Socializing the results and obtaining buy-in
- Establishing ongoing benchmarking and scoring processes such that customers can be scored for churn propensity each month
- Measuring the benefit of a trial champion/challenger comparison between existing retention processes and analytically targeted retention processes

As an initiative, these activities deliver incremental value to the business. By the end of the project, assuming everything went well, the organization is disproportionately better off as compared to the investment made. Through delivering the initiative, new processes, competencies, and assets may be (and often are) created.

Because these projects almost always create competitive advantage (sustainable or not) in some form, the vast majority of organizations prefer to internalize their execution. Leveraging an external group normally leads to a variety of issues, including:

- A failure to internalize the competencies developed
- Limited sustainable competitive advantages due to the external group selling its services to other competitors

Success is normally measured in the direct value created, regardless of whether it is tangible or intangible. New assets will almost always be created as part of the initiative.

Operational Activities

Critically, though, should the process stop, that incremental value will disappear. And so, that growth initiative transitions into an operational activity. Not surprisingly, this often involves a direct migration from the discovery environment into the operational environment. Often, the two are highly linked, with the migration from a growth initiative into an operational activity covered within the same program of work. Importantly, this is not always the case. One of the biggest reasons teams fail to deliver real value from business analytics is because this migration *does not occur.*

Operational activities, when ineffectively managed, often consume the vast majority of an analyst's hours in the day. It is easy to see why when processes are not automated; in these situations, analysts need to manually extract, process, score, and deliver data to the right systems, all of which takes significant time. In many ways, however, these activities are the lifeblood of the team: Where a growth initiative delivers incremental value, operational activities ensure that those returns are maintained.

When compared against growth initiatives, operational activities tend to be more process driven, have no fixed end date, and leverage existing assets, capabilities, and processes. The transition from growth to operational often involves moving from a project-based view of activity to a process-based view of activity, which is repeated as often as needed. For most predictive models, this involves moving from a modeling process to an ongoing scoring process. For reports, it often involves moving from exploratory data analysis to an operational reporting process.

The frequency with which these processes are executed varies by application. For many organizations, scoring processes are often executed on a weekly or monthly basis. In the case of management reporting, it may be as frequently as on a daily basis. Using the same churn example, the same analyst might (on a monthly basis):

- Run standardized data management processes on the data warehouse to get and transform the necessary input variables
- Score new data to create churn predictions by customer
- Run additional standardized data management processes to deliver the results back into the data warehouse
- Create a variety of standardized reports on the results for archival and analytical purposes

By doing these activities as frequently as is needed, the value captured through the initial growth project is preserved. Because the assets have already been created and there is little additional intellectual property created, many organizations are willing to consider using external consultants to support these activities. The decision whether to use an external party for these activities often comes down to how closely linked they are to other types of initiatives, how much internal knowledge is needed to execute them, and what time commitment is needed.

For example, monitoring the accuracy of models on an ongoing basis may not be worth outsourcing. The decision whether to redevelop a model is often based on how well an existing model is performing. When models degrade past a predefined point, the team will often start a new growth initiative to develop new challenger models. Using an external party to do this monitoring may actually introduce inefficiencies by extending the time inaccurate models are left in-market. For each month an inaccurate churn identification model is left operational, the organization is losing customers it could have otherwise preserved. Additionally, because a well-designed monitoring process requires minimal time investment to operate, using external resources may needlessly increase costs.

Success is normally measured in terms of process completion. Because assets and processes already exist, the focus is normally on ensuring that they complete successfully on a set schedule.

Research Initiatives

Sometimes, business analytics is applied to answer a specific question and, once answered, no further activities are needed. A good example is product rationalization. In an organization plagued with too many products with too low an average profitability, reducing the number of products on offer is a quick way of improving profitability. Identifying this short-list is typically a one-off activity—once the products are identified, it is simply a case of eliminating them and potentially establishing customer migration paths. Beyond that point, nothing needs to be deployed or repeated on a regular basis.

This forms a classic case of a research initiative. The primary characteristic is that the initiative delivers insight, not direct value. It may be instrumental in providing the information necessary to create value but in itself it does not create the value.

Another example lies in process redesign where existing processes are profiled and optimized. It may be that scoring processes are taking far too long to complete. A research initiative might produce a variety of recommendations that could include the creation of an analytical datamart, greater use of automated model building technology, or leveraging in-database scoring technology. Should nothing further be done at this point, the team would continue to operate as usual. It is not until new processes are built and deployed that the team can benefit from any efficiency improvements.

Research projects often form the basis for additional incremental investment. Common applications include:

- Feasibility studies to determine the potential return from developing a new competency or extending an existing competency

- Process redesign studies, aimed at mapping existing processes and identifying opportunities for efficiency improvements

- Roadmapping studies, aimed at identifying a tactical and strategic growth path for the team and/or organization

Unlike growth initiatives, these projects do not always need to be internalized. It is often irrelevant whether an internal group or an external group does the work. As long as they are appropriately managed, the important thing is the answer, not the process itself. As such, the decision whether to internalize the project or outsource it largely comes down to resourcing availability.

Success is normally measured by the quality and usefulness of the answer provided.

Enabling Initiatives

The final type of initiative business analytics teams often execute is the creation of a process or asset needed either for a planned growth initiative or to deliver evolutionary efficiency improvements. These types of initiatives rarely deliver much (if any) tangible economic value to the organization. Instead, they are normally necessary prerequisites to creating tangible economic value.

A common example is the creation of a standardized analytical datamart. In the absence of such a datamart, a team of analysts may spend excessive amounts of time duplicating data management processes. In practice, this usually involves multiple people within the team extracting the same data and replicating the same data transformations, simply because they are not aware that their peers are doing almost exactly the same work. Normally, this leads to wasted time, data quality issues, and overly long projects. Creating a standardized analytical datamart takes a relatively substantial amount of time but offers a number of advantages, including:

- The ability to standardize data extraction, transformation, and cleansing processes
- The ability to automate processes
- A reduction in the total time spent across the team managing and manipulating data
- An increase in the breadth of information included within models through sharing of derived variables among team members
- Simplifying the application of analytics into new areas of the business

The analytical datamart delivers productivity gains to the team, improves the quality of team members' output, and increases their scope of focus, but it does not directly deliver any tangible value to the organization. It will often, however, allow the team to develop new competencies and create evolutionary growth initiatives through applying existing competencies throughout other areas of the business.

These types of initiatives share a number of characteristics with growth initiatives. They create a variety of assets and processes, they have a fixed end date, and they have a series of well-defined deliverables. The key difference is that whereas growth initiatives deliver incremental value to the *business*, enabling initiatives often deliver incremental value to the *team*.

Much like research projects or operational activities, these projects can be executed by an external party. Many organizations use external consultants to help with the creation of analytical datamarts, to improve process efficiency, or to help build monitoring frameworks. Because these types of activities rarely deliver direct competitive advantage in the form of organizational-level value creation, the risk of another organization capitalizing on the insight captured by the external party is relatively low.

Success is normally measured by how well the assets created deliver the internal benefits expected.

Mapping Tactical Initiatives to Strategic Advantage

The initiatives discussed so far clearly have a role to play in creating sustainable competitive advantage. However, this relationship is not always self-evident. Something that may appear counterintuitive is that while there is often a relationship between the degree of innovation delivered by an initiative and the level of competitive advantage offered, there is often no such clear relationship to the degree of value offered.

The reason for this is simple: As value is usually measured primarily by tangible return, it matters little whether this value is created by innovating or by simply applying an existing competency to a new problem. An organization applying predictive analytics in one context (such as cross-sell models) has the potential to get substantial returns by applying the same competency (predictive modeling) in a different context (such as retention modeling).

Developing a totally new competency (such as social network analysis) may offer equivalent returns (such as through viral marketing), but the risk and resourcing required to support a new competency are far higher. Importantly, though, while innovation does not necessarily lead to greater value, *it is frequently linked to sustainable competitive advantage.*

The reason that innovation activities tend to be highly related to competitive advantage is because, if successful, they fundamentally change the ability of the organization to transform inputs into economic return. This is somewhat of an abstract concept; it is helpful to look at some very real examples.

Consider a telecommunications company focused on analytical marketing. Most apply various forms of predictive analytics to support direct marketing and retention activities. This usually involves analysts building and managing models which are then used to score the company's customer base on their interest in new products or alternative products, and their likelihood of churn. These processes are often relatively standardized but still fairly heavily dependent on manual intervention at various stages within the value chain.

For example, processing jobs may fail due to changing input data structures, requiring direct intervention. Or, jobs may run and it may not be until the results are examined that analysts realize that the data warehouse failed to load the latest customer data. Or, as is surprisingly often the case, the final scores need to be manually transferred to a staging area where IT resources will eventually pick them up for manual import into the data warehouse.

On any given day most analysts need to perform a number of duties, including:

- Defining and managing analytical data processes
- Developing and comparing new models through various champion/challenger processes
- Deploying models in a way that allows ongoing scoring of new customer data
- Benchmarking existing models to identify the point at which they have degraded beyond acceptable limits
- Providing ongoing management reporting and ad hoc analysis

For many organizations, deploying models tends to be fairly time consuming and manually intensive. To give an indication of how significantly this can vary, higher-performing organizations may take days to weeks to get a new model into production. However, organizations on the upper end may take as long as a year to get a new model into production. This delay can create a number of issues.

These models, once executed, deliver direct economic value, whether it is in the form of increased revenue, decreased customer churn, or reduced rates of fraud. However, all models degrade over time; as customer demographics and market conditions change, the relevancy of the initial assumptions and data decreases and the scoring accuracy correspondingly drops. This varies heavily by industry and application. Whereas marketing models may have effective lifetimes of up to a year, fraud model lifetimes may be as short as months or even weeks. The difference lies in the behavioral patterns of the people being targeted. Whereas most people are fairly comfortable in their living patterns, fraudsters often deliberately try to vary their behaviors to avoid detection.

It is within this context that innovation plays a role. The same company may decide that it is going to fundamentally reinvent its model development and deployment processes. Rather than using a one-size-fits-all strategy, management may decide that they want to focus on interacting on a more personal level with their customers. To support this, they decide that using one cross-sell model for their entire customer base is inefficient, mainly because using one model means treating everyone exactly the same. Instead, they apply a microsegmentation model, creating thousands of groups of statistically similar customers. Each of these groups represents a set of customers with similar behavioral patterns, allowing the organization to tailor its offerings and communication to suit the unique characteristics of that specific group.

Through high-performance computing and automated model selection and comparison, they then develop a unique model with potentially a unique algorithm for each microsegment. This usually means moving from one model to thousands. The reason for doing this is a powerful one; by increasing the granularity of their models, organizations significantly increase their aggregate classification and predictive accuracy. Statistical modeling works best when individuals within the sample being analyzed are similar and have similar behaviors. As a simplified example, it is a lot easier to predict the behavior of an individual within a room when presented with a mobile phone if you know everyone in the room is a toddler; more than likely, you are going to end up with a broken phone.

If, however, you include a number of highly technical individuals between the ages of 25 to 32 in the mix, it suddenly becomes a lot harder to predict any one person's interest if all you have is the name, gender, and living location of all participants. By statistically grouping individuals based on common behavioral and sociodemographic patterns, you improve the homogeneity of the sample and, correspondingly, improve the accuracy of the final model.

By completely rebuilding their processes from scratch, organizations may go from dealing with a handful of models to hundreds (if not thousands) of unique models. And, by streamlining their deployment processes, they may also reduce the time needed to get a model into production down from weeks to days.

This, fundamentally, is competitive advantage made real. By innovating relative to their existing processes and their peers, organizations are able to:

- Respond to changing market conditions faster
- Deal with customers on a more personally relevant level
- Better transform information into insight

Unfortunately, nothing is free. For a team that is totally saturated, innovation may be seen as impossible. Innovation is not easy; it is time consuming and risky and requires developing new competencies. These all require resources—resources that are not necessarily immediately available. That does not mean it cannot be achieved. It just means that it requires an understanding of how evolutionary improvements can allow innovation.

Evolution versus Innovation

Given that context, how does a team that is already saturated move from being overworked to innovating, delivering incremental growth, and obtaining further investment? The trick is in understanding the balance between innovation and evolution.

Within the context of business analytics, innovation is *the process of delivering a fundamentally different approach, often involving high amounts of disruption*. Two useful examples are:

1. *The creation of a completely new organizational competency.* For example, a team focusing on building predictive cross-sell models might extend its capabilities into social network analysis or campaign optimization.

2. *The end-to-end recreation and replacement of existing processes.* This might be the comprehensive replacement of nonstandardized data management processes and decentralized modeling storage tables with an analytical datamart and scheduled data management, quality, and transformation processes.

In contrast, evolution is *an incremental improvement or extension on existing processes or capabilities, often involving adaptation or modification*. Two useful examples are:

1. *The extension of an existing competency into a new application.* For example, a team focusing on building predictive cross-sell models extends into building predictive retention models.

2. *An incremental improvement to an existing process.* This might mean modifying an existing modeling process based purely on a logistic regression to accommodate and benchmark multiple algorithms.

In practice, these two approaches are points on a spectrum, not clearly defined outcomes. What is important, though, is that generally speaking:

- Innovation activities offer the opportunity for greater competitive advantage but carry higher risk, higher resourcing requirements, and a lower probability of success.

- Evolutionary activities carry lower risk, lower resourcing requirements, and a higher probability of success, but often offer a lower level of sustainable competitive advantage.

Successfully innovating may lead to substantial performance or efficiency improvements. Unfortunately, this often requires significant resource investment, sometimes beyond what a team is capable of providing. Because of this, the most effective teams understand the need to balance their innovation and evolutionary activities. Getting the freedom to innovate often requires delivering a series of evolutionary improvements first. However, focusing on too many evolutionary activities may lead to an underperforming team.

Understanding the risk/reward structure of activities is essential. Much like an effective investment strategy, by considering the degree to which activities in aggregate balance innovation and evolution, managers can ensure an appropriate level of gearing and return on investment.

Establishing a Road Map

Under the context of a single initiative, the framework discussed so far provides a good starting point for a manager to understand:

- Where internal and external value is being created

- Which activities must be internalized and which can potentially be given to external parties

■ How strongly the team is geared toward high-risk/high-reward activities

Something that we have not yet considered is how these initiatives are originally defined. Implicit in this framework is the assumption that managers already know all the activities they could be working on. Defining and executing on this road map is probably one of the most important things a manager can do; it not only keeps the team focused, it acts as a reality check for ongoing value delivery.

Every analytics team inevitably deals with the tricky balance of innovation and delivering business as usual. The importance of this balance cannot be understated. Focusing only on business as usual almost inevitably leads to a team that is overworked, has retention issues, and eventually lags the competition. However, focusing only on innovation and building new competencies generally leads to a schism between the business and the analytics team. This is largely because while innovation is often very high-value, it also tends to be very resource intensive, consuming significant resources for a business benefit that is often visible to only a small part of the organization.

Defining a road map helps to explicitly balance these two competing priorities. A good road map provides a baseline to balance allocating resources to delivering business as usual against providing a realistic, staged progression toward building new competencies and innovating. Equally important, it provides a series of relatively short-term tangible goals that provide motivation and measurement of progress (not to mention an early indicator if anything is going wrong.).

Fundamentally, a good road map provides a number of valuable outcomes:

■ It creates a vision that helps drive the team past business as usual.
■ It provides focus around a communication and delivery strategy for economic value to the business.
■ It focuses attention on a series of milestones, increasing the probability of successful delivery.

As established in Chapter 2, analytics is one of the few business activities that can deliver renewable value. The flipside of this coin is that, given the large number of potential applications of analytics, there are inevitably more applications than there are resources available to support the delivery of those applications. As with most things, being an effective manager requires a high amount of prioritization and allocation of limited resources.

As such, a roadmapping process involves four steps:

1. *Scanning*—the open identification of the broadest set of potential economic opportunities for analytics
2. *Prioritizing*—short-listing these opportunities based on their likelihood of successful completion and their likely economic value to the business
3. *Analyzing gaps*—identifying the dependencies and interdependencies between specific activities and current coverage across people, process, technology, and data
4. *Mapping*—creating expected delivery time frames, order of execution between these opportunities, and expected investment/value delivery milestones

A practical guide to doing this requires more space than is available within this book. However, it is important to be aware that this is a critical part of establishing a high-level delivery plan. Without this road map, it is exceedingly hard for a manager to prioritize activities to maximize organizational value.

As such, the overview provided in this chapter is primarily intended to provide a basic understanding of what is typically involved. Some of the most important points to consider when developing a road map are:

- *Be timely.* Ensure that there is not a significant gap between opportunities that deliver direct economic value.
- *Be pragmatic about delivery.* One year is too short to create a vision, but a five-year time frame is well beyond the ability of most organizations to commit to.
- *Be realistic about resourcing.* Most teams, when starting out, have the capability to deliver no more than one or two initiatives every six months.

Scanning for Opportunities

As covered in Chapter 4, *it is important that these opportunities be aligned to some form of economic return to the business.* Although understanding customer satisfaction is a great enabler for further work, it rarely delivers any direct economic value. It is what is done with the information that delivers the economic value. This could include targeted retention programs or product redesign. What is important is that while customer satisfaction profiling may be a heavily analytical activity, on its own it does not deliver any direct economic value. As such, although the programs that leverage its results may be included, the customer satisfaction survey itself should not end up on the opportunity list.

In practice, it is not surprising for an imaginative team to come up with hundreds of potentially valuable applications of analytics within any given business. This should be an open activity and a fun process—any and every idea is valid. The point is to consider every opportunity, regardless of what is realistic or possible. True innovation comes from thinking the unthinkable, and if you preemptively discount creative ideas, you can very easily kill significant value in the distant future.

Prioritizing Opportunities

Balancing this is the reality that in the absence of a large analytics team, most organizations struggle to deliver more than one or two new initiatives every six months. And the number of initiatives the team can work on is in turn largely dependent on the size of the team and the degree to which it is committed to doing business as usual.

The next step involves examining the full list of potential opportunities and short-listing them based on their likely economic value to the business and their likelihood of success. At this point, it is highly unlikely that the true value will be known; it is a rare group that is able to immediately quantify the value of something that it has never done before.

Because of this, estimation is critical. Although there is no single best approach, a useful starting point is to estimate the relative scale of likely economic value and use that as a starting point for prioritization. Often, this involves very heavy assumptions. This is fine; the point of the process is simply to create a short-list to start working from, not to commit to an immovable five-year plan.

Analyzing Gaps

Once these opportunities have been prioritized, the next step is to consider any existing gaps between current and required people, process, technology, and data. The point of this exercise is both to identify the interdependencies between opportunities and to identify any enabling initiatives that also need to occur in parallel.

Three common examples of enabling initiatives are the creation of an analytics datamart, building a monitoring and measurement platform, and creating automated modeling and scoring processes. The first is almost inevitably a precursor to doing any team-based analytics, the second essential for building credibility and optimizing existing activities, and the third essential for productivity improvements. However, although these are often critical enablers, none of them delivers any form of direct economic return to the business. These enabling initiatives most likely will not be considered of value externally, but they are often essential for longer-term growth.

Mapping Opportunities

At this point, all that remains is to outline these growth and enabling initiatives in a road map. This can take any form that makes sense, but one example is presented in Figure 6.1.

The road map should be over a horizon sufficiently long that it identifies the strategic value being created by the analytics team. However, there should also be sufficient growth initiatives delivered in the short term to demonstrate organizational value.

Applying the Road Map

This road map often forms the starting point for business-level discussions. It helps identify the:

- Focus of the team
- Types of value the team will be creating
- Investment schedule required to deliver value

DATE:	STAGE 1: ESTABLISH				STAGE 2: EXTEND				STAGE 1: DIFFERENTIATE			
	201X: Q1	201X: Q2	201X: Q3	201X: Q4	201Y: Q1	201Y: Q2	201Y: Q3	201Y: Q4	201Z: Q1	201Z: Q2	201Z: Q3	…
ENGAGEMENT OPTIMIZATION										Activate offer optimization processes		
FRAUD DETECTION AND MANAGEMENT								Identify application fraud				
NEXT-BEST OFFER							Deploy propensity models					
SINGLE VIEW OF CUSTOMER					Deliver DoE-based marketing	Deliver single view of customer						
TEST AND LEARN			Establish champion/challenger						Deploy real-time offer testing			
SELF-SERVICE INFORMATION		Automate reports / self-service					Provide campaign tracking				Provide real-time performance monitoring	
INFRASTRUCTURE AND DATA	Create analytics datamart			Extend datamart to support SVoC				Extend datamart to support optimization				

Figure 6.1 Creating the Delivery Map

Once created, it defines the execution plan for the team. By making it possible to link activity to value, it acts as a communication tool to help managers sell the value of their work. And, by clarifying the speed at which the team will be creating organizational value, it helps managers ensure their work is adding value to the organization at a sufficiently frequent rate.

Obtaining Organizational Commitment

A road map not only defines direction; it also acts as a powerful tool to drive organizational commitment on the use of business analytics. Because initiatives within the road map are aligned with the creation of value, the road map provides a business-focused framework to confirm contribution to strategic goals.

Organizational commitment to the use of business analytics is arguably the single biggest enabler in delivering competitive advantage. Without this commitment, business analytics often fails to gain traction, is used in an ad hoc fashion, and rarely leads to the development of true competencies. Although some organizations have the benefit of leaders who already understand the value of business analytics, many do not. And, in these organizations, one of the roles business analytics managers need to play is that of a *change agent*, helping to facilitate this transformation.

A road map helps this transformation. Rather than deal in technical terms, it frames things within a business context. Initiatives are described in terms of the value they create, not the activities they involve. By outlining initiatives in business terms, it makes business analytics more approachable for those who may not understand the detail.

In addition to these benefits, a road map also establishes a longer-term vision. It helps describe where the organization *will be* through the use of analytics, not just how things will change *now*. Creating and socializing this road map helps managers get explicit organizational commitment to the application of business analytics, not just today but well into the future. Senior sponsors can be identified and their support obtained. Without a road map, it is often extremely challenging for a manager to get strategic commitment. Individual initiatives may garner support, but the fate of business analytics within an organization often collapses to the value of the current initiative.

If every initiative were a growth initiative, this would not present a problem. However, establishing competitive advantage often requires the creation of new assets, new competencies, and new processes, not all of which will lead to organizational value. Although these enabling initiatives are still critical, without identifying *how* they will lead to future value, the organization will often be reluctant to commit the resources necessary to deliver them.

Measuring the Frequency of Value Creation

A road map allows a business analytics manager to objectively consider the speed at which value will be created. Markets move fast, and a balance needs to be maintained between creating sustainable competitive advantage and delivering short-term returns.

By examining time frames, reviewing how much tangible value is being created over a variety of horizons, and considering who will benefit from the initiatives, managers can reduce risk and increase the odds of political success. The three key things to remember are:

1. The larger and more complex the project, the greater the likelihood of slippage.
2. Perceptions dictate reality.
3. Credibility and value come from visibility and delivery.

First, complex projects are notorious for experiencing delays. The bigger the project, the higher the odds that issues will arise during the delivery process. By ensuring that value is created on an incremental basis and not reliant on a single complex project, a manager can often improve the consistency of the team's ability to create value.

Second, perceptions dictate reality. Regardless of all the great work being executed within the team, if nothing is delivered in a reasonable time frame, the external perception will likely be that the team is not delivering any value. A road map helps ensure that the team is delivering value on a regular basis by explicitly identifying when and how value will be created. For most organizations, a "reasonable time frame" is under a year, mainly because:

- It aligns with planning cycles, financial years, and accounting drives.
- Staff retention issues and project delivery time frames often make it difficult to demonstrate value beyond that horizon.

By overlaying these time frames on the road map, managers can get an instant feel of how their value-creation schedule will fit in with organizational perceptions. And, if a mismatch occurs, they can take early corrective action.

Finally, regular delivery creates trust and credibility. As discussed in the example earlier in this chapter, one of the single most damaging things a team can do to its reputation is fail to deliver. Ensuring a regular and reliable delivery schedule is the first defense against this perception forming.

DELIVERING TO THE PLAN

Once created, this road map defines the initiatives the team will deliver along with the value considered worthwhile by the organization. Delivering this value, however, is often challenging. Most teams need to deal with:

- A lack of sufficient resources
- Methodological uncertainty
- Varying levels of confusion around process ownership

Virtually every team is resource constrained to some degree. Understanding how to do more with less is an essential criterion for success. Equally, analytics teams often need to deliver projects outside their historical experience. Almost by definition, developing a new competency involves creating new skills. Planning for this and minimizing uncertainty is therefore a critical skill for a business analytics manager to develop.

Finally, the team will often be dealing with highly complex processes that span multiple groups within the organization. Without explicit management and role definition, this complexity runs the risk of delaying or derailing the delivery plan. By applying various strategies to align ownership against delivery, a manager can increase the odds of success.

DEALING WITH RESOURCE CONSTRAINTS

The key challenge for most teams is balancing time spent on operational and research activities against time spent delivering growth and enabling initiatives; because of their repetitive nature, operational activities tend to consume consistent amounts of resource time. While they are essential in maintaining existing value, they don't normally create any incremental value for the organization.

The Catch-22 of Business Analytics

Delivering growth initiatives in the face of having highly limited resources is a critical challenge for a team looking to create value. Unfortunately, every time a team delivers a growth initiative, it needs to allocate more time to support the ongoing resulting operational activities.

Because of this necessary relationship between value creation and ongoing value maintenance, business analytics teams will usually continue to add value until they reach saturation point. At that point, all their available resource time will be consumed maintaining the value they originally created. Once they hit that point, their ability to create new value becomes severely constrained.

In an ideal world, this would not present a problem. By the time the team hits saturation point, additional investment is relatively easy to arrange as the organization:

- Has strong management commitment to the use of business analytics
- Understands the value that business analytics brings
- Is already leveraging business analytics in multiple areas of the business
- Is actively looking for new areas to apply business analytics

The reality is often starkly different: The number of organizations globally that have such clarity of focus is relatively small. For the vast majority of analytics teams, many of which are either newly created or trying to establish some momentum, their environment is far more challenging. The organization often:

- Does not have clear management visibility over the use of business analytics and instead makes decisions based on gut feel
- Is unclear about how advanced forms of analytics can actually add value
- Is using business analytics only in highly siloed and "under-the-covers" applications, if at all
- Does not have an overarching approach, strategy, or culture around applying business analytics

Because of this, teams get trapped in a Catch-22: They cannot justify further incremental investment into the team without demonstrating the potential for additional value, but they cannot demonstrate the potential for additional value because they do not have resourcing to support an investigation! For most teams, getting trapped in this situation and being unable to get out of it is a death knell. Almost inevitably, this stagnation starts impacting people at both personal and professional levels.

Their interest levels fall due to a lack of challenge, their career growth starts being impacted, and their internal visibility drops. Eventually, this manifests as a decrease in staff retention, further increasing the pressure on the group as the higher performers (often with substantial amounts of knowledge) leave the group, increasing the workload on the remaining team members. Unless broken, this cycle eventually leads to the business analytics team becoming increasingly irrelevant, misunderstood, and perceived as being of low value to the organization.

Understanding Tactical Revolutions

Given unlimited resources, anything is possible. For many teams, though, the only realistic way to start creating and delivering new value is to somehow free up enough time for additional projects. It is in these situations that evolutionary improvements are most valuable. By taking a pragmatic look at where resource time is typically consumed over the course of a week, it is often fairly easy for a manager to identify potential opportunities for improvement.

The key thing is that these improvements do not need to be revolutionary: They simply need to free up small, incremental amounts of time each week that can then be reinvested in creating more evolutionary improvements. Eventually, enough time is freed up to support a new growth project, which in turn becomes justification for the additional resources needed in the first place.

A critical enabler in this process is having access to a measurement and monitoring platform that provides comparative measures between initiatives. Without this, it is often a guess as to where the biggest efficiency improvements lie; we will examine what this means in more detail in Chapter 7.

A good example of how to create these efficiencies lies in data preparation. The vast majority of any business analytics project is spent dealing with data. And, in most teams, there is more than one project in flight, often using the same source data but creating different analytical processes. Commonly, these team members are dealing with extremely similar, if not exactly the same, transformed data. However, because they are working independently, they often manage their own data extraction and transformation processes.

Even if these processes take only half an hour per person per week, consolidating them into a single shared process gives additional resourcing headroom that allows them to spend more time focusing on streamlining their processes and freeing up additional time. If there are five people on the team, standardizing their processes may free up to two and a half hours each week!

Creating these tactical revolutions is not easy. The biggest dangers are:

- Not having a clear understanding of the end game
- Putting too much focus on process efficiency and not enough on value delivery
- Setting goals too high

Without understanding what the final goal is, it is extremely hard to identify incremental improvements that consistently move the team in the right direction. With so many opportunities for improvement in every team, it is critical that the team navigate the most efficient path toward the desired end state. And, if that end state is poorly defined, it is dangerously easy for a team to spend significant amounts of time improving activities that, although still beneficial, do not help the team move toward any strategic goals. Having access to a monitoring and measurement platform is the best defense against this risk.

Another temptation to watch out for is an exclusive focus on process improvement. Although a full-time focus on making processes more efficient will inevitably mean a faster delivery cycle, business unfortunately does not stop in the meantime. A full reinvention can take anywhere from months to years and, if too much time is spent exclusively on this reinvention, the rest of the business starts to question the value of investing in a business unit that delivers no apparent value.

Setting goals too high can also slow delivery and delay the reinvention cycle. The best opportunities for tactical revolutions are those that require the least amount of effort to achieve a measurable process efficiency improvement. This does not necessarily mean focusing on the activities that, if optimized, would provide the biggest benefit. If the team is lucky, they are one and the same. However, in most situations, the biggest opportunities for improvement often require the biggest amount of time investment. By focusing on these, the danger is that the delivery time frame might shift from months to years, often leading to staff retention issues and further setting the team back.

Delivering a Tactical Revolution

Combating these common pitfalls is relatively simple and involves remembering these three key points:

1. *Leverage the road map.* Tactics are the steps, but strategy is the outcome.
2. *Keep delivering value.* Without ongoing value, it is easy to lose organizational support.
3. *Be persistent.* Reinvention is an incremental process of continuous improvement.

When we get into our car to drive to a new destination, we normally use a GPS or a paper map; we know where we want to go, we just need to know the steps to get there. Business analytics is no different: In the absence of a road map, a business analytics team will almost inevitably end up focusing purely on business as usual or responding tactically to the business, never really developing any new competencies in a repeatable capacity or delivering any true efficiency improvements.

A business analytics team should be creating tangible value for the business. This is important, as most organizations classify groups into either cost centers or profit centers. In the main, profit centers attract investment whereas cost centers attract cost-cutting. Given the competitive advantage business analytics offers, allowing the perception that a business analytics team is a cost center is counterproductive at best, and value destroying at worst.

Because of this, the onus is on the business analytics team to demonstrate constant value delivery. If every initiative over a two-year horizon involves process efficiencies without any incremental value creation, the broader perception within the business is likely to be that the business analytics team does not directly add value. Once this perception is entrenched, investment minimization becomes the major focus.

Creating a tactical revolution requires balancing these incremental process improvements against ongoing value delivery. In practice, this is a challenging process. Given how saturated most teams are, the thought of taking on more work is beyond daunting. However, no matter how difficult it may appear, it is one of the most direct routes to attracting additional investment.

Finally, it is critical that the team remembers that creating a tactical revolution is a marathon, not a sprint. Given explicit organizational sanction and investment, a total reinvention can be relatively rapid. In some cases, it can take as little time as under a year. Unfortunately, for the majority of organizations this process takes far longer. However, by picking incremental improvements, delivering them consistently over time, being persistent, and constantly expanding the scope of its operations, it is possible for the team to deliver a true tactical revolution.

PLANNING FOR SUCCESS

Successful delivery requires both a strategic plan and a tactical plan. Although business analytics initiatives have many similarities to other disciplines, there are a few key differences that when successfully managed increase the probability of successful delivery. These are:

- The temptation to rely on ability rather than management
- A failure to acknowledge the high degree of uncertainty involved in business analytics
- Ignoring the importance of turning discovery processes into operational processes

Often, analytics teams are highly skilled. Because of this, it is tempting to allow team members to operate largely independently with relatively little oversight. Although this can work, it is very easy for teams to become far too focused on their daily activities at the expense of what they are trying to deliver. Because of their background and ability, analysts will often find a multitude of ways to solve the issues they come across. This is missing the forest for the trees; although they *are* keeping the project moving, they may not always realize that deadlines are slipping. This may introduce significant delays and, in the absence of management supervision, they may believe that there are no problems with the project. Even though it might be a bit delayed, things are still moving. Keeping an eye on the overall delivery plan is critical if delays are to be avoided.

Analysts often need to deal with a high degree of uncertainty. At an analytical level, almost every problem is different and requires a relatively unique solution. Like any discovery-styled project, delivering an analytics project comes down to making assumptions at the start of the project, testing them, and, if they prove to be incorrect, testing alternative approaches. Planning for this is critical; if insufficient time is built into the initial plan for this discovery process, it will be impossible to meet the projected deadlines. Equally, if expectations are not managed internally, this standard approach can be misinterpreted as confusion and uncertainty. When inappropriately managed, this discovery process can create significant delivery delays and damage internal credibility.

Finally, the value of business analytics comes from executing on the insight generated by the analytics team. By definition, this means that the team's discovery processes must be able to be operationally deployed. As discussed earlier, when this is not taken into account it is possible for analysts to develop processes that cannot be operationally deployed, often necessitating a complete redesign of their activities.

Monitor Ongoing Effort and Apply the 80/20 Rule

Because of the complex interdependencies involved in creating insight, it is extremely easy to focus on the problem and not the steps leading to that problem. Generating a report or creating a predictive model is often a relatively straightforward activity. And if that is the key input into the final outcome, it is tempting to plan around the expected time needed to deliver it.

Unfortunately, it is often the case that *getting to that point* requires significant effort. Sourcing the right data can take weeks of negotiation and investigation with other business units. Structuring and cleansing the data can take further weeks. And, once the report or model has been built, deploying it into the data warehouse can be a struggle as well.

Comparatively, creating the asset often takes the least amount of time in the overall value chain. Treating the initiative as a project and explicitly defining all the required activities helps uncover these dependencies. Failing to do so runs the risk of missing some key activities and introducing significant delays.

Another common problem is focusing too much on the detail, often at the expense of the outcome. It is always possible for analysts to improve the accuracy or presentation of the final results—models can always be improved and reports made more attractive. This incremental improvement is seductive: By investing just a little more time and trying something else, the analyst will almost always be able to make things better. Without any other time constraints, it is easy to spend a significant amount of time on these incremental improvements.

Beyond a certain point, though, diminishing returns start to occur and increased amounts of effort often translate into smaller and smaller amounts of accuracy or insight. Managing these activities is critical; within a business analytics context, the *value* delivered is the key measure of concern. A good-enough model is worth far more than an excellent model if the first is acted on and the second is not—until the insight is executed, no value is created. Having a project plan and outcomes-based monitoring structures helps create a buffer against these types of slippages; it encourages analysts to balance accuracy against delivery.

Plan for What You Do Not Know

Creating insight is an uncertain process. Although high-level activities can often be defined in advance, the detail of what will be involved is hard to identify ahead of time. This is largely inevitable; analytics typically involves creating insight from real-world behaviors. The world is a complex place and unlike largely deterministic systems such as the physical sciences, peoples' behaviors vary significantly.

Although trends do exist (often making these behaviors predicable), these trends will change depending on the people being examined and the context within which they are operating. Because of this, it is very difficult to know what specific technical challenges will need to be overcome when creating insight from the data. Not only that, but the insight often needs to be used by people who cannot articulate how they will use it until they can see what it will look like.

These uncertainties directly impact how the insight is generated. There may be measurement issues that require data cleansing and manipulation. There may be methodological or data challenges that preclude certain types of technical approaches. There may be misunderstandings among other groups within the organization of what form the outputs will take, requiring changes to the look and feel of the outputs. As if that were not enough, it is almost inevitable that delivering a series of models or insights leads to the creation of new insights and potential modeling opportunities.

A key part of any business analytics initiative is establishing the high-level methodology that will hopefully lead to the target outcome. This is often a series of broad activities that are believed to be required in order to achieve the desired outcome. Experience normally plays a heavy role in identifying these activities. Because it can be hard to identify these detailed activities ahead of time, planning for what you do not know is critical. Two key things to remember are:

1. No one knows everything.
2. Analytics is a voyage of discovery—uncertainty is par for the course.

Those involved in delivering value through business analytics are probably dealing with people with unclear requirements, data that is incomplete at best (and often downright incorrect), and problems they have never solved before. And yet, they are tasked with solving these problems quickly, efficiently, and robustly.

The degree of uncertainty involved in most business analytics projects is surprising to people familiar with other disciplines such as data warehousing, engineering, or even the legal profession. While every profession has its own degree of uncertainty, it is rare to be involved in one where:

- The definition of *success* is uncertain.
- The materials being used are totally undefined.
- There exist no generally acknowledged specific best practices to solve problems.
- Most problems are almost totally unique. (For example, modeling churn in prepaid mobile handsets is almost a totally different problem from modeling churn in postpaid mobile handsets, even though it is arguably the same customer demographics, the same industry, and the same hardware!)

Creating a project plan helps manage these issues in two ways:

1. It minimizes uncertainty within the team.
2. It identifies whether the target methodology is working or struggling.

By explicitly defining the major steps within the overall methodology, the broader team gets an understanding of how the problem is likely to be solved. Although team members may not be clear on the specifics of the detail until they start working on it, understanding the overall approach helps by providing them with some guidance around what the outputs of a particular stage should broadly look like. Additionally, clarity of direction helps combat the morale issues often associated with working with unknowns.

However, not all methodologies work. Uncertainty means that sometimes the plan will be wrong. By defining the high-level steps involved with the project, managers can explicitly track progress and quality of output. If insufficient progress is being made, it may be necessary to go back to the drawing-board and develop an entirely new methodology. Given early enough identification, this may be possible without impacting the final delivery date. In the absence of a defined delivery plan, this may be impossible.

Plan for the Transition into Operational Use

The value of business analytics comes from the action taken on the insight that has been generated. Because of this, growth initiatives need to focus not only on discovery, but also on how that insight will be turned into something that can be operationally executed.

A great example of how failing to plan for transition can create issues again lies in data management. Data is usually messy, unstructured, missing, or just plain incorrect. A classic example I once dealt with was trying to reconcile transactional revenue against profitability in an organization's general ledger.

After spending hours being unable to work out why my summations did not match the top-line numbers I had been provided, I finally bit the bullet and gave someone a call. His response? "Oh, yeah, we don't use that field—it's wrong!"

Although effort varies, it is not uncommon to see over 80 percent of team members' time spent simply trying to manage the data they are using. Included in this is time spent:

- Extracting data from data warehouses and other source systems
- Cleansing and standardizing the data
- Sanity-checking the numbers to make sure they make sense
- Transforming the data and creating various useful derived variables (such as moving averages, changes in measures between time periods, and so on)
- Deriving aggregations and summary tables
- Creating training tables to be used for predictive modeling
- Creating scoring table structures to be used for ongoing prediction

That is a lot of work! Unless explicitly monitored and managed, it is dangerously easy to develop discovery processes that *cannot* be operationally deployed. A common example is when teams use interactive tools such as Microsoft Excel to do data management—although this may create great insights, it can be extremely difficult to take those insights and turn them into automated processes that are integrated into operational customer relationship management, ordering, inventory management, or fraud detection systems.

When this occurs, teams face a significant dilemma. They may have created insight that is robust, interesting, and highly valuable. Unfortunately, because that insight cannot be automated, they must do one of three things:

1. Commit a resource to running the insight processes on demand for an indefinite period into the future.
2. Redevelop their insight processes from scratch to support automation and systems integration.
3. Write off their time and effort and sacrifice the value they have created.

The first choice leads to a drain on resources. The second leads to significant delays and requires more investment. And, where the third choice limits any additional investment, it also prevents teams from creating any value.

Because of this, it is essential that the team plans *how* operational deployment will occur at the *start* of the project. Although the final solution will probably not yet be known, a solution that cannot be executed is worthless. Planning usually involves:

- Defining a series of approved insight-development tools and processes that allow for operational deployment
- Ensuring the team is allocating time to planning and delivering the operational deployment processes within the project plan

By including operational deployment in the planning stage, a manager can help drive a team toward an outcomes-based view of delivery rather than a development-based view of delivery.

Establish Ownership Early

Teams also sometimes fail to deliver because of a general misalignment between outcomes and responsibilities. Most business analytics projects are relatively complex and involve people from across the organization; it is not uncommon to see representatives from various execution groups, IT, and the business analytics team in any successful project.

Achieving a successful outcome requires treating every initiative as a project in its own right. This means more than just acknowledging that people are "working on things"; it means creating a project delivery plan that explicitly defines:

- Roles and responsibilities
- Specific activities that will be carried out
- Staged milestones and scheduled progress reports
- Delivery time frames and expected outputs

Failed initiatives often have a generally relaxed approach to managing activities. Conversely, the teams that deliver successfully tend to appreciate the importance of applying varying levels of project management to their activities.

This does not mean activities need to be micromanaged. Although some teams find it useful to create extremely granular project plans, it is often more important that the plan clarify responsibilities. When it does not, it often leads to:

- Misunderstandings about what is required by when
- A lack of clarity around who is responsible for what
- Failing to consider necessary prerequisite activities and their associated time commitments

Managing this complexity requires clarity, not only in terms of responsibility but also motivational factors. Basing success on outcomes rather than activity drives successful behaviors. By focusing attention on the value rather than the effort, team members are encouraged to work toward value creation rather than insight generation. When this clarity is not provided, teams often experience delays because people:

▪ Are unsure who is ultimately responsible for different activities

▪ Spend excessive time focusing on activity rather than value creation

▪ Are not clear on what the final outcome is

Teams facing these challenges fail to consistently deliver value. Through chance or heroic effort, they may deliver enough value to guarantee their existence within an organization. However, they also often experience high turnover, regular project delays, and a general perception within the organization that analytics is valuable but unreliable.

Establishing ownership early makes it easier for managers to co-ordinate across multiple teams. For example, a functional group within the organization will need to execute on the findings to realize the value. To execute on the findings, IT will need to have made them available through the relevant supporting systems. To make them available, the business analytics team will need to have generated the insights and created an automated scoring process to ensure they are up to date.

Even in this simple example, three separate teams within the organization need to change their processes to support execution. Change requires time and effort, and, if sufficient notice is not pro-vided, it may be impossible for other teams to change their processes in time. Creating a project delivery plan, socializing it, and getting commitment to it helps ensure that the changes required will be scheduled into their prioritized activities. It also establishes an under-standing of how their commitments fit into the overall value chain, helping combat a belief that it does not matter if they are late.

As with every project, clearly defined ownership over specific activities is critical. Otherwise, delays constantly creep into the plan because people are mistakenly waiting for others to deliver things they are not even working on. Managing this complexity is critical, and the absence of a formally defined plan is a short path to project failure.

Set Appropriate Success and Reward Measures

Also important is aligning success and reward measures against desired outcomes. By doing so, a manager can drive positive behaviors. To highlight why this is so important, it is useful to examine the creation of a model that identifies fraudulent behavioral patterns. One approach would be to design incentive structures to reward model accuracy or speed of delivery. Unfortunately, these incentive structures run the risk of creating countervailing forces against value creation.

It is a foolish analyst who would argue that accuracy is not an important measure. However, within the context of business analytics, *action* is arguably more important—without action, there is no value. Given that projects allow limited resources and finite delivery time, project teams inevitably need to make decisions about where time and effort are spent. By rewarding accuracy as the primary measure of success, a manager can unintentionally reward inaction; team members may prioritize increasing the accuracy of models over successful execution because that is where their incentive framework drives them.

Similarly, rewarding speed of delivery can unintentionally create bad behavioral patterns. Although efficiency is important, so is quality of output. If speed is the primary measure of success, teams may be driven toward establishing "minimum acceptable" delivery outcomes because that maximizes their incentive structures. This obviously carries an opportunity cost. Although outcomes are being produced, better outcomes might have been achieved given the right incentive structures.

Setting an appropriate reward system is a critical success factor for a business analytics manager: By driving team focus toward outcomes over activity, managers draw attention to what is important. In practice, this often means designing reward and bonus structures around the degree to which value is created. Examples could include improvements in profitability, customer retention rates, or the proportion of accepted offers within an acquisition process. Creating an appropriate incentive framework helps ensure the focus is on value creation rather than low-level activity.

PRACTICAL EXAMPLE: SOCIAL NETWORK ANALYSIS

One recent example of the importance of effective up-front planning I was involved in revolved around using social network analysis to predict viral churn in telecommunications. Key to successful delivery was:

- Creating a flexible planning framework
- Relying on rapid, iterative delivery
- Focusing on creating reusable standardized processes

The background of the project was fairly straightforward. The company in question was interested in knowing whether it was possible to identify who was likely to churn based on customers' relationships with those who had churned in a prior period. Making things slightly more complex, the company was interested in testing the validity of the approach using only social network data. As such, we were not provided any customer information, or usage patterns over time, or any other factors that would normally be used to predict churn.

Making things even more complex, we had agreed that we would deliver the entire project within six weeks, including all data management, analysis, knowledge handover, and presentations. As if that were not enough, I was also dealing with an application of analytics that the team had had no experience doing before. And although I had previously dealt with similar applications, such as agent-based-modeling and relationship-driven marketing, I was acutely conscious that my level of direct experience was relatively low.

As such, I decided to build the entire approach around planning for the unknown. While I had a large degree of confidence in the high-level activities I had identified that we would need to go through, I started from the assumption that the detailed activities would likely be informed by the discoveries we would make through doing the project. So, rather than try to identify every specific action we would take through the six weeks, I built our project plan around the milestones that we would need to hit in order to deliver in time. For this specific project, those milestones were:

- Identifying the communities within the overall network
- Calculating a variety of centrality measures within each community and deriving relationship structures
- Developing a predictive model to identify propensity for churn
- Scoring the test datasets and presenting the results

Rather than tie delivery to each of these milestones, I set a series of expected outcomes for each week's close. That way, given the level of uncertainty we were dealing with, I would have very early signals if we were either going down a dead end or having delivery issues.

This became a critical enabler. Due to a variety of data and platform issues, we ended up slipping significantly in the first three weeks. However, because we had the early warning detection in place, we had the ability to quickly reprioritize, request additional resources, and rework the project plan to conduct activities in parallel, ensuring that by the time we hit the week before we were scheduled to deliver, we were running just under a week behind.

Another critical success factor was the focus the team put on creating modularized, reusable processes. Toward the end of the project, we had quite a large number of people working independently to create their own steps within an overall modeling chain. We had no room in the project plan to serialize our activities and, to make things even more complicated, we were needing to test the overall process multiple times each day for predictive accuracy.

By making sure everyone was designing his or her individual processes to be self-contained and working from a series of standardized tables, we managed to collapse what would have otherwise taken roughly three weeks into less than a week, an estimated time savings of over 66 percent. And, we did so with no loss in accuracy or any team-level confusion. One of the final things we did was have one person package up the entire process for handover and documentation. Importantly, she was able to do this within less than a day, despite never having seen or understood how the other 80 percent of the analytics worked.

SUMMARY

Committing to delivering the value in the form of an execution plan is essential. As we have seen:

- An innovation approach typically offers competitive advantage at a higher risk and time investment.
- An evolutionary approach typically offers incremental improvements at lower risk and time investment.

- The value created is independent of whether the approach is innovative or evolutionary.
- Operational activities tend to maintain existing value.
- Growth activities tend to add to existing value.
- In order to maintain the value returned, growth business analytics activities typically transition into operational.

Delivering sustained value through business analytics requires *delivering regular incremental value* at the same time as *committing to a road map*. It requires a *strong focus on planning, execution, and measurement* to deliver real returns and justify ongoing investment. And, delivering the above often *requires creating tactical revolutions*, leveraging the time freed through small evolutionary improvements to deliver *growth initiatives*.

For most teams, this involves the following five steps:

1. Deliver evolutionary activities within the business-as-usual space to free up a beachhead of time.
2. This time is then invested in evolutionary growth projects, typically leveraging existing competencies to deliver new sources of value.
3. Once measured, the value delivered through this growth project is used to justify additional resourcing.
4. This additional resourcing is then applied toward innovating operational processes, freeing up significant amounts of time and creating competitive advantage.
5. Once these efficiencies are delivered, the newly streamlined team starts focusing on innovation growth projects aimed at creating a new competency, transitioning it into operational activities, and reapplying it in new areas of the business.

Once the value has been defined and the benefits communicated, *committing to a delivery plan* becomes an essential part of achieving success through business analytics. The final piece of the puzzle involves measuring the benefits.

In the next chapter, we will investigate the core characteristics of an effective measurement framework, examine some of the major types of measures of greatest interest to analytics teams, and consider a few of the more advanced measurement techniques.

 ## THE CHECKLIST: DELIVERING THE VALUE

Key Considerations

Creating the Road Map

Where could analytics be applied to create value within the organization?

What would be the likely return and benefits for each of these initiatives?

How long would it take to deliver each of these initiatives?

Which of these initiatives would be most worth delivering?

What are the interdependencies between these initiatives?

What existing assets and competencies would each of these initiatives leverage?

What assets or competencies are required by these initiatives that do not already exist?

Understanding Value Creation

How frequently will value be delivered?

What is the balance between growth and value maintenance?

What is the balance between innovation-focused and evolutionary-driven initiatives?

How will ad hoc queries be managed?

Where will the efficiencies come from to allow the additional workload?

What is the plan for transitioning each growth initiative into an operational activity?

How realistic is the road map?

Which key stakeholders need to agree with the road map?

How will their agreement be achieved?

Delivering the Value

For each initiative, which team member will be responsible for what?

For each of these outcomes, how will success be measured?

For each of these outcomes, what will the reward structure look like?

For each initiative, who outside of the team will be responsible for what?

CHAPTER 7

Delivering the Measurement Framework

INTRODUCTION

As noted in Chapter 6, a measurement framework is a critical enabler for delivering tactical revolutions. Without understanding time allocations and where things *could* be improved, it is often impossible for managers to create the efficiencies necessary to free up time for innovation.

This alone is a good reason to establish a measurement framework. However, a good measurement framework does more than that. It also helps quantify *actual* return, not just *planned* return. Although the business case developed in Chapter 4 is essential, at best it only represents promises and intentions. This is usually a prerequisite for getting organizational commitment—without quantifying the expected returns, investment is unlikely.

A business case builds interest and hope. And demonstrating ongoing returns builds trust and credibility. Because of the high degree of linkage between business analytics and strategic advantage, this trust is an essential component in transforming organizational culture. By being able to demonstrate and quantify real and renewable tangible returns, managers make their lives far easier.

Trust helps build a belief that additional initiatives will deliver incremental value. Credibility helps streamline the capital allocation process. And, both help obtain commitment to strategic objectives, not just short-term tactical returns.

A measurement framework is the final essential component of successfully selling the value of analytics. It demonstrates in agreed, comparable terms the value of business analytics. It measures the effort expended by the team executing various activities, allowing managers to deliver ongoing internal efficiency improvements. And, possibly most importantly, it does so with a minimum of overhead requirements, significantly increasing the ability of the team to scale.

In this chapter, we will review the various types of measures of interest to a business analytics team. We will consider the importance of identifying these during the planning stages, and not just as an afterthought. We will also examine some of the most important characteristics of a good measurement platform. Finally, we will explore some of the more advanced forms of measurement, focusing on quantifying aspects that are sometimes hard to measure.

WHY A MEASUREMENT FRAMEWORK IS ESSENTIAL

Committing to value creation is one thing; proving it is another. Obtaining investment almost inevitably requires some form of business case. If an organization is not able to articulate and communicate the value being created through the use of business analytics, it will find it difficult to make any form of significant investment.

Once this case has been successfully communicated, the team needs to execute on its suggestions. Unfortunately, execution is not sufficient to guarantee ongoing success—although the team may create significant value, unless it can quantify that value to the business in a way that is trusted and believed, it may as well have done nothing at all.

Establishing a measurement framework is critical for a number of reasons. It helps build trust and credibility within the organization, clarify attention where it is needed, and maintain focus where competing priorities arise, as they almost always do.

Specifically, a measurement framework helps:

- Justify ongoing investment
- Optimize internal activities
- Establish and defend priorities

Delivering a business case and obtaining organizational commitment are only the first steps in truly unleashing the value of business analytics. Because competencies are usually applicable across many business problems, the real value comes from releveraging existing competencies at low cost in other areas.

As discussed in Chapter 6, although competencies and tools are largely reusable, every growth initiative adds to the ongoing effort required to support operational activities and maintain value. Even though effort can be minimized through effective use of technology, it still exists. Because of this, being able to justify ongoing investment is critical. At some stage, this investment will be needed if the team is to preserve its value.

When teams are unable to directly measure the value they create, credibility suffers. From an external perspective, significant amounts of time, money, and effort may have been spent for little apparent return. Without this credibility, teams are often unable to source the funding they need to cover their ongoing incremental growth.

A measurement framework also plays a critical role in focusing attention on evolutionary improvements to where it is needed. Business analytics teams conduct a wide variety of activities ranging from the technical to the strategic. Because solving business problems often requires translating strategic issues into mathematical concepts, team members will normally be involved in data management, conceptual mapping, asset development, group communication, and systems integration and asset deployment. Each of these activities has varying degrees of opportunity for efficiency improvement. If managers are not able to quantify the time and effort expended against each of these, it is difficult (if not impossible) for them to identify where optimization activities would have the greatest impact.

A final important role of a measurement framework is blocking deviation from strategic objectives. Business analytics plays two roles: strategic enabler and tactical value creator.

Although maintaining a strategic view helps deliver growth initiatives and create competitive advantage, the temptation is always there to focus on providing operational insight and sacrifice strategic growth for immediate return. By establishing a measurement framework and tracking the relative value created through operational activities and growth initiatives, managers can explicitly communicate the trade-off the organization will be making by detouring from its business analytics road map. Without this measurement, many organizations struggle to maintain focus. Solving an immediate pain almost always trumps making things easier in the future.

Establishing a measurement framework is a critical enabler in building trust, prioritizing internal optimization targets, and maintaining focus. Regardless of how effectively the value is defined, how well this value is communicated, and how well the organization commits to delivering it, things almost inevitably fall apart if effort and value creation are not tracked. Even in successful teams, this can be a significant problem.

Overworked and Under-Resourced Team

Failing to measure value creates a variety of challenges for an analytics team, the most discouraging of which involves a general inability to convince the organization to invest in the team. A good practical example of how this can manifest involves some work I did with an insight team.

The team as a group was extremely capable—the manager had a clear vision of the benefits business analytics could provide to the organization, his team members had a strong set of supporting competencies, and their analytics platform had the core tools they believed they needed. They also had an unwavering focus on adding value to the business; without fail, they would manage to service requests from the business in record time. On paper, everything was perfect.

Unfortunately, delving into a little more detail with them uncovered a rather uncomfortable reality. Although they were exceedingly good at servicing the business, the time they were spending providing operational support was eating into what they *really* considered exciting and motivating: business innovation and the creation of competitive advantage. This was creating friction within the team—although the team understood the importance of establishing its value to the business, its morale was suffering.

The obvious answer was for the manager to go and appropriate funding for additional resources. Rather confusingly, though, when he put in a business case to hire two more individuals, his case had been knocked back for being a lower priority. What was especially confounding was that requests from the business for insight had been increasing at a rapid rate over the past two years. Despite broad acknowledgment from multiple areas of the business of the importance of business analytics, his repeated attempts to obtain additional investment had been blocked.

When I met with him, he was understandably confused. On one hand, various functional groups in the business insisted that they would not be able to do their jobs without the insight his team was providing. Regardless of whom he spoke with, there was no doubt about his team's value. On the other hand, despite his team's critical role in keeping the business operating, the people who controlled the capital obviously did not see enough value in adding additional headcount to justify direct investment.

This lack of additional funding was creating very real issues. Critically, he was at serious risk of losing individuals due to frustration —their workload had been increasing for a number of years and although they had managed to do a phenomenal job of increasing efficiency to deal with the increased levels of demand they were facing, there was an upper limit to what any individual team member could deal with. Additionally, his team was comprised of very bright individuals—their job satisfaction was heavily tied to creative thinking and innovation. By focusing almost purely on operational activities and ad hoc responses, many of them were starting to feel constrained and in danger of stagnating. He was painfully aware that unless he could break through this deadlock with his funding committee, he was in serious danger of his team imploding.

The answer lay in what he was doing, or more accurately, what he was *not* doing. Despite spending significant time adding value to the business, he had no way to *quantify* either the value he was creating or the effort his team was expending creating this value. Without this direct relationship between value creation and effort expended, he was struggling to communicate *how* additional resources would add incremental value to the business. And although this relationship had been more than adequately demonstrated, his inability to provide specific measurements meant that he was unlikely to ever get any real traction with the people who controlled access to funding; they could see the value, but they could not understand how more resources would create more value.

The solution was fairly straightforward. By working with the already-supportive external teams to identify the relationships between his team's insight and the external teams' value creation, he could directly measure the value his team was creating and thereby create specific financial arguments to justify incremental investment.

Linking his activity to organizational value creation was the first step. One of the things we quickly identified was that unless he put in place a framework to measure ongoing value creation, it was likely that he would end up in the same position in next year's budgeting cycle. In parallel, we also created an automated measurement platform to capture the value created *and* establish it as a standard necessary requirement within any new operational activity or growth initiative. By making the measurement framework a mandatory part of any project executed by his team, he ensured that he would always be able to demonstrate his team's value-add, removing his most significant barrier to obtaining additional funding.

In a Nutshell: What You Need at a Minimum and How to Do It

Measuring the value of business analytics is a critical enabler to demonstrating real return and optimizing internal activities. When measures are not tracked, teams often fail to convince stakeholders of their value. Equally, delivering substantial and regular process improvements, reducing needless work, and identifying bottlenecks is extremely challenging, if not impossible. Tracking value also helps teams defend their focus by quantifying what the trade-off would be should their attention be diverted.

The most common types of measures tracked by an analytics team are:

- Business measures
- Analytical measures
- Technical measures

Business measures are primarily concerned with demonstrating the value of business analytics. Analytical measures help divert focus from where it is not needed. Technical measures help identify bottlenecks and prioritize technology and process reengineering investment.

A good measurement framework limits focus to tracking important and realistic measures instead of every measure. This helps ensure a minimum level of tracking overhead as well as making it easier to include these measures in all future initiatives.

Delivering this framework requires access to a common platform that often leverages off-the-shelf reporting toolsets. It should encourage management by exception and maintain a focus on standardizing outputs and processes. Finally, the quickest path to success is to ensure a high level of automation across all non-value-added activities.

ROLE OF THE MEASUREMENT FRAMEWORK

Delivering initiatives is often difficult. Managers need to deal with high levels of uncertainty and they are often working with fewer resources than would be ideal. Effective project management almost *demands* a ruthless approach when it comes to prioritizing activities. Limiting scope creep is not optional; it is mandatory.

Under this delivery pressure, why would a manager commit to the additional work of creating a measurement framework? After all, every hour of effort spent tracking measures is an hour that could be spent on something else. This is an especially valid question given that a measurement framework does not directly relate to value creation or risk mitigation.

While a simple view may suggest that it is extra effort for little return, a measurement framework plays an essential role. As stated earlier, it helps the team:

- Justify ongoing investment
- Optimize internal activities
- Establish and defend priorities

Organizations are in a constant battle against scarcity—at any given time, there are normally many more opportunities than there is capital. From a strategic point of view, business analytics initiatives are simply one of many potential sources of return. Although they align well against short-term value creation *and* the creation of competitive advantage, they still need to be prioritized against every other potential initiative. Without a measurement framework, it is impossible to demonstrate *real and sustainable* value creation, not just *planned* value creation. And, without these measures, it can be extremely difficult to justify ongoing investment.

Another advantage of business analytics is its ability to scale. Because it leverages mathematics and systems-based technologies, process scalability is dictated not by the amount of manual labor but by the degree of investment in technology and capital. This is attractive for a variety of reasons: Leveraging technology enhances individual productivity, it allows the use of highly fungible goods, and it creates repeatability. However, understanding *where* these efficiencies can be created requires a good understanding of where the bottlenecks exist. A measurement framework helps quantify the relative effort expended across the entire value chain, focusing optimization activities and investment to where they provide the greatest benefits.

Finally, the life of a business analytics manager is one defined by constantly balancing short-term demands against strategic value. Responding to requests from the business for insight usually builds goodwill and helps resolve immediate issues. These are often symptoms of a broader problem. Such firefighting requests are usually due to operational processes failing to integrate the insight provided by analytical assets. If these assets had been integrated into the operational processes in the first place, it is unlikely that the analytics team would have needed to manually create one-off insight.

Creating this strategic value usually requires the team to divert focus away from solving these short-term issues. And, without clear reasoning *why* the team is refocusing its efforts, it is very easy to destroy all the goodwill that has been built over time. A measurement framework helps the team provide empirical and quantifiable evidence of the value of growth initiatives, defending its decision to reduce emphasis on supporting operational insight processes.

Justify Ongoing Investment

As discussed in Chapter 2, a significant value of business analytics lies in its reusability across the organization. Competencies, once developed, can be applied to multiple business problems, creating an ongoing source of highly renewable value. Importantly, though, this does not mean that *no* ongoing investment is required: Growth initiatives usually require some degree of incremental investment. At a minimum they require diversion of existing resources to support them. Often, they will also require acquisition of new tools or assets.

As discussed in Chapter 6, almost every growth initiative eventually transitions into an operational activity if the value created is to be maintained. In practice, this inevitably requires some degree of incremental investment. Although the required competencies may have already been developed and the required tools already purchased, moving from a growth initiative to an operational activity typically requires:

- The creation of required data structures in the operational data warehouse

- Promotion or migration of discovery data management processes to operational data management processes

- Migration of analytics assets from the discovery environment into the operational environment

- Training operational support staff in how to interpret and best leverage the new insight that is provided to them

These are not free—more often than not, these activities require the organization to spend varying amounts of operational expenditure to support them. While business analytics offers a highly reusable and cost-effective way of creating value, it also requires investment. Demonstrating how business analytics has actually created *real* value (as opposed to *planned* or *future* value) is a critical part of getting access to this capital; trust and credibility are two of the shortest paths to success.

In order to invest in business analytics, the organization needs to understand the value that will be created. More than that, however, it also needs to trust that that value is real and that the team has sufficient credibility to deliver that value. A business case makes a useful contrast: It demonstrates *where* the value *is planned* to come from and *who* will be responsible for that value, but *it does not prove the value.* Proving that the value is real requires execution and measurement; it is not until the expected return has been accrued that it is real. And, having trust that the team will succeed requires history; knowing that the team has delivered successfully previously helps build trust that it can do it again.

A measurement framework helps build this trust. By explicitly measuring the real value created from a business analytics initiative, a manager can demonstrate to the organization that business analytics is delivering *real* value. And, when it comes to requesting additional investment for the next growth initiative, the organization can trust that the manager will be able to deliver it.

Optimize Internal Activities

Reapplying competencies across multiple business problems requires an ability to scale. While business analytics offers an extremely cost-effective approach, the team will eventually need additional resources. Time needs to be spent applying a given competency to a new business problem. New assets need to be created, monitored, and managed. And, processes frequently need to be reengineered to support operational analytics.

Meeting this internal demand and delivering incremental value requires managers to increase their scope of work. Practically speaking, there are only two ways they can do this:

1. Hire additional resources.

2. Do more with existing resources.

Getting access to additional headcount is notoriously difficult in most organizations; unless there is an extremely convincing reason why additional people are necessary, most managers struggle to hire more staff. And, even when they are given approval to hire additional resources, finding those resources is not always easy; getting people who are skilled in advanced analytics *as well* as experienced with applying advanced analytics for business value creation can be a challenge.

Because of this, managers usually need to develop a series of strategies to do more with their existing resources. For many teams caught in the Catch-22 discussed in Chapter 6, the reality is that they are heavily overworked, without any approval to hire additional staff. Solving this requires the manager to identify and deliver efficiency improvements. And doing so is nearly impossible without some form of measurement framework.

A measurement framework helps in two ways:

1. *It identifies efficiency bottlenecks,* allowing managers to focus their reengineering efforts where they will make the biggest difference.

2. *It provides visibility of value-creating time and effort,* allowing managers to prioritize their overall projects.

Taken as a whole, a business analytics team conducts a wide variety of activities. Any of these activities may benefit from focused reengineering. By profiling how they are executed, a manager can usually identify potential efficiency improvements. However, not all of these improvements are equal—some will have greater impact than others.

Without being able to understand the team's effort distribution, managers are flying blind. Their only source of information is often anecdotal and, in most situations, highly specific and not necessarily generalizable. For example, they may see one of their team members spending most of her time trying to clarify requirements within a specific group in the organization. A simple extrapolation from this might suggest that cross-team communication is the biggest hindrance. However, it might be just that particular group in the organization that has difficulties clarifying what it is they do; the rest of the team members might spend most of their time struggling with data quality.

A measurement framework helps cut through this uncertainty by providing a manager with visibility over the team's distribution of effort across various activities. By understanding where their team members spend most of their time, managers can identify the areas with the biggest *potential* for improvement. Critically, this is extremely difficult (if not impossible) without some form of measurement framework.

A measurement framework also allows a manager to understand the linkages between activity and outcomes. Because a good framework tracks not only effort but also where the effort was focused, it becomes relatively simple for a manager to investigate which activities were and were not linked to value creation. Understanding these relationships allows managers to make objective decisions about where to focus their teams for maximum organizational return. Without this visibility, it is often easiest for them to make the decision based on who yells the loudest.

Establish and Defend Priorities

A final important reason to establish a measurement framework is to give managers the ability to maintain strategic direction in the face of competing pressures. In most organizations, the team provides extremely useful insight to other business units. However, the analytics team is also ideally working to a road map that will lead to the creation of sustainable competitive advantage. Because of this, managers often need to balance satisfying internal demand for insight against the creation and application of new competencies to deliver measurable organizational value.

As has been stated repeatedly throughout this book, business analytics teams are often resource constrained. Time spent responding to ad hoc requests for insight is time taken away from other work. Establishing a measurement framework helps combat this by quantifying what is being sacrificed when focus is diverted from the road map. By being able to quantify the historical value of growth initiatives and current value of operational activities, managers can strengthen their arguments against taking on additional work that may be difficult to link to direct organizational value.

MEASURING WHAT IS IMPORTANT

Building an effective measurement framework need not be complex. Although a multitude of different measures *may* be useful, often only a small number of these are *really important*. An effective measurement framework aims to do three things:

1. Measure the value being created.
2. Focus attention on underperforming assets.
3. Identify areas that may benefit from optimization.

The most effective measurement frameworks are often the simplest. By tracking only what is important, the team can spend less time developing a needlessly complex reporting platform. By keeping the number of measures monitored low, the team makes its analysis simpler. And, by focusing attention on the measures that most impact success, managers drive optimizing behaviors away from activity and toward outcomes.

When the right measures *are not* tracked, teams often struggle to understand what is adding value, how much value they have created, and where they should be investing resources. Conversely, if *too many* measures are tracked, teams often fail to deliver any measurement framework at all. Because building a measurement platform takes time away from growth initiatives, it is often difficult for managers to justify a significant time investment from their team. After all, every hour spent building the platform could be an hour spent creating tangible or intangible value for the organization.

Specific measures will vary by application, but the most effective teams consider three broad classes of indicators:

1. Business measures
2. Analytical measures
3. Technical measures

Business measures have already had significant attention within this book, specifically in Chapter 4: They encompass the measures most directly associated with return. When accurately measured and trusted by the organization, they act as the justification for further investment in business analytics. At their core, *they demonstrate the ability of business analytics initiatives to create value.*

Analytical measures are usually the indicators that analysts are most familiar with. They encompass a variety of measures representing the accuracy and changing behaviors of the assets created by the team. Although rarely of interest to the broader organization, they normally play a vital role within the analytics team by helping focus redevelopment attention to where it is most needed. And, by doing so, *they help streamline team activity by taking away attention from where it is not needed.*

Technical measures are directly linked with the team's ability to optimize its internal processes; they aim to quantify activity, access, and productivity. Much like analytical measures, the broader organization often has little interest in these measures. However, they play a critical role in the team's ability to drive tactical revolutions: *When successfully tracked they often define where optimization activity needs to occur.*

An effective measurement framework tracks a minimum of measures across all three, balancing the need for management visibility against the overhead created by any measurement process. We will consider this in more detail later, but it is essential to remember that automated measurement should be leveraged wherever possible. Doing so reduces effort and overhead. Common examples include automatically extracting information from logs or creating data management processes to automatically track campaign response rates.

Business Measures

Business measures help demonstrate the value of business analytics. Their defining characteristic is their focus on what has been achieved, not the effort expended in getting there. Importantly, these measures provide comparability. Because they are standardized across different potential approaches, *they can be compared against the outcomes being delivered by current processes.*

Value creation is relative; without being able to relate it to the value being created currently, any measure is meaningless. These measures provide the greatest insight when they can be compared against the value being delivered by existing activities. We will examine this in more detail later in this chapter; for now, it is important to remember that each of these is necessarily a *relative* measure, not an absolute measure.

The two primary classes of business measures are financial outcomes and activity outcomes.

Financial Outcomes

Financial outcomes primarily track the economic contribution of growth initiatives to the organization. They give managers the ability to quantify the tangible value of the assets they have created. By focusing on economic outcomes, they translate what are often fairly abstract activities into something the financial side of the organization can relate to.

Unsurprisingly, the vast majority of these are the measures discussed in Chapter 4. They should relate directly to what was put forward in the business case. Some common examples can include:

- Gross revenue generation
- Gross cost avoidance
- Simple return on investment
- Realized rate of return
- Net economic value

When these are compared against the measures estimated in the business case, there is one key difference. Because they represent historical measures, they represent *real* value, not *discounted* value. Put another way, they do not have to include the time cost of money—for most organizations, a direct calculation is sufficient. Occasionally, some organizations will require the team to factor in the effects of inflation across the investment period to provide a real measure for value creation. However, this level of rigor is rarely used in practice.

Activity Outcomes

Activity outcomes provide a number of non-economic measures, often aligned with key performance indicators tracked by specific stakeholders within the organization. They aim to capture the direct outcomes associated with operational activities. Although they often play a role as an input into economic calculations of return, they rarely represent direct economic measures. Instead, they normally play a role in building internal political support. Because they map directly against specific target activities, they help demonstrate personally relevant value to concerned external stakeholders.

Whereas financial measures are usually common across organizations and applications of business analytics, activity outcomes vary significantly. Because they are aligned with operational activities, indicators are heavily dependent on the business problem being solved. Examples could include:

- The proportion of offers accepted through direct marketing activities
- The number of accurately and inaccurately identified cases of fraud
- The number of times a report is accessed by the organization
- The final quality of a given good as measured by deviation from ideal design
- The level of accuracy of a demand forecast

Common to all of these is that *they are activity-based measures of the level of success being achieved by the process.* For example, the manager of a direct marketing group may specifically be tasked with improving the organization's relevancy of marketing communication. Because many countries place limits on how frequently customers can be contacted, this becomes an important consideration for a marketing group interested in optimizing their allowed contacts.

Because every unsuccessful contact prevents the organization from making another offer that may be more relevant, increasing the proportion of offers accepted represents a direct demonstration of activity improvement. By applying more accurate predictive models, this acceptance rate might increase, delivering greater revenue *as well as* improving one of the primary metrics of concern for the direct marketing manager.

Quality improvement provides another useful example. A Six Sigma black belt might be tasked with improving product quality, as measured by how significantly a given manufacturing process deviates from an ideal process. A combination of analytical techniques (including design of experiments and relational modeling) might identify the major factors influencing process deviation as well as the process characteristics that would lead to ideal product quality. Applying analytics in this situation not only reduces costs through wastage but also improves some of the measures of most concern to the Six Sigma black belt. Where tracked, these improvements directly help the Six Sigma black belt, demonstrating the value of analytics and helping to create another internal supporter.

Analytical Measures

The main use of analytical measures is to direct internal attention where it is needed. Their defining characteristic is their focus on the assets created and managed by the team. When used effectively they help the team prioritize redevelopment and redesign effort.

These measures primarily focus on the *quality* of assets: They track the inherent characteristics of the assets being examined and provide managers with an understanding of how the assets are changing over time. Without them, managers are often unable to determine:

- How well assets are aligned with organizational objectives
- How effectively assets are performing
- How much the environment within which the assets operate has changed and how these changes will affect the assets

Tracking these measures makes it easier for managers to prioritize redevelopment effort. When these measures *are not* tracked, teams will often invest unnecessary time redeveloping or updating existing assets. To help illustrate why these measures are so important, it is useful to examine a typical team's monitoring activities.

Predictive models, like any other asset, degrade over time. Because they are based on identifying statistically significant common patterns within a customer base, they remain valid only for as long as those behaviors remain constant. As those behaviors change, the accuracy of a model degrades.

Behaviors inevitably change for a variety of reasons. At a macroeconomic level, the environment itself creates changes in customer sentiment, living patterns, and sociodemographic composition. At a microeconomic level, customer acquisition leads to organizations expanding into new segments and withdrawing from other segments. At a product level, technology can create new markets or kill existing ones, rendering existing models irrelevant when customer preferences and perceptions change. And, similar to Heisenberg's uncertainty principle, even the use of analytics can change the behaviors of those being modeled as they come to expect that they are being modeled.

The speed of this change varies significantly by domain. Behavioral changes can occur over relatively long periods of time, often in the order of a year or more. Fraud patterns, however, can change in the order of weeks; because the target groups are usually actively trying to mask their identifiers, they will render models useless as soon as they know how they are being identified.

For managers, tracking the quality and reliability of models is critical because it affects their ability to determine when a model's accuracy has degraded past a useful threshold. If a model is allowed to degrade too far, it may actually produce results that are worse than a random guess. However, refreshing or redeveloping models too frequently creates significant opportunity costs. The team could have spent that time creating new competencies or developing new assets.

Although quality measures will vary by application, algorithm, and asset type, some of the most common quality measures include:

- *Accuracy measures*—the ability of the model to make *correct* predictions

- *Improvement measures*—the ability of the model to make *better* predictions than existing processes

- *Deviation measures*—the degree to which underlying data is changing over time

Accuracy Measures

Accuracy measures help managers track, understand, and compare the ability of models to make correct predictions. They are often used to help managers decide which approach to use out of a collection of models or processes.

Models create a prediction based on a series of either business rules or statistical inferences. When these predictions are incorrect, they can be incorrect in two ways: They can either predict that the event *will* occur and it *does not* (also known as a *false positive* or *Type I error*) or they can predict that the event *will not* occur and it *does* (also known as a *false negative* or *Type II error*). Understanding the likelihood of each of these errors is essential when their cost to the organization is disproportionate.

One example of how these errors can affect the value of a model lies in a model built to identify fraud. If the expected value of a fraudulent transaction is extremely high, the organization would normally want to *minimize false negatives as much as possible*. Given the high cost of a missed detection, it may be better for the organization to deal with false positives and spend additional amounts on investigation rather than experience the significant losses associated with a missed detection.

However, if the expected losses from a missed detection are relatively low and investigation resources are heavily constrained, an organization may decide that efficient identification is the most important outcome. The most valuable model in this context might be one that has a high number of correct predictions *and* the *smallest number of false positives*. Minimizing false positives is important because each false positive represents an investigation that will not lead to a successful prosecution, limiting the effectiveness of the resource-constrained investigations team.

Improvement Measures

Improvement measures help managers measure the degree to which analytical assets add value beyond alternative (and existing) processes. Because they are a relative measure that can be directly compared against alternative challenger processes, they are often used to set a lower threshold below which models need to be redeveloped or refreshed.

A new predictive model should, in principle, provide better predictions than current processes. This establishes the minimum level of predictive accuracy a model needs to achieve. By analyzing the frequency with which an event occurs in the general population when current processes are applied, a manager can set a floor that represents the organization's level of accuracy should nothing change. For example, if 5 percent of all offers are accepted through direct marketing activity using current processes, the model should at least achieve an acceptance rate higher than 5 percent. If it does not, the champion process offers an equivalent or better outcome.

Because this measure represents the model's level of accuracy above existing processes, this improvement is often referred to as *lift*. As models degrade, this lift decreases. Eventually, the model will be only as good as or worse than the processes it replaced.

Tracking how lift changes over time is a vital consideration in working out the ideal time to refresh or redevelop a model: If it is redeveloped too frequently, the value created by the refresh may be less than the value created through a new growth initiative. If left too long, the value being lost through inaccurate models may outweigh the value being delivered through growth initiatives.

By tracking these measures, managers can make an objective decision on the optimal point in time to refresh or redevelop models. Additionally, they can establish various processes and business rules to automate notification processes, reducing the time spent by their team analyzing model accuracy.

Deviation Measures

The final types of commonly captured quality measures are deviation measures. These measures help managers understand how rapidly their external environment is changing around them. They are often used as an input into deciding how frequently models need to be redeveloped.

Models are fundamentally constrained by the stability of their inputs. When the current data being used no longer follows the same statistical characteristics of the data originally used to develop the model, the outputs of the model can no longer be trusted. Determining when the data to be scored has deviated beyond an acceptable point is usually a subjective judgment based on experience. However, without tracking the degree to which inputs are deviating from their original values, it is impossible for an analyst even to be aware of how substantially the assumptions underpinning a model have been violated.

By tracking these measures, analysts have the ability to visualize how greatly the underlying data has deviated from the original sample. And, by seeing this, they can make an informed judgment about whether the model's assumptions need to be reevaluated and the model potentially redeveloped.

Consider a model developed to identify the propensity of customers to be interested in bleeding-edge technology products. When the model was initially developed, the organization's original customer base might have been younger and extremely technologically savvy. Since the model was developed, however, the organization may have expanded into new markets, acquiring more conservative customers.

As the initial model was developed using a different type of customer base than the organization now has, the assumptions and relationships identified by the model may no longer be applicable. By examining a variety of deviation measures, including average customer age, purchasing patterns, and segment distributions over time, an analyst may quickly identify that the likely reason for the model's degraded performance is a changed customer base. And, because the organization's current customers might be driven by different behavioral patterns, the original set of inputs into the model might no longer be applicable.

Because of this, the analyst may decide that rather than try to refresh the model, it might be better to simply redevelop it from scratch, potentially saving a week's worth of work and achieving a better outcome. Critically, this decision would have been extremely difficult to make in the absence of objective deviation measures.

Technical Measures

Technical measures help identify how processes and technologies could be optimized. Their defining characteristic is their focus on the *activity* of and *effort* spent by the team. When used effectively they act as a major consideration in prioritizing enabling initiatives and delivering tactical revolutions.

The two major resources available to business analytics managers are their team and the tools they use. Understanding how well their resources are operating and identifying bottlenecks is a critical component of effective delivery. By being able to quantify these bottlenecks managers can identify the areas that would benefit most from additional investment.

These measures primarily focus on measuring the effort expended by the team, usually cutting across:

- Technology effort
- Development effort
- Operational effort

Technology effort measures are primarily concerned with profiling and understanding systems-level bottlenecks in an objective and rigorous manner. They usually act as a critical input into identifying and prioritizing which platform and environment components require upgrades and the order in which they will provide maximum benefit.

Development effort measures are primarily concerned with profiling and understanding the time taken to develop new assets. They usually act as a critical input into identifying potential areas of process improvement, often through mentoring, process optimization, developing new assets, or acquiring new tools.

Operational effort measures are primarily concerned with profiling and measuring the time spent conducting operational activities. This often includes responding to ad hoc queries from the business, running scoring processes, or providing operational reports. They usually act as a critical input into prioritizing activities, developing alternative operational processes, or acquiring new tools to facilitate operational delivery.

Technology Effort

Technology effort measures capture the distribution of processing time in the analytics platform, spanning both the discovery and operational environments. Often, these are quantified by analyzing processing logs and other platform-related reporting systems.

These measures exclude all the time spent by the team directly interacting with the platform. Instead, they measure system effort. The most common measures in this category are:

- Total execution (or real) processing time
- Data transfer time
- Data processing time
- Computation (or CPU) time

Execution time is usually the total amount of time a job needs to be completed. It is for this reason that it is also often referred to as *real time*. In isolation, it rarely indicates anything other than the jobs that take the longest time to finish. Although it helps to prioritize optimization effort based on sheer scale, it rarely identifies *why* processing jobs are taking a long time. For that, the other three measures are essential.

Data transfer time tracks the time needed to move data from source systems to the analytical environment and vice versa. Excessive time spent in these activities often indicates inadequate network infrastructure or inappropriately designed network architectures. Some common examples include traversing low-bandwidth public networks or inappropriately scoped interconnection bandwidth (e.g., 100 Mb Ethernet vs. fiber channel). Common solutions include rearchitecting network architectures, moving to incremental data updates rather than retransferring entire datasets every time source data is updated, or limiting the amount of data being transferred to only what is necessary.

Data processing time tracks the amount of time needed to transform and process data within the analytical platform. Excessive time spent in these activities often indicates storage architecture issues or data architecture issues. Some common examples include inappropriately architected storage platforms (e.g., NAS vs. SAN, RAID 5 vs. RAID 1+0, etc.) and poor data management processes (such as creating needless copies of data, excessive intermediary data processing steps, or inefficient data quality processes). Common solutions include migrating to alternative storage platforms, optimizing data management processes, or migrating to 64-bit platforms to increase the amount of memory addressable by the platform.

Computation time tracks the total amount of time spent by the platform performing computational activities. Although it may seem that execution time should match computation time, that is rarely the case; bottlenecks in other areas of the platform may make execution time significantly longer than computation time. For example, data normally needs to be transferred and transformed as part of most analytical processes. When this creates the bottleneck, the CPU sits idle while it waits for the data management processes to finish. Because of this, a complex data processing job that may take hours to execute may only involve minutes of actual computation time.

Excessive time spent on these activities often indicates inadequately sized platform processing capability. Some common examples include having too many users accessing the analytics platform or using inappropriate CPU or platform architectures. Common solutions include migrating to parallel processing/grid platforms or migrating to more appropriately architected hardware platforms.

Development Effort

Development effort measures aim to capture the amount of time spent creating new assets. They represent an internally focused activity measure and provide critical insight into opportunities for process improvement.

When these measures are not tracked, managers often struggle to identify and prioritize how processes should be improved. Without having visibility over the effort being expended by their team developing new assets, it is exceedingly difficult for a manager to make an objective decision about where to start optimizing or improving efficiencies.

The most common measurement process to capture development effort involves:

- Identifying the major repeatable activities in developing different classes of assets. These include problem definition, data preparation, documentation, model development, deployment, and so on.
- Establishing lightweight tracking systems to keep track of the elapsed time spent in each of these activities.
- Establishing aggregate reporting systems to aid in analyzing where time is spent.

One of the important considerations in capturing these measures is ensuring they provide the necessary level of insight without creating excessive overhead. The ideal system requires no time from the analyst to update. The time the analyst spends working is automatically tracked and captured. Unfortunately, this ideal is usually unattainable, forcing analysts to actively track the time they spend in various ways.

One approach is through the use of timesheets. When using this approach, activities are given specific tracking codes and team members are required to document, at a minimum:

- The amount of time spent working on the activity
- The client or project requesting the activity

In an organization already required to use timesheets, leveraging this approach often makes sense. However, this is not always the case; although timesheets usually allow managers to track time spent at a very granular level, they do not always fit within an organization's culture or working processes.

Another approach involves defining standardized workflow processes, implementing supporting systems, and transparently capturing the time spent within specific activities. When used effectively, moving through the various steps within the workflow automatically captures the date and time the step was completed. By aligning activities against high-level measures, managers can leverage the workflow system to create insight on what tasks are taking the longest time.

Operational Effort

Operational effort measures aim to capture the amount of time spent conducting operational activities. Much like development measures, they are an internal activity measure and often form a key input into identifying opportunities for process optimization and improvement.

The key difference between these measures and development measures is that where development measures can be aligned against specific initiatives, operational measures often have no ending date. Instead, they represent a level of relatively stable time consumption against which initiatives need to be balanced. Capturing these measures often involves using the same approach as capturing development effort.

The primary reason for tracking operational measures is to give managers the ability to objectively balance responding to ongoing business issues against creating value. When appropriately managed, the analytics team helps provide insight to the organization *as well as* creating new value for the organization.

When these activities spiral out of balance, managers create a variety of challenges for themselves. If operational activities consume *too much* time, managers become limited in their ability to create new value through growth initiatives. The value delivered by the analytics team stabilizes and eventually stagnates. However, if *too little* time is spent on operational activities and the focus is purely on growth initiatives, the organization often fails to maintain the value created by the analytics team.

ESTABLISHING A MEASUREMENT FRAMEWORK

Holistically, the measures described so far provide a useful framework to quantify value, manage risk, and identify opportunities for improvement. Because of this, they are an essential management tool. But they need more than just definition—they need to be captured in a way that:

- Ensures that they are relevant
- Minimizes the overhead imposed on the team
- Is consistent between initiatives

A measurement framework is useless if the things it is meant to measure are not relevant or are impossible to capture. Creating an effective and useful measurement framework requires focusing on what is relevant and useful both to the organization and to the analytics team.

It is also important to consider the overhead involved with tracking measures. Every additional activity takes time away from already-overworked resources; unless the benefits outweigh the overhead, the framework will become a secondary priority. Although ignoring the measurement framework may provide short-term productivity benefits, it only hurts the team in the long run.

A good framework gives managers the ability to compare effort across different initiatives and activities. By having comparable measures, it becomes easy for a team to prioritize attention. This level of comparability and focus cannot be built on an ad hoc basis—it should be planned.

Success Starts in the Planning Stages

An effective measurement framework requires forethought. Ongoing success requires more than asset delivery—it also requires the team to demonstrate the value it has created to the rest of the organization. Ensuring this understanding requires that:

- The *right* measures are used.
- Those measures are *captured*.

Considering the measures to track up-front ensures that managers get an empirical view of how their value chain contributes to organizational return. Establishing standardized tracking processes as a standard part of every initiative ensures that measures *will* be captured.

When these processes are considered a secondary priority, teams often track a subset of measures and have their attention distracted before they can deliver. Equally, if different measures are captured between different initiatives, it is often impossible to make comparisons. Planning the execution of a measurement framework and not treating it as an ad hoc, secondary activity is not optional for effective management: It is a critical step in demonstrating the real value of business analytics to the organization.

A good practical example lies in a growth initiative focused on identifying and reducing fraud. If the project plan does not specifically include operational performance monitoring components, the team will likely leave them exposed on project completion. Once the project is completed, it is extremely unlikely that the team will manage to convince key stakeholders of the value of spending additional time on what is apparently an already completed project. Specifically, if the team tries to create these measurement processes *after* the project has been delivered, it runs two risks:

1. There may be a significant delay between project launch and when the measures start to be captured.
2. The team may have its attention diverted before it delivers the measurement framework.

A delay between project launch and when the measures start to be captured inevitably leads to the team being unable to articulate the true total value of the initiative. Among other risks, this inevitably means that managers will undersell the true value of business analytics to the organization.

Additionally, although a measurement framework helps managers *justify and communicate* the value of business analytics, it does not help *create* value through business analytics. As discussed earlier, one of the key roles of an effective measurement framework is as a supporting tool to build credibility and encourage organizational transformation. Because of this, a measurement framework is often of greatest value to the business analytics manager.

When the measurement framework is separated from the initiative and treated as a discrete project, it usually needs to be prioritized against other activities. And, if these other activities include value-creating growth initiatives, it often becomes hard for managers to justify working on an enabling initiative that does not create competitive advantage or a new competency. Because the organization has already realized the value from the project, delivering the measurement framework usually ends up being delayed indefinitely.

A better approach involves treating the creation of measurement processes as an integral part of the project. Following this philosophy, delivery would include establishing tracking measures across the analytical environment, the investigations team, and the recovery team, possibly measuring:

- Improvements in predictive accuracy and classification accuracy
- The increase in cases managed by the investigations team
- Any reductions in case management time
- Any changes in capital recovered by the recovery team

By establishing these monitoring and measuring systems *as part* of the project, the analytics team will be able to measure the total value created, not just a subset of the value created.

Mitigating these risks is relatively simple; managers simply need to:

- Consider what the outcomes will be up front
- Ensure measurement processes are included as part of the initiative

By defining and measuring the value being created, managers link their team's activities to worthwhile organizational outcomes, thereby greatly simplifying the process of building internal credibility and obtaining additional investment.

DELIVERING THE MEASUREMENT FRAMEWORK

Once the framework has been defined and planned, all that remains is to execute. Given the right supporting tools and philosophies, putting plans into action is relatively straightforward. All that is required is:

- For measurement processes to run without direct interaction
- A platform to support presentation, investigation, and understanding

Manual interactions, when inappropriately used, create significant inefficiencies. If every measure needs to be manually collated, interpreted, and formatted for presentation, the team's ability to scale is severely constrained. Ensuring measurement processes can be and are automated is a critical step in effective execution.

Equally important is the ability to create insight. To act, managers need to have access to good information; although capturing information is essential, so is having the ability to review those measures and make decisions. Doing so requires a platform designed to support effective performance management.

In an ideal world, the measurement framework goes beyond these two minimum characteristics. The most effective measurement frameworks often integrate the abilities to delegate tasks, create workflows, and monitor outstanding issues. However, focusing on automation and the platform is a useful starting point to provide managers with an effective performance monitoring tool.

Developing a Platform for Measurement

Capturing the right variety of measures is one thing; understanding, visualizing, and acting on those measures is another. Using this information to create internal value is no different from any other area of business analytics. The value lies in the action taken based on the insight, not in the measurement itself.

In order to effectively action the insight provided by these measures, a manager must be able to:

- Quickly scan and visualize current performance
- Identify measures that are outside of acceptable patterns
- Directly compare the quality of various assets and the time invested in delivering initiatives and operational activities

Doing these tasks effectively involves applying the same rigor and attention as in any other business analytics application. A good measurement platform makes it as easy as possible to create insight, define direction, and execute action. Normally, this involves:

- Leveraging reporting toolsets
- Managing by exception
- Standardizing outputs and processes

Reporting toolsets are designed to make it as easy as possible to create standardized visualizations on a repeatable basis. Technologies such as dashboards and charts that allow drill-through are ideally suited to supporting performance management within an analytics team. They allow managers to get an instant view of overall performance with a minimum of effort.

Rather than try to work with a variety of nonstandardized spreadsheets that usually resist automation, effective teams often use mature performance management toolkits to support team and process management. Not only are the tools built to specifically support these types of activities; when selected appropriately they are often integrated with the team's discovery environment, increasing productivity and reducing the effort required to create these operational management reports. And, because they normally rely on automated data management processes, they require little operational effort to maintain once built.

Such a platform provides a major productivity benefit. Automation allows management by exception. Rather than manually investigating a wide variety of measures for potential improvements, the system itself can be configured to watch for unacceptable levels of performance. Once identified, notifications are automatically sent to the relevant individuals, allowing managers to focus their team's attention where it is most needed. By making effective use of dashboards and other key indicators, the team can prioritize focus by creating rules that flag activities that:

- Are in danger of stalling or already stalled
- Usually take the greatest effort or longest time to complete
- Are taking longer to complete than would normally be expected based on historical patterns

Tasks that meet these criteria often present the greatest challenges as well as offering the greatest opportunities for improvement. Because of this, they also deserve the most focus. This automated prioritization reduces uncertainty, clarifies focus, and encourages a philosophy of intervening primarily to optimize inefficient activities, and not just to play.

Leveraging a reporting platform also encourages the standardization of measures and reports. By presenting the "business on a page," managers can quickly identify inconsistencies and ensure consistency across measures. When measures are calculated and reported in a standardized format, managers can make:

- Direct comparisons of effort between activities and processes
- Objective comparisons between the quality of and value created by various assets
- Effective decisions about where best to invest resources and capital

When measures and visualizations *are not* standardized, managers may:

- Struggle to understand the true effort expended executing various activities and focus optimization efforts in the wrong areas
- Under- or overestimate the quality of and value created by various assets, potentially damaging their internal credibility
- Invest resource and capital in the wrong areas, using organizational resources for no real benefit

Establishing a standardized monitoring platform helps managers in a variety of ways. It reduces delivery times by making it easier to incorporate monitoring processes into initiatives. It helps prioritize attention where it is most needed. Probably most importantly, it makes it easy to communicate the organizational value being created through business analytics.

Automation Makes the Difference

Monitoring operational activities can be an extremely time-consuming process. This is especially true as an organization increases the complexity and sophistication of its business analytics initiatives. Logically, every initiative creates additional monitoring workload.

Many organizations start out applying a small number of models and assets to support specific problems. For example, an organization facing high levels of customer migration may decide to proactively contact customers at risk of churning. To improve the accuracy of its targeting processes, it may leverage retention models built using predictive analytics. To support this, the analytics team goes about creating a retention model and works with the outbound customer retention team to embed this asset within its operational targeting processes. And, once embedded, the organization obtains a competitive advantage over its peers that are *not* using predictive models.

In isolation, measuring the various business, analytical, and technical measures associated with this change may be fairly simple. There is one model, one process, and one possible outcome. Given enough will, an analyst could probably collate all the necessary tracking information manually. In the short term, this approach may be sufficient.

Unfortunately, it cannot scale. Over time, the predictive model may degrade in accuracy, possibly due to:

- An overall increase in the level of sophistication of business analytics within the industry
- Changing customer behavioral patterns
- Technological convergence creating higher levels of product substitutability across historically separate technologies

Because of these possibilities, the organization may decide to redevelop *and* expand its use of business analytics to reestablish competitive advantage. One way of doing this is to increase the granularity of the models applied, taking into account how different groups of customers exhibit different behavioral patterns before they churn. A common approach involves applying statistical segmentation models to group similar customers together. A unique retention model is then built for each segment that takes its unique characteristics into account within the segment's specific model.

In practice, this involves moving from one retention model to many. And, although manual processes and heroic effort may suffice to measure the outcomes from one process, it is unlikely that they will scale to be able to deal with many, let alone potentially hundreds, should the organization subsequently decide to move to a microsegmentation modeling process.

Managing this complexity requires committing to a philosophy of automating everything that *can* be automated. Doing so encourages a culture of efficiency. Some processes, once defined, can be automated without any loss of insight or organizational value. Common examples include data management activities, standardized report creation, and customer or account scoring processes. Automating these types of processes allows major productivity improvements with little risk.

The effort expended in executing these automatable processes is, by definition, non–value adding. Leveraging automation increases efficiency and scalability without any loss in organizational value. The most effective teams understand the importance of identifying and automating these non-value-adding activities. They maintain a strong philosophy throughout their activities of creating automatable, standardized, and reusable processes wherever reasonable.

By developing this culture, these teams ensure that they will be able to scale as requirements increase, regardless of whether it is by drilling to ever-greater levels of modeling detail or by applying an existing competency to new areas of the business.

By contrast, it is extremely difficult to automate discovery, research, or model building processes without usually reducing insight or value. Doing these effectively requires experience and creativity, something automated systems-based processes are ill-suited for—having analysts do these activities usually leads to better outcomes.

ADVANCED MEASUREMENT CONCEPTS

Creating an effective measurement framework is relatively straight-forward. It simply requires a fair amount of forethought, planning, and focus on execution. Beyond that, it also requires an appropriate supporting toolset, designed to facilitate standardized reporting and management by exception. For many teams, creating this platform forms a substantial enabling initiative in its own right.

However, good measurement frameworks need not end there. Similar to how leveraging simulation techniques can provide greater insight within a business case, there are a variety of advanced concepts that, when applied, expand the scope of a measurement framework's coverage to deal with various other business issues.

Two of these extensions are often of serious interest once the groundwork has been laid:

1. The creation of test-and-learn strategies

2. Dealing with information that resists being directly measured

Thus far, we have focused primarily on internal and outcomes-based measures. There also exists another class of measures that can be extremely valuable to an organization: testing measures. Testing measures are heavily related to outcomes-based measures; the key difference is that whereas an outcomes-based measure focuses on the final results, testing measures leverage a variety of techniques to provide an indication of what the outcomes are likely to be *prior to applying them.*

They often form a key input into optimizing execution strategies. Because they give an indication of how effective a variety of new processes are likely to be before they are executed, managers can take advantage of the best features of each of these processes, creating a totally new process and achieving a better outcome than would otherwise have been possible.

Another common challenge is dealing with information that is hard to quantify, hard to observe, or otherwise hard to visualize. By applying well-known statistical techniques such as sampling, managers can track measures that otherwise might have been impossible to capture.

Test-and-Learn Strategies

The best-performing organizations understand the importance of continuous improvement. For these types of organizations, measuring performance goes beyond outcomes and internal efficiencies; tracking testing measures can be a powerful tool to optimize business execution. They help make the organization more effective, increase overall predictive accuracy, and do all this without touching the vast majority of the organization's customers.

By applying test-and-learn strategies, measurement processes can help an organization identify effective approaches prior to using them against its entire target group. When applied, organizations can learn and optimize at relatively low cost prior to committing to a particular path.

Establishing a comprehensive test-and-learn–focused culture is complex, but establishing the groundwork is fairly straightforward. Two areas worth considering are:

1. Establishing champion/challenger processes
2. Applying statistical techniques such as design of experiments

Champion/challenger processes form the bare minimum when it comes to benchmarking various processes. They are so named because they compare a variety of potential processes against a single, current champion process. Good practice suggests that a process should be changed only if a new process produces a better outcome; if it does not, the initial process should be retained.

One of the nice things about this relatively simple concept is that it applies regardless of whether one is considering changing customer contact strategies, applying new analytical assets to support retention activities, or creating new rule sets for the detection of fraud. However, making this comparison is often harder than it first appears. Although the concept is simple, execution often requires fairly significant process and platform reengineering.

Design of experiments takes this approach a step further: It allows an organization to apply a structured and rigorous approach to understand the relationships between different choices and different outcomes. Once mapped, the results can be used to optimize the final execution strategy, delivering an optimal outcome. And, importantly, the technique helps the organization do so in a way that is cost-effective and efficient.

Champion/Challenger Processes

Champion/challenger comparisons within business analytics applications usually make comparisons between potential predictive models and execution processes.

Predictive models, as discussed in Chapter 3, create a series of probabilistic predictions using a variety of behavioral and environmental characteristics. Critically, these models inevitably degrade over time as behaviors and conditions change. Degradation speed is neither constant nor common—the speed at which a model loses accuracy is dependent on the inputs, techniques, and algorithms being used. Because of this, what may have been the best model during development may not be the best model in six months' time.

Champion/challenger processes compare the level of ongoing predictive and classification accuracy between a variety of challenger models and the current champion model. To provide a real-world measure of accuracy, these models are usually applied against the previous period's data, giving a direct comparison against what the models predicted and what actually happened. This gives managers visibility into how well or poorly the champion and challenger models are performing.

If a champion model consistently underperforms one or more challenger models, the team may decide to replace the current champion with a new model, turning the current champion model into a challenger model and promoting the best challenger model to be the new champion. The old model is often retained because although it may not be the most accurate at a point in time, there is no reason why it might not increase in accuracy as time passes. Often, this promotion/demotion process is done as a stopgap measure to provide short-term accuracy improvements while the team goes back to either respecify or redevelop a new set of candidate models.

Following this approach provides a number of significant benefits. First, it gives the team an understanding of whether any decreases in accuracy are due to the unique characteristics of the champion model or whether they are due to broader behavioral or environmental issues. If only the champion model's accuracy is dropping, it may be that there are flaws in the assumptions underlying the model. Alternatively, if the challenger models are also degrading, it may be that there are more systemic issues that may require a fundamental reassessment of what is happening. If the issues are isolated to the champion model, promoting the best-performing challenger may be a good enough solution.

Second, it gives the team the ability to extend the life span of its models, reusing already-developed assets wherever possible. The time saved can be reinvested into new growth or enabling initiatives, delivering more value or creating sustainable competitive advantage.

And finally, by integrating all valuable analytical assets into a single environment, teams reduce the time it takes to deploy new models. When good champion/challenger measurement processes are not applied, teams often need to search through archived material to find the models they would consider. Because of the often significant lag between when models are developed and when challenger models become an attractive proposition, reintegrating these assets into current processes may be time consuming and complex. When this work is conducted during the original project, teams ensure that the work is done while they are still familiar with it.

Predictive models are only one area that benefits from champion/ challenger processes. Because business analytics is so reliant on execution, it is rare that execution processes cannot also be bench-marked. The approach is broadly similar: Existing processes or target-ing rules provide a set level of performance and accuracy. While a new approach may offer a variety of potential improvements, most orga-nizations are keen to ensure that these improvements are real and achievable before they conduct wholesale process reengineering or rule redevelopment.

The principal difference between benchmarking predictive models and benchmarking execution processes is that unlike predictive models, execution processes require a significant amount of manual interaction to complete. Although a model can be easily applied against historical data to provide an indication of predictive accuracy, the only way to test a new execution process is to actually try it in-market. A good example lies in debt collection.

For many debt collection groups or agencies, their first set of chal-lenges involves:

- Making contact with the debtor
- Agreeing on a payment plan with the debtor

Making contact with a debtor can be difficult. Often, the starting point is for the collection group to decide which contact channel to use. The debtor may be potentially contactable via e-mail, SMS, mobile telephone, or even multiple fixed-line telephone numbers. Depending on the chosen channel, this contact could take many forms. At its simplest, it may involve an automated dialer that patches the debtor through to a call-center operator if the debtor picks up the phone. More complex (and relatively duplicitous) techniques may involve sending an SMS containing the name of someone of the debtor's opposite sex to the debtor's mobile phone along with a request to call the person back. In this case, the return number naturally goes back to the debt collection agency.

Once contact is made, the agency works toward agreeing on a payment plan with the debtor. It may choose to do this aggressively, taking the role of a supporter, or it may use other psychologically driven approaches. And, if the parties manage to agree on a payment plan, the agency may have the option of using a variety of techniques to maintain contact and ensure regular repayment. It may send a regular SMS, send a single formal letter reminding the debtor of his or her commitment, or use any other combination of follow-up communications.

Some of these approaches may offer better results than others, either in isolation or in combination. Importantly, the only way to test the effectiveness of each of these is to actually execute it. Because of this, organizations keen to extend their measurement framework to operational activities often need to build sufficient flexibility into their execution processes to deliver and track different processes with a minimum of effort. In this case, the simplest example involves having sufficient flexibility in the organization's contact management processes to separate customers into two groups, run the champion and challenger processes in parallel for a certain period of time, and then analyze and report on the comparative results.

This ability to compare the relative benefits of various alternative processes using outcomes-focused measures provides a wide variety of benefits. First, it allows organizations to optimize yet another area of their business. Second, it helps encourage a culture of continuous improvement. Finally, it acts as a major enabler for the next level of complexity—identifying truly optimal processes.

Design of Experiments

Running single champion/challenger operational processes is an excellent first step. Unfortunately, it is highly limited—simple logic identifies that the organization is constrained in how many changes it can consider at once. Even worse, if multiple changes are applied at once, it is impossible for the organization to isolate the impact of any one of these changes on its own or identify how the changes are interacting to make outcomes better or worse.

Returning to the debt collection example, the organization could test whether contacting via voice over mobile or via SMS on first contact provides the best recovery outcomes. In isolation, this helps provide useful information. It gives a quantifiable comparison that can be used to select between the two processes. Unfortunately, this is only one possible consideration; not only are there many other potential contact channels but there are also a wide variety of other changes that could also be tested. So, although the organization gets excellent visibility over how choosing a voice call over an SMS affects outcomes, testing each change in turn will probably take it an excessively long time. And, even if it manages to work its way through every possible change, the organization still has no understanding of how different options potentially interact to improve or hurt results.

To streamline this comparison process, the organization may decide to try to come up with an "ideal" test process. This process may involve changing a wide variety of activities, including the channel and communication strategy being used. Adopting this approach lets the organization change multiple things at once, hopefully increasing the speed of its test-and-learn strategy. Not only that, but because these changes are made simultaneously, the outcomes implicitly include any interaction effects created by having multiple changes at the same time.

Unfortunately, although the organization can measure the effect the new process has on outcomes, it has no way of understanding which changes within the process are actually driving the improvements. Realizing these benefits requires total process reengineering, significantly increasing risk and training requirements. Equally, it has no way of knowing whether the subset of changes it has selected was the best set of changes to select. Other changes might have had better results. Testing this, however, is challenging. It increases cost by requiring the organization to exhaustively test every possible combination of changes.

Clearly, each approach provides various advantages and disadvantages. Luckily, there exists a third, analytically driven approach that greatly simplifies this testing strategy. Commonly referred to as *design of experiments* (DoE), this statistically driven process helps uncover the often complex relationships between various factors and the target outcome. Fully understanding the practical application of this exercise requires significantly more detail than can be provided in this book. However, it is extremely useful to understand what it is and what it delivers. When used effectively it is an extremely powerful tool in optimizing execution processes.

The core philosophy behind the approach is to combine statistical sampling with predictive modeling to identify the strength of relationships between activities and outcomes without requiring these activities to be tested exhaustively across an entire customer base. That is a lot to take in, so it helps to examine each element specifically.

Understanding the impact of a particular activity on the outcome requires testing that activity in the market. For example, an organization may be able to make an offer to a set of 100,000 customers by e-mail, by SMS, by phone, or by physical mail. Depending on the customers being targeted, each of these may or may not be attractive. Typically, some channels will be more attractive to the customer than others. Understanding how the use of each of these channels affects offer acceptance rates requires testing them on customers. A naive approach may involve picking one channel at random and testing it on the entire customer base. The risk with this approach is that if one channel is preferred above all others, there is only a one-in-four chance of picking it at random. So, three times out of four the organization could have achieved a better outcome.

A slightly more sophisticated approach might involve splitting customers into four groups and testing a different channel on each of the groups. While this would provide valuable insight into the best channel for the next campaign, the organization will still achieve a suboptimal outcome for its current campaign. Although 25 percent of customers will be approached using the best channel, 75 percent of customers could have been approached with a better channel.

The final (and most efficient) approach involves using sampling theory to identify the minimum number of customers needed to be contacted to achieve a statistically valid understanding of channel effectiveness. In practice, this might be as low as roughly 1,000 per channel, requiring the organization to initially contact only 4,000 customers out of 100,000. Once the best channel has been identified, it can be used for the remaining 96,000 customers, achieving a better outcome than any other approach.

Predictive modeling takes this a step further. In the case of channel selection, each choice is fundamentally binary. Either customers are contacted using that channel or they are not. However, other choices may be linear or continuous, allowing the organization to choose from a potentially infinite number of potential options within the same activity. A good example lies in the degree of discount offered within a promotional activity. The organization could offer a 5 percent discount, a 10 percent discount, or any discount level up to an internal limit of 50 percent. Obviously, this involves a trade-off—one would expect that the higher the discount, the greater the probability of offer acceptance. However, the greater the discount was, the lower the campaign's profitability would be. Understanding the relationship between the discount being offered and probability of acceptance allows the organization to make an objective decision based on overall profitability on how much discount to offer.

Predictive modeling helps quantify this relationship. By using the same sampling approach across some key points within the desired range, the organization can create a model that quantifies how substantially acceptance rates increase as the discount rate increases. Importantly, the organization does not need to test every possible discount level. By being smart about the increments it tests, it is possible to interpolate the results to provide an estimate of how much a 1 percent increase in discount affects acceptance rates. Equally, because advanced forms of predictive modeling can be used, there is no requirement that these relationships be linear. It may be that because the targeted customer base has a psychological barrier of 25 percent, any discount offered that is greater than 25 percent may have negligible effect on increasing acceptance rates.

Individually, each of these is relatively simple. However, things become more complex when multiple activities can be changed and each activity has a few potential choices. For example, the organization may be able to select from four potential channels and offer one of five different discount levels. Making things even more complicated, there may actually be a relationship between these choices. Using the right channel may actually decrease the level of discount required. Because of this, testing the individual activities in isolation may not be enough. Understanding the complex interaction effects requires testing combinations of choices. If 1,000 customers need to be tested for each possible combination to provide a representative sample, testing every possible strategy requires testing 20 (4 channels × 5 discount levels) different execution strategies. Already, this requires contacting 20,000 customers, or 20 percent of the customer base. Making things even worse, the organization may also be able to choose from three different templates and two different bonus gifts should the offer be accepted. All of a sudden, rather than requiring 20,000 customers to test against, the organization now needs to test 120 (4 channels × 5 discount levels × 3 templates × 2 bonus gifts) different potential combinations. This would require 120,000 test customers, more customers than the organization can contact in the first place!

Combining sampling and predictive modeling in an economical manner is the power of using design of experiments. By following a statistically valid sampling approach, the organization can scatter its sampling across these combinations to significantly reduce the number of customers needed to be contacted while still providing a statistically valid approach. A key advantage is that the technique provides specific guidance on how to balance these constraints to achieve the best outcome possible. Equally, it allows organizations to focus sampling coverage across specific areas of interest, giving them the ability to meet real-world constraints while still achieving the most insight possible. This is often extremely useful in situations where there are set limits on the number of customers the organization can contact. Despite this hard constraint, design of experiments allows the organization to extract as much insight as it possibly can.

Applying Statistical Sampling

A final important consideration for many organizations involves dealing with measures that are inherently hard to quantify. A common perception is that there are certain things that are impossible to measure; while this is sometimes true, it is not as often as people believe. A core tenet of business analytics is that the insight is applied to create value. This value by definition must have some form of real-world impact. And, if it has some form of real-world impact, by definition it is measurable, even if that measurement is not necessarily direct or easy.

At best, the organization may be able to identify a specific numerical measure. However, this is not always required. Often, all the organization needs is an indication of whether things are improving. Measures do not necessarily need to be precise; as long as they are representative and repeatable, it is possible for an organization to identify changes over time. And, in many cases, that may be enough; whether the percentage of satisfied customers is 50 or 55 percent is relatively unimportant compared to whether customer satisfaction levels are increasing over time. In this situation, it is the *comparison* that is important, not necessarily the *absolute value*.

Sampling plays a significant role in many of these situations. Understanding how customer satisfaction levels are changing is a common example. An organization may have a target of increasing customer satisfaction levels in the belief that happier customers leads to more business. In most situations, this is a reasonable goal; the literature suggests that not only is it cheaper to sell to an existing customer but that happier customers tend to purchase more. Measuring this customer satisfaction, however, is difficult: Although customers may purchase things, they rarely tell you how they are feeling about the transaction.

One option would be to change selling processes to require front-line staff to ask every customer what he or she thinks of the organization. While this might theoretically provide total coverage across every transaction, it also runs the risk of irritating customers, unintentionally *decreasing* customer satisfaction levels. A more effective approach may involve using sampling theory to identify a statistically representative subset of customers and approaching them specifically. When this sample is appropriately defined, their responses will correlate highly with overall customer satisfaction levels, giving the organization an understanding of overall satisfaction levels without requiring it to contact every customer.

PRACTICAL EXAMPLE: THE ONGOING GROWTH OF AN ANALYTICS TEAM

A measurement framework can be a powerful tool to attract ongoing investment when used effectively. One of the best examples of how much this can help involves a team I worked with that, over the course of a number of years, rarely had any real issues obtaining additional investment from internal decision makers. In contrast, many other groups within the organization often struggled to seek funding and in many cases had their budgets cut over the same time period.

By defining and tracking the value they were creating, the team members successfully transformed the organization from one that was dubious about the value of business analytics into one that regularly sought the use of business analytics within its operational processes. To understand how the team did this, it is necessary to understand where it came from.

Although the organization had historically been applying analytics to support a variety of operational processes, its usage of analytics was heavily fragmented and rarely repeatable. There were multiple teams within the organization that were functionally aligned and charged with leveraging analytics to add value.

Despite this, the organization's overall level of success in applying analytics to create value was relatively low. Delays were common, there was a great deal of uncertainty as to whether analytics was actually adding value, and many operational teams were relatively unwilling to change their processes to leverage the insight being created.

After a number of years of operating this way, the organization took on new management who, as part of their cultural influence, were strong proponents of the use of business analytics. Although this was a critical enabler in getting various operational teams to reexamine their processes, in itself it was not enough to get the organization to broadly adopt the use of business analytics.

It was about this time that one analytics team within the organization had the fortune to be put under a manager who understood the importance of communicating the value of business analytics to the organization. Rather than try to solve all of the organization's problems at once, team members took a pragmatic position and identified a key area of high value to the business: the ability to provide insight about the organization's customers. While difficult to link to tangible value, this had significant intangible value to the outbound marketing arms of the organization: Being able to classify customers into different groups based on their behavioral patterns gave them the ability to treat groups differently.

The manager realized early that delivering the model was not sufficient. In order to get real traction with the operational arms of the business, the team needed to embed its assets within the other teams' standard processes. At first call, this involved ensuring that the team's customer grouping models were embedded as a standard piece of information everywhere from the data warehouse right through to the organization's customer relationship management systems. By making this information another "fact" within the organization, its origins became irrelevant. It was extremely useful information and as such it was willingly adopted.

Usage provided the first step; equally important was measurement. Although marketing execution was far more important than their customer grouping models in influencing financial outcomes, something they *could* measure was activity in the form of the number of campaigns using their insight. By tracking this information, team members took this initial success and used their data to convince key decision makers that insight was adding value. This small step helped overcome some of the doubt that surrounded further investment in business analytics. And, by pairing this with a detailed business case identifying how their next initiatives would create *economic* value, they established a reason to make a real investment, thus breaking the cycle.

Over the next few years, the team built a repeatable model that involved:

- Defining the value it was going to create in the form of a business case
- Delivering the project and tracking the value created
- Communicating this value with the broader business and evangelizing the use of business analytics
- Identifying new sponsors and business problems to solve

To support their ongoing growth, team members augmented their outcomes-focused measurement framework with one that also tracked technical and analytical measures. These acted as a major driver in identifying where they needed to focus their process and activity optimization effort, ensuring that they would be able to scale at least as fast as business demands were growing, if not faster. It also meant that they were able to prioritize their asset redevelopment efforts, limiting their attention to only the areas that *needed* focus.

As an example, they highlighted the major benefits from effectively leveraging a measurement framework. They:

- Successfully demonstrated the value of analytics to the organization
- Achieved ongoing funding and investment support
- Knew where best to spend effort in improving their activities

SUMMARY

Being able to quantify real-world measures is critical. Without this ability, teams often find it difficult to:

- Maintain strategic focus in the face of competing priorities
- Build trust and internal credibility
- Seek additional investment
- Optimize their internal activities, giving them the ability to scale

By establishing an *effective measurement platform* and maintaining a focus on *automating everything that can be automated*, managers can overcome these challenges with minimal incremental workload. And by applying more advanced techniques such as *experimental design* and *sampling theory*, managers can boost the effectiveness of analytics even in highly complex situations.

For most teams, this involves the following five steps:

1. The team identifies the types of measures of most interest, ensuring that they are comparable between initiatives and processes.
2. The team establishes a performance measurement platform to support visualization and management by exception.
3. Creating automated measurement processes for these measures becomes a standardized delivery milestone for specific types of initiatives.
4. The outputs of these measures are used to justify the value being created and target optimization activities.

5. Execution and monitoring processes are extended and/or modified to support champion/challenger processes and possibly experimental design.

Establishing a measurement framework forms the final part of a comprehensive strategy to achieve success through business analytics. It acts as the monitoring component, supporting the target outcomes identified through:

- Defining the value
- Communicating the value
- Committing to it

In the final chapter, we will bring this entire framework together into a hypothetical example, providing an illustration of how it can work in practice.

 THE CHECKLIST: MEASURING THE VALUE

Key Considerations

Planning the Measures

What needs to be demonstrated to the organization to justify future investment?
What needs to be tracked to identify potential internal efficiency improvements?
What operational initiatives are currently ongoing?
What growth initiatives are planned?
What assets are used by the analytics team?

Identifying the Measures

What business measures need to be tracked?
What analytical measures need to be tracked?
What technical measures need to be tracked?
For each of these measures, how would they be quantified?
For each of these measures, how would they be captured?
For each of these measures, who would find them useful and valuable?
How will capturing these measures be automated?
How will these measures be reported?

Measuring the Value

How do existing initiatives need to be modified to support capturing these measures?

How will future initiative planning be modified to ensure these measures are captured?

Who will be responsible for ensuring these measures are captured and reported?

CHAPTER **8**

Bringing It All Together

INTRODUCTION

We have covered a lot so far. Within the previous seven chapters, we have considered:

- How analytics fits into strategic planning and the creation of competitive advantage
- The various tactical challenges teams face, along with typical organizational and management structures
- Strategies and techniques to help define the value of analytics
- The importance of cultural patterns and thinking preferences in developing a communication strategy
- Techniques to break free from being overworked, types of initiatives, and how to plot tactical activities into a strategic road map
- How to build an effective measurement framework and use it to justify ongoing investment in analytics

Following the philosophies outlined in this book makes it easier to achieve success. However, it requires diligence and commitment. Unless the team can change its own approach, it is unlikely that it will be able to change the broader organization.

The reality is that teams rarely enact this change overnight; change is hard, and biting off more than one can chew is a recipe for disaster. Instead, many teams try to improve things incrementally, focusing on the areas that they feel are most lacking and that will have the greatest impact. In many ways, it is the same as eating an elephant—the trick is to do it one bite at a time.

As a closing example, we will consider how these elements can be applied together as a single framework. By necessity, this is a hypothetical example. Though the example draws from a wide variety of real-world experiences, it is hard to step through a real end-to-end experience without making it too easy to identify the team in question. Instead, this example blends a variety of case studies into a single narrative, highlighting the individual successes experienced by different teams.

SARAH'S CHALLENGES

Sarah sighed; this was not quite what she had signed up for when she had accepted the position. Running the analytics team had sounded like a great step forward when they had approached her about the opening. In retrospect, she probably should have paid more attention to the barely concealed look of relief in her ex-boss's eyes when he had given his farewell speech—and his vaguely sympathetic look when he shook her hand and wished her luck just before he had left the building for the last time.

She had been wracking her brain for weeks now, trying to figure out why things were not working. When she had been the lead modeler, things had been far simpler. She had her requirements, she knew her data, and she had always been good at building accurate models. She was sure that part of the reason she got the position was because she was always able to answer any question her team or clients had, regardless of how hairy it was. Being the "expert" was fun, if sometimes a bit stressful. She had always been overworked, but given how busy they all were, it seemed logical that the organization would hire more people.

Her manager's resigning had been a shock, but it was not entirely unexpected. He had been frustrated for quite a while. Despite his best efforts, the team had not had much luck working with the direct marketing team. She was not quite sure of the details, but her best guess was that their insights were seen as threatening. The direct marketing group had spent over six months developing a segmentation model that, to her, did not make much sense—it was based totally on assumptions and guesses. She had built a demonstrably better segmentation model using self-organizing maps that, when correctly plotted, could highlight countless fascinating customer characteristics. She had even demonstrated how to interactively explore and create these charts with the direct marketing team members, but for whatever reason, they had never picked it up and used it.

It made sense to everyone in the organization that she should have her manager's now-vacant role. She was the most experienced analyst and understood their data better than anyone else. The interviewing process had largely been a formality; she knew she had the job as soon as she had applied. Unfortunately, nine months on, if she were being honest with herself, not much had changed. There was still a fair degree of animosity between her team and the direct marketing group. They were still overworked. Even worse, she was not only trying to do her current job, she was also still doing her old job!

One of the first things she had done after accepting the position was to meet with the head of direct marketing to try and calm the waters. Surprisingly, she had found him very reasonable and more than happy to look for various ways their teams could work together. Unfortunately, despite that positive initial meeting, not much had progressed since then. There had been a few meetings where she had shared the accuracy of the models her team had built, but somehow, they inevitably seemed to get sidetracked away from the value her team was providing into tangential discussion about how the models had been built, what the assumptions were, how the people had been selected, and whether the models could be trusted. She had tried repeatedly to explain the statistics and methodology behind these, but there was just never enough time; they always ran out of meeting time before they could cover the necessary groundwork.

Reducing her team's workload had been another priority. During her first-ever planning cycle, she had gone to the appropriation committee to request an additional employee, on top of one to fill her now-vacant position. She had wanted to make sure she explained things thoroughly, so she outlined in specific detail the number of models her team members were working on, the hours they were frequently working, and the new techniques they were keen to test and what they would be able to do if they were given an additional resource. The committee had listened politely and nodded throughout her presentation, but when it came down to allocating capital, they had denied her request to increase headcount. Frustratingly, they had also told her that because of the imminent rollout of their new operational customer contact management system, she would likely need to increase her team's productivity by around 25 percent.

Most depressingly, her own personal workload had gone up by almost 100 percent. She had thought that by moving into a new role, she would be able to focus on fixing all the problems her ex-manager could not. Given that she had left a vacant position behind her, all the work she had previously been doing would easily fall to the new hire. Sadly, it had not worked out that way—she was still the only person who understood her team's data and, as such, still answered all of the team members' questions on a daily basis. She had hired a replacement modeler, but given the sophistication of her approach and the complexity of their data, he still was not really productive after nine months of focused effort. And management was still coming to her every time they needed an answer to a particularly hairy problem.

On a professional level, she was concerned that the organization's competitors were gradually outclassing it. She went to conferences, she researched, she networked, and she knew what was cutting edge. Unfortunately, she also knew that her organization was not even close. On a personal level, she was starting to become seriously concerned that she might not last another year in her new position. She was acutely conscious that unless she could start demonstrating how she was improving things, there was a very real chance that she might be demoted back to her old role. It was enough to make her feel sick.

THE LIGHT-BULB MOMENT

"And that's where I'm at."

The barista dropped a coffee cup on the floor, making them both jump at the crash, loud even over the din of the café. After a few days of deliberation, Sarah had decided to eat her pride and give Kate, a colleague of hers, a call. Years ago, Kate and Sarah had worked together on the same team, forming the core of the team's insight-generation abilities. Kate had been interested in more responsibility and, given that their then-current manager did not appear to have any interest in moving, she had decided to look outside. She had taken on a role as the senior modeler within another organization and, in the six intervening years, had managed to work her way through to leading the team, and eventually to reporting directly to the chief marketing officer. At the time, Sarah had been somewhat jealous of Kate's rapid career progression, but she also knew that she enjoyed what she was doing; greater responsibility and more money would have been nice, but it was not something she had been expressly looking for.

Things, obviously, had changed. As hard as it had been for her, she had decided to give Kate a call to try to find out why her organization had been so different. She also wondered whether there might be a role for her there.

Kate had listened to her story with a sympathetic, understanding, and at times amused look on her face. She still knew most of the people Sarah worked with and, when she heard Sarah's description of the direct marketing manager's inability to grasp basic statistics, she outright laughed. If nothing else, Sarah felt somewhat relieved at being able to get all this off her chest.

"It's a challenge," Kate commiserated. "I know exactly what you mean—I was in the same situation when I took over managing my team. It took me forever to work out how to turn things around."

Sarah sat back in her chair. "How'd you do it? I feel like I'm missing something. I keep explaining everything but nothing seems to stick. Everything seems to take five times as long as I think it should. It doesn't matter how much I push, nothing seems to change!"

Kate nodded. "Let's take a step back, and apologies in advance if this sounds somewhat rude. What's the value you're bringing to the company?"

Sarah thought for a bit and responded, "Insight. We bring understanding. We help answer questions no one else can. No one else in the company has as good an understanding of our data—we're the only group that can actually tell you everything any given customer has."

"Okay," Kate responded, "so how does that help add value to the organization?"

"By making it easier to make decisions."

Kate shook her head. "That's not quite what I mean. How are you contributing to the bottom line?"

Sarah sat back again. "Well, that's not our responsibility. We just provide the insight—it's up to the other groups to actually do something with that insight. I mean, we don't control the execution, we're service providers. We work with our customers to help them achieve better results."

"Do you see the issue now?"

Sarah looked a bit confused. "No, not really. That's not my job—I run the analytics team, not the execution. If they're not succeeding, it's not my fault."

Sipping her coffee, Kate responded, "That's true in principle. But, it's not how people actually decide to fund things. The problem is that unless you can link what you're doing to something that impacts the bottom line, you're probably not going to get what you're looking for."

Sarah started to get a bit angry. "Look, I know it's been a while, but we just don't work that way. It may be different where you are, but we still treat analytics as being separate from everything else. My job doesn't go that far—I only have control over insight, not execution."

Kate nodded and, sitting back, responded, "Sure, I know. It was the same when I took over the team. I kept looking at how I could answer everyone's questions better, convinced that if I could just give better insight, everyone would understand how important analytics was. I wasted months making sure the models my team was producing were the best they could be. I didn't get anywhere."

Kate took another sip of her coffee. "It took me close to a year to realize that no one cared. At the end of the day, the only thing anyone cared about was how much money we made. To be frank, I felt a bit silly when I realized that I'd been chasing the wrong goal all that time—what mattered wasn't my models, it was my *outcomes*."

Sitting forward, she continued, "Even though I didn't have any control over how people used the insight we were creating, the decision whether to invest in my group was still based on how much value we were creating. Focusing so much on the analytics instead of the outcomes, I didn't even realize that we were actually adding very little value to the organization. Look at it from their perspective: I had a team of five people plus me, none of whom were cheap. Everyone agreed that we were important, but everyone also agreed that the company wasn't anywhere near effective enough at selling through our call center. For the cost of one additional person on my team, they could hire three temps in the call center. Which do you think they did?"

Sarah's face dropped. "I didn't think of it that way."

Kate smiled. "Don't feel bad—neither did I. It took me ages to realize that what I believed wasn't the whole picture. Don't get me wrong, good models are still important—if we can't trust them, we can't use them. It's just that I finally understood that running my team wasn't as separate from running a business as I thought."

"So, what did you do?"

Kate paused. "A lot. It's different—you need to look at things differently. You need to shift from looking at the detail to looking at how what you're doing is going to be used. You need to convince people that what you've produced is 'true' and worth using. You need to prove that you've succeeded. It's a lot of work."

"Where do I start?"

"You need to understand the value of what you're producing. It's more than 'insight' or 'efficiency'—you need to be able to quantify it. If you can't describe it financially, most people will think it's worthless. That's probably not true, but when they control the money, you live in their world. And, once you can break down the worth of what you're doing, you need to convince them that what you're saying is true. You need to build trust."

"What else?"

Kate sat back again. "Well, you still have to deliver. If you don't, you might as well start looking for a job somewhere else right now. Probably the worst thing you can do is build expectations past the point where you can deliver. If you do that, it doesn't matter whether you create any value or not; you'll hang yourself. And, you need to prove what you have achieved—if you can't measure the difference you've made, you'll struggle to get people to trust you next time."

Sighing, Sarah said, "Makes sense. I just don't see how I can do it. I'm already overworked because my team can't get up to speed. I'm doing at least three jobs at the moment. Maybe I should start looking now."

Kate laughed. "Don't give up—I was in the same boat. They hired me because we had been such a great team, you and I; I didn't understand their business, but I did know how to get results. When I got promoted, I was doing my old job as well as my new job. I was so tired some nights, I barely knew where I was!"

"So what did you do?"

"Nothing too complex—I just looked for every efficiency improvement I could find. Sounds easy, but the trick was actually doing it; I annoyed more than a few people when I 'reprioritized' helping them below solving my own problems. It was a hard decision—I got into quite a few arguments about why we couldn't help everyone who needed answers yesterday. The only reason I think I didn't get fired was because I could explain where I believed we'd be in a few years. Luckily, we got there. If we hadn't, I'd probably be begging you for a job right now!"

Sarah nodded. "You know, I was hoping that you might be hiring. That's why I called."

Kate smiled and responded, "I thought that might be the case. Don't give up, though. I think you're close. If you can't get things working over the next six months or so, give me another call and we'll see what we can do."

TRANSFORMING THE ORGANIZATION

Sarah sat back in her chair. It had been a long year, but things were finally looking up. Her second set of models was going into production, she had finally gotten approval for additional headcount, and possibly most importantly, her company's customer relationship management strategy actually had requirements for analytical integration as an explicit component. She was expecting vendor responses any day now.

Her meeting with Kate had been a watershed moment. She had felt positively broken the first few days afterward, but once she had managed to pick herself up off the ground, she had realized that Kate was right. Until she could demonstrate the value she was bringing to the organization in a way management could relate to, she was only going to be spinning her wheels.

The first thing she had focused on was understanding how her team's insights were being used. It was somewhat disconcerting when she realized that they were not being used at all; despite the quality of her team's answers, the other teams they had been working with were not actually using the knowledge her team had been providing. When she had caught up with her counterparts, she had found that this was so for a variety of reasons. For some of them, it was just too hard to change how they were working. For others, it was because they wanted to justify decisions they had already made. And, still others had accepted her team's results just to demonstrate that they had involved all the right people in the organization, a political "tick in the box" without any intention of using the hard work her team had provided.

Once she had gotten over her frustration, she used the information she had obtained to start prioritizing her support. As irritating as it was, despite everyone always insisting on getting answers as quickly as they could, very few of them were actually interested in the results her team had provided. Tracking her team's time gave her the ability to start prioritizing its focus. Previously, because everything had been equally important, she had tried to make sure the team had delivered everything asked of it as quickly as possible. By understanding how much time her team actually had available and scheduling work around her team's ability to deliver rather than simply trying (often unsuccessfully) to deliver everything, she had managed to reduce its workload significantly.

Needless to say, people had complained. Luckily, though, she had been able to justify her prioritizations by being able to point to her existing commitments and the time those commitments would require. It had been an uncomfortable few months, but being able to point to hard quantitative information on why she could not support everyone had been invaluable.

In parallel with understanding the reality of how she was helping the organization, she sat down with her team to try to brainstorm some ways that the team could add value to the organization. It had not started as well as it could have. Most of the ideas that were thrown around, although attractive, were focused on intangible benefits. Making other people's jobs easier was a nice objective, but she could not afford to focus too much on creating value that could not be measured. In the end, she had created a road map with her team that identified the ways that it would be able to create real innovation as well as the steps it would need to take to get there. With a bit more work, she had also managed to map those steps back to specific forms of economic value that the team would create while getting there. The first of these was the delivery of a series of retention models to support the outbound marketing team.

The outbound marketing team was an interesting group. Whereas most of the teams she had dealt with were not really interested in using her team's insights, the outbound marketing group had shown strong interest. Their main problem was that they simply could not take advantage of the information her team had been providing; because they were so operationally focused, this group had little understanding of how to coordinate the supporting systems they needed to do their work better.

A key point of meeting with each of the teams she regularly worked with was to look for potential execution champions. Based on what she had found, the outbound marketing group was possibly the best, assuming she could solve their operational execution issues.

It had not taken much to convince them of the value she could provide. She had started out by benchmarking her models against the group's existing processes, demonstrating that she would likely be able to give at least a few percentage points' improvement in their levels of retention. Although she still did not have the ability to deploy her models into operational processes, the group had been more than willing to test out her targets in-market using spreadsheet-based call-lists. Exporting her recommended retention targets had been simple, as had comparing her results against the group's.

As she had expected, her results outperformed the group's existing selection processes. Because one of their key performance indicators was their retention effectiveness, that improvement was more than enough for them to justify changing their approach. Unfortunately, while they were happy to do things differently, they could not see how they would be able to work off spreadsheets as an ongoing operational process.

At first, this had stumped Sarah; although they were more than willing to change, their existing processes were blocking them. After thinking about it for a bit, Sarah realized she had everything she needed. She used the uplift she would be providing to build a business case and went to her investment committee to appropriate funding for IT support. Even if she did not have the right tools, she still had access to significant IT resources, some of which could be used in the short term to translate her models into something their customer relationship management system could understand and execute. It was not the most efficient solution, but it still held up within the business case.

To make sure she hit all the angles during her presentation, she ran through not only the expected financial return and resourcing requirements but also the strategic value she would be creating. Their market was becoming increasingly competitive and churn was an issue across the board. By being more effective at retaining their existing customers, they would achieve a significant advantage over their competitors. And, it would provide a critical enabler to becoming more responsive to customer complaints. To make sure everything was crystal clear, she also outlined the key steps to getting there and how things would change compared to their existing processes.

The presentation went better than she had expected. While there had still been a bit of concern about how she was going to manage the personal uncertainty these changes might create in the call center, the overall support had been high. They had allocated the money and she had gotten to work.

A few months later she had all the evidence that she needed. Her counterpart in the outbound marketing group had been equally happy—the group's effectiveness had increased twofold. Critically, she had seen in advance that she would need to be able to demonstrate the value they had created if she was to ever get access to funding again. So, as part of the deployment process, she had made sure that the outbound marketing group had kept in place their existing processes. Their manager had been reluctant to do so at first; because he had already seen the value of her models, he could not understand why he should keep a relatively inefficient process running. It was only after she had explained that they still needed to prove the ongoing value of the new approach that he had seen the light: By tracking both in parallel, they had indisputable evidence of the benefits of their new processes.

An interesting by-product of their measurement processes was that she found her team members had been spending far too much time managing data. Despite all the effort she had put into standardizing her data within their shared network drives, her team members seemed unaware of what data already existed. When she had investigated this a little more, she had discovered that although she understood where everything was, no one else did. She had been so focused on making sure her team was getting some runs on the board that she had not realized how much individuals were struggling or how nonstandardized the data management routines she had built actually were.

Because of this, her first order of business once she had demonstrated some success was to hire someone to simplify the team's data. She had run the numbers and, based on her estimates, she would save roughly a day's work per team member if she could simply consolidate the team's data into a single environment. By definition, this would require a common analytical platform, something that she had not even considered a year ago. Though she had not understood the importance of moving from a tools-based approach to a platform-based approach a year ago, times had changed. It was not just a case of this being a good idea; it would actually save her days of effort every week—days that could be invested in her next project, creating more value and justifying further investment in business analytics.

It had not been an easy year, but it had been a fun one. Probably most importantly, Sarah no longer felt the need to give Kate a call for anything other than a cup of coffee.

SUMMARY

Analytics is often challenging, and business analytics even more so. True success requires being able to deal with the most granular of details right through to the highest level of strategy. It requires the ability to deal with not only the technical but also the political. Success comes from execution, evangelism, and encouraging change.

Given this breadth, it is not surprising that so many teams struggle. However, it need not be this way. By understanding the importance of selling the value of analytics, it is possible to stack the odds in one's favor. By understanding how analytics creates value and focusing on communicating this value, it is possible to create compelling reasons to change. And, by having a strong execution plan and tracking success, it is possible to build trust.

Success in selling the value of analytics comes down to four things:

1. Defining the value
2. Communicating the value
3. Committing to delivering the value
4. Measuring the value

We have considered each of these in turn, investigating how each leads to success. We have reviewed the most common mistakes and how to overcome them. Possibly most importantly, we have established the bare minimum that needs to be considered.

These lessons are not hypothetical; the most successful teams are already applying the insights contained in this book. They have transformed their organizations, reshaping them so that they differentiate themselves in the market. They have achieved commitment, recognition, and value.

The returns that come from selling the value of analytics are real. All that remains is for you to take advantage of it.

Glossary

Advanced analytics
A subset of analytical techniques that among other things often uses statistical methods to identify and quantify the influence and significance of relationships between items of interest, group similar items together, create predictions, and identify mathematical optimal or near-optimal answers to business problems.

Agent-based modeling
A computationally driven modeling approach that simulates the local interactions of autonomous agents with the goal of monitoring global outcomes.

Aggregation
A process by which variables are summed based on a classification or temporal hierarchy. Common examples include totaling all sales for a given time period or geographic region.

Algorithm
A finite series of well-defined steps that achieve a desired outcome. These steps may be deterministic or include random or probabilistic elements.

Analytical perspective
A communication approach that focuses on an objective assessment of the facts, relying heavily on logic, rigor, and rationality.

Analytics
A data-driven process that creates insight. These processes incorporate a wide variety of techniques and may include manual analysis, reporting, predictive models, time-series models, or optimization models.

Analytics platform
A technology platform that provides standardized tools, the ability to collaborate, and the ability to migrate insight into operational processes.

Anchoring
A cognitive tendency to focus on specific data points at the expense of the overall trend.

Assets
Items of economic value created by a team through the application of competencies and tools. Within a business analytics context they are normally intangible in nature and often include models, processes, and electronic documentation.

Average revenue per user (ARPU)
A measure commonly used in telecommunications to calculate the revenue value of various customer groups. Increasing ARPU is a common goal within the telecommunications industry, often through increasing total share of wallet through cross-selling products or up-selling to existing and potential customers.

Base rate bias
A cognitive tendency to over- or underestimate the likelihood of specific events.

Big data
A colloquial term referring to exceedingly large datasets that are unwieldy to deal with in a reasonable amount of time in the absence of specialized tools. They typically require unique approaches for capture, processing, analysis, search, and visualization.

Business analytics
The process of leveraging all forms of analytics to achieve business outcomes through requiring business relevancy, actionable insight, and performance management and value measurement. These business outcomes may be of tangible or intangible value of interest to the organization.

Business intelligence
A broad classification of information systems–based technologies that support the identification and presentation of insight. Common historical usage referred primarily to reporting-focused systems, but usage of the term has been broadened by some to include all forms of insight generation (including exploratory data analysis and predictive analytics).

Business planning
An intermediate level of strategic planning, typically focusing on the individual strategies that will lead to the broader organizational strategies.

It may include the creation of competitive differentiation, cost minimization, or vertical integration.

Butters's Law
The trend for the amount of data carried by a single optical fiber to keep pace with Moore's Law. It was defined by Gerry Butters while at Bell Labs.

Campaign optimization
A process involving operations research that maximizes a target marketing outcome given a variety of channel and offer options for each customer and a series of fixed constraints, often involving communication restrictions.

Catch-22
A term popularized by Joseph Heller in his 1961 book, *Catch-22*, referring to a no-win situation involving circular logic.

Centrality measures
A variety of statistics often used in social network analysis to calculate individuals' relationships with other people in their network.

Champion/challenger process
A process that benchmarks alternative processes against the currently selected process. If an alternative, challenger process outperforms the current, champion process, the champion process is usually replaced with the challenger process.

Churn
A term that refers to a customer going to a different provider. Depending on the context, it may refer to a total migration away from the organization in question or to a reduction in consumption.

Competencies
Reusable and generalizable skills held by a business analytics team. A common example is the ability to build predictive models.

Competitive advantage
A strategic advantage held by one organization that cannot be matched by its competitors. This advantage may or may not be sustainable and, if not, may eventually be replicated by its competitors.

Contagious churn/viral churn
A situation where individuals cancel their service because people in their network have canceled theirs. Common reasons include being made

aware of better options and pull-through by leveraging positive network externalities.

Converting
A planning technique within Porter's SWOT analysis that involves transforming weaknesses or threats into strengths or opportunities.

Cost leadership strategy
A strategy that focuses on achieving the lowest perceived market price while taking into account the value received from the good. This lower price point can then be leveraged to achieve a majority market share.

Cross-sectional modeling
A variety of methods that focus on analyzing time captured across entities at a specific point in time. Common applications include identifying differences between groups or relationships between outcomes and causal factors, and creating predictions.

Cross-sell
A process by which new, non-overlapping products are sold to existing customers.

Data cleansing
The process of detecting, removing, or correcting incorrect data.

Data management process
A series of well-defined steps that take source data, conduct a series of operations on it, and deliver it to a predefined location.

Datamart
A shared repository of data, often used to support functional areas within the business. It is sometimes used as the direct access layer to the data warehouse.

Data quality
A broad term that refers to the accuracy and precision of data being examined. Data that exhibits high quality correctly quantifies the real-world items it represents.

Data warehouse
A shared repository of data, often used to support the centralized consolidation of information for decision making.

Decision tree
An algorithm that focuses on maximizing group separation by iteratively splitting variables.

Departmental platform
A centralized analytics environment based on a defined set of tools that supports a department or functional unit within an organization.

Derived variable
A variable not included in the original data but based on the underlying characteristics of the source data. Common examples include calculating a three-month moving average and calculating recency, frequency, and monetary statistics.

Design of experiments (DoE)
An experimentation process by which the impact of various influencers on items of interest can be tested in an efficient manner.

Differentiation strategy
A strategy that focuses on building unique competitive differentiators within the broader market. This differentiation can then be leveraged to charge higher prices, increase customer loyalty, or otherwise create barriers against competitors.

Discounted value
The value of an item after taking into account the cost of time.

Discovery environment
A logically defined and usually separate area within an analytics platform that provides users with the ability to create assets and generate insight.

Enabling initiative
A business analytics initiative focused on creating processes or assets needed either for a planned growth initiative or to deliver evolutionary efficiency improvements.

Enterprise platform
A centralized analytics environment based on a defined set of tools that supports the entire organization.

Enterprise resource planning
A variety of software-based systems that aim to standardize processes and information management within organizations, typically focusing on operational processes including finance and accounting, supply chain and logistics, inventory management, and resource management.

Environmental determinism
The belief within strategic planning processes that the ideal strategy is determined by the environment in which the organization operates.

Strategic planning therefore involves identifying the optimal fit for the organization within its environment.

Ethernet
A high-speed networking standard used for local area networks, typically capable of speeds up to 1 gigabit per second.

Evolution
Within the context of business analytics, the incremental improvement or extension of existing processes or capabilities, often involving adaptation or modification.

Fiber channel
A high-speed networking standard often used for storage networks, running on both twisted-pair copper and optical fiber.

Functional planning
The most granular level of strategic planning, typically focusing on the operational activities needed to achieve the objectives outlined at the business level. It normally revolves around processes and resources, and activities at this level are the most specific, often dealing with detailed execution plans and individual resources.

Future shock
A term coined by Alvin Toffler in his book, *Future Shock*, first published in 1970. It describes the confusion and shattering psychological stress resulting from too much change over a relatively short period. Symptoms include distress and disorientation.

Gains chart
A visual representation of lift.

Gearing
The degree to which investments are split between high- and low-risk investments.

Grouping model
A type of model specifically focusing on grouping similar individuals or entities together based on multidimensional information. A common example is a customer segmentation model.

Growth initiative
A business analytics initiative focused on creating value. It tends to have fairly well-defined deliverables and fixed time frames with expected end dates, and to involve the creation of new assets and processes.

Hax and Wilde's Delta model

A way of looking at competitive advantage that seeks ways of maximizing the customer value proposition to achieve maximal customer bonding. It describes three broad strategies: best product, total customer solutions, and system lock-in.

Hedonic pricing analysis

An econometric technique that aims to identify and quantify the underlying factors that drive demand in a heterogeneous market. A common example is within real estate, where prices, location, distance from main roads, number of bedrooms, and overall square footage all contribute to the final price the market will bear.

High-context culture

A grouping of individuals with a tendency to rely on cultural norms and implicit communication when communicating. Cultural history and understanding is often extremely important.

Ideation

The process of generating and communicating ideas. It includes the innovation process and should eventually lead to commercialization.

Imputation

The process of estimating likely values for missing data taking into account the statistical characteristics of broader population, often simultaneously trying to minimize the bias introduced through estimation.

In-database processing

A technique involving migrating logic processing away from a generalized computing tier and into the database. A common example in analytics is transforming analytical processing steps into native database execution logic and deploying this logic into the database.

Independent variables

A term referring to the inputs used within a model. They are typically unrelated to each other but should exhibit some form of causal relationship toward the outcome being examined.

Information theory

A branch of research pioneered by Claude E. Shannon that focuses on the quantification of information.

Innovation

Within the context of business analytics, the process of delivering a fundamentally different approach, often involving high amounts of disruption.

Intangible value
The immeasurable worth of an asset of outcome to an organization. Common examples include job satisfaction and the ability to make better decisions.

Intentional planning
A structured planning process that includes a series of predefined planning steps and a deliberate consideration of various influences, and focuses on a horizon that extends relatively far into the future.

Internal rate of return
A more advanced financial measure that estimates the interest rate needed to make the net present value of benefits equal the net present value of costs.

Join
See *Merge.*

Kryder's Law
The trend for magnetic disk storage to double annually, leading to significant ongoing increases in storage capacity. It was defined by Mark Kryder while at Seagate.

Lift
A common statistical measure that represents the degree of improvement one or more alternative classification processes offer over an existing process.

Linear programming
A technique within operations research that maximizes or minimizes an objective function through varying inputs given constraints. It relies on the assumption of a linear relationship between inputs and outputs.

Low-context culture
A grouping of individuals with a tendency to explicitly communicate concepts and avoid relying on "things left unsaid." Cultural history and understanding tends to be less important.

Market failure
An economic condition where the allocation of goods by the market creates an inefficient outcome. In the absence of intervention, the free market will achieve a suboptimal result. Common examples include the creation of negative market externalities such as pollution or the abuse of shared public grounds, known as the "tragedy of the commons."

Matching
A planning technique within Porter's SWOT analysis that involves mapping strengths to opportunities, looking for ways to create competitive advantage.

Merge
A process by which two or more tables are combined into one, matching them using one or more common fields. A common example involves combining customer data with purchasing data to create a single table that incorporates all available information.

Microsegmentation modeling
A segmentation approach that creates very high numbers of segments, often in the thousands.

Model
An abstracted view of reality. Within analytics, it often refers to a mathematically or logically defined function that helps simplify multidimensional information into a small set of useful measures.

Model deployment
The process by which models are migrated from a discovery environment into an operational environment and used to provide ongoing scoring processes.

Model development
The process by which models are created.

Monochronicity
The perception of time as linear discrete units. Typically, monochrons exhibit a preference for doing things in a sequential manner, focusing on managing time explicitly.

Monte Carlo sampling
A process by which samples are repeatedly drawn with replacement from an existing population. Typically, Monte Carlo sampling is used as an input generation process to run a variety of simulations and capture the resulting outputs.

Moore's Law
The trend for the number of transistors on an integrated circuit to double roughly every two years, leading to significant ongoing increases in computing power. It was defined by Gordon E. Moore, cofounder of Intel.

Multivariate analysis
A form of statistical analysis that includes more than one variable at a time.

Net present value
A more advanced financial measure that calculates net return taking into account the time value of money.

Network-attached storage
A storage device on a network deployed in such a way that it appears as a discrete file server available to multiple clients on a network.

Neural network
An algorithm that conceptually mimics the learning patterns of biological neural networks through adaptively adjusting a series of classification functions in a nonlinear nature to maximize predictive accuracy given a series of inputs.

Nonparametric statistics
A branch of statistics that makes no assumptions on the underlying distributions of the data being examined. In general, the tests are far more generalizable but sacrifice precision and power.

Organizational benefits
Benefits that accrue to the broader organization.

Operational activity
An ongoing process focused on preserving existing value. These activities tend to be more process driven, have no fixed end date, and leverage existing assets, capabilities, and processes.

Operational environment
A logically defined and usually separate area within an analytics platform that provides users with the ability to deploy assets into processes and workflows to support operational activities.

Operations research
A subset of analytical techniques that apply mathematical optimization techniques to identify optimal or near-optimal answers to business problems. It is often used to support inventory optimization and supply-chain optimization, and to optimize the allocation of scarce resources.

Opportunistic planning
A relatively ad hoc planning process that forgoes strongly defined processes for flexibility and tactical delivery. Managers applying this form of

planning often seek incremental tactical improvements that broadly lead toward an often generally described end state.

Opportunity cost
The cost of the next-best choice to someone who has picked from a series of mutually exclusive options. It represents the option forgone.

Optimization model
A type of model that aims to maximize or minimize a target outcome through identifying the best inputs or settings to use given a series of constraints. Common examples include optimizing production or delivery schedules to minimize total cost or routing time.

Organizational planning
The highest level of strategic planning, typically focusing on identifying the markets where the organization will or will not compete, targeting acquisitions or creating key competencies and cultures.

Parametric statistics
A branch of statistics that assumes the data being examined comes from a variety of known probability distributions. In general, the tests sacrifice generalizability for speed of computation and precision, providing the requisite assumptions are met.

Payback
A simple time-based measure that quantifies the period of time needed to recoup the cost of investment.

Performance management
The application of technology, process, and psychology to manage behavior and results and facilitate the delivery of strategic and tactical objectives.

Personal benefits
Benefits that accrue to individuals within the organization.

Personal perspective
A communication approach that focuses on the personal impact of changes, paying specific attention to the intangible benefits and interpersonal relationships that will be created.

Petabyte
An SI-defined measure of data storage equal to 1,000 terabytes, or 1,000,000 gigabytes. For comparison, a single commercial single-sided dual-layer DVD can store up to approximately 8.5 gigabytes.

Polychronicity
The perception of time as a continuous flow. Typically, polychrons exhibit a preference for doing multiple things at once and focus on the holistic, preferring not to manage time explicitly.

Porter's Five Forces
A framework to consider industry structure as defined by Michael Porter. It aims to identify attractive industries based on the threat of new entrants, the threat of substitutable products, the bargaining power of consumers, the bargaining power of suppliers, and the degree of competitive rivalry within the industry in question.

Positioning approach
A process espoused by Michael Porter that involves considering the impact of Porter's Five Forces when determining the attractiveness of a given industry. By doing so, planners can position the organization within its environment.

Predictive modeling
A process by which the underlying relationships behind an outcome are identified, quantified, and used to create predictions for new information. These are often statistically based. A common example is using information about customers who have canceled their phone service to statistically identify and quantify the major leading indicators that suggest someone will cancel. These indicators are then translated into a scoring process and used to score existing customers, helping to identify those who are at a high probability of cancellation. Once identified, they can then be contacted before they cancel, potentially making a unique retention offer to discourage them from going to a competitor.

Pricing analytics
The application of analytics to specifically support calculating optimal prices and understanding the relationship between prices and demand through price elasticity models.

Process perspective
A communication approach that focuses on the sequential activities that need to occur, paying specific attention to the changes that will need to be implemented.

Propensity model
A type of model that specifically focuses on creating predictions around the likelihood of an individual performing a particular action. Common

examples include the propensity of an individual to default on a loan or to purchase a given product.

Proxemic factors
A broad grouping of spatial and nonverbal communication influencers. These include spatial proximity, posture, touching, visual characteristics, volume, and odor.

Radio-frequency identification (RFID)
A low-power technology that supports low-cost wireless communication between readers and devices. Because of its low-cost structures, it is used to support a wide variety of asset management problems ranging from tracking casino chips to monitoring usage of toll roads.

RAID 0+1
A storage technique that involves striping information across multiple physical disks without parity and then mirroring the array onto another array, delivering speed and redundancy at the cost of available storage. *RAID* stands for *redundant array of inexpensive disks*.

RAID 5
A storage technique that involves striping information across multiple physical disks while preserving redundancy through parity bits. *RAID* stands for *redundant array of inexpensive disks*.

Ratemaking
A variety of techniques that specifically focus on calculating premiums, taking into account the frequency and severity of loss-making events.

Recency, frequency, monetary (RFM) analysis
A technique commonly used in marketing applications to profile customer spending patterns. It derives a series of variables to identify how recently each customer spent money, how frequently they spend money, and how much money they spend with the organization in question.

Relational model
A type of model that aims to identify relationships of interest and quantify the strength of relationship between individuals or entities. Common examples include market-basket analysis and social network analysis.

Reporting
A process by which insight is presented in a visually appealing and informative manner.

Research initiative
A business analytics initiative focused on delivering insight. While these initiatives often enable value creation, they usually do not create any direct value in and of themselves.

Resource-based view of the firm
A way of looking at organizational value creation with the goal of identifying resource-based competitive advantages, consolidated by Birger Wernerfelt. It aims to create competitive advantage by identifying and leveraging resources that are valuable, rare, inimitable, and nonsubstitutable.

Return on investment
A simple financial measure that subtracts the investment expended from the total returns generated, giving a simple net financial return.

Road map
Within the context of business analytics, a defined set of staged initiatives that deliver tactical returns while moving the team toward strategic outcomes.

Scoring process
A process by which a predefined model is applied against new data, creating a new variable for each record that contains the result of the model. A common example is calculating the propensity of every customer to churn within a given time period.

Scoring table
A table containing new data that is to be fed through a scoring model.

Segmentation
A process by which entities within a population are grouped into segments that have common characteristics. This grouping process may be manually, algorithmically, or statistically based and will often take into account anywhere from a handful to hundreds of common attributes across all the entities.

Segmentation strategy
A strategy that identifies subgroups within the market and treats these groups differently. This targeted treatment can then drive offer relevancy and increase offer attractiveness.

Sensitivity analysis
A form of simulation modeling that focuses specifically on identifying the upper and lower bounds of model outputs given a series of inputs with specific variance.

Simulation
A process by which processes or models are run repeatedly, using a variety of inputs. The outputs are normally captured and analyzed to conduct sensitivity analysis, provide insight around likely potential outcomes, and identify bottlenecks and constraints within existing processes or models.

Simulation modeling
An analytical technique that often involves running models repeatedly, using a variety of inputs to determine the upper and lower bounds of possible outcomes. This simulation process is also sometimes used to identify the likely distribution of outputs given a series of assumptions around how the inputs are distributed.

Single view of customer (SVoC)
A consolidated view of all customer information within an organization.

Social network analysis
The application of analytics to analyze relationships between individuals, often to help with contagious churn or viral marketing.

Six Sigma process improvement
A business management strategy focusing on quality control testing and optimizing processes through reducing process variance.

Strategic perspective
A communication approach that focuses on the holistic impact of business analytics, paying specific attention to the strategic implications of change.

Strategic planning
The process by which organizations identify a desired outcome, the resources required to support that outcome, and the plan to achieve the outcome. Typically, strategic planning is an important step in identifying the creation of new competitive advantages.

Storage-attached network
A storage device on a network deployed in such a way that it appears to be locally attached to the operating system.

Stress testing
A form of simulation modeling that focuses specifically on identifying the response of a model under specific, often highly negative scenarios. Common examples include testing the profitability of a bank given catastrophic levels of mortgage defaults or modeling extreme macroeconomic conditions.

Strongly defined process
A series of steps that is clearly defined, is repeatable, can be automated, and leads to the creation of value.

Supply-chain optimization
A process, often leveraging operations research, that aims to improve the efficiency of a given supply chain. Common targets include minimizing delivery time, reducing total cost of delivery, minimizing inventory held on-hand, and minimizing the total number of distribution centers needed.

SWOT analysis
An input into a strategic planning process defined by Michael Porter. It focuses on identifying an organization's *s*trengths, *w*eaknesses, *o*pportunities, and *t*hreats.

Tactical revolution
The process by which deliberate incremental improvements can be leveraged to create sufficient free time to allow the delivery of growth initiatives.

Tangible value
The quantifiable and measurable worth of an asset or outcome to an organization. Common examples include financial improvements and saleable market value.

Team platform
A centralized analytics environment based on a defined set of tools that supports a business analytics team.

Terabyte
An SI-defined measure of data store equal to 1,000 gigabytes. For comparison, a single commercial single-sided dual-layer DVD can store up to 8.54 gigabytes.

Time-series analysis
A variety of methods that focus on analyzing time-stamped information, often with an emphasis on identifying relationships between events and outcomes as well as creating predictions.

Tools
The basic building blocks through which most assets are created. They can be internally developed or purchased off the shelf, but without an appropriate set of purpose-built tools, a business analytics team is unable to create any new assets.

Total cost of ownership
A simple financial measure of the total costs of an initiative, covering services, software, hardware, support agreements, internal transfer pricing, training, and all other associated costs.

Training table
A table containing data that is used to develop a model.

Transformation
A mathematically defined way of taking data and altering it based on a generalized mapping function, often with the goal of creating a different way of looking at the data in an easily reversible way. Common examples include taking the natural logarithm or exponentiation.

Trending
A process by which underlying trends are identified within time-related data. These trends may be manually, algorithmically, or statistically identified and extrapolated into the future to aid planning.

Type I error
A term that refers to incorrectly rejecting a null hypothesis. It is also sometimes termed a "false positive" and used when an outcome is incorrectly identified as having happened, such as when a customer is incorrectly identified as having committed fraud.

Type II error
A term that refers to failing to reject a null hypothesis when it is false. It is also sometimes termed a "false negative" and used when an outcome is incorrectly identified as not having happened, such as when a customer has committed fraud but has not been accurately identified.

Univariate analysis
A form of statistical analysis that focuses on one variable at a time.

Up-sell
A process by which customers are upgraded to more expensive products, replacing their existing products.

Value
The intrinsic and extrinsic worth of an asset or outcome to an individual or organization.

Viral marketing
The application of direct marketing with the goal of leveraging individuals' personal networks to promote a message, increase mindshare, or drive pull-through sales through positive network externalities.

VRIN resources
Resources that lead to competitive advantage as suggested by the resource-based view of the firm. Their main characteristic is that they are valuable, rare, inimitable, and nonsubstitutable.

Walrasian auction
A conceptual simultaneous auction where all bidders submit their price sensitivity curve to a central agent, who then optimizes distribution to ensure demand equals supply. It is characterized by perfect information and zero transaction costs.

Weakly defined process
A series of steps that leads to the creation of value, is based on guidelines, and relies on the skill and ingenuity of the analyst to be completed successfully.

Welfare economics
A typically normative branch of economics that focuses on optimizing aggregate utility in general equilibrium through the application of micro-economic techniques such as income redistribution and market regulation. Pareto optimality occurs at the point where no individual can be made better off without making another individual worse off.

About the Author

Evan Stubbs has over 10 years' experience helping organizations extract value from business analytics. A recognized expert in innovation, Evan has a background advising as a management consultant with KPMG Consulting, providing architectural strategy with Deloitte, and managing innovation within General Motors's research and development activities.

Over the course of his career he has delivered projects as diverse as identifying viral churn within telecommunications through social network analysis, implementing an analytics-based policy planning tool kit within the public sector, and creating a human–machine interface and entertainment system for a concept car. A champion for innovation and improvement, he advises organizations across multiple industry sectors and assists companies in achieving best practices in analytics.

Index